the WILD COAST

the WILD COAST

A KAYAKING, HIKING AND RECREATION GUIDE FOR NORTH AND WEST VANCOUVER ISLAND

by John Kimantas

whitecap

Edited by Elaine Jones
Proofread by Joan E. Templeton
Cover and interior design by Jacqui Thomas
Photography and maps by John Kimantas
Front cover kayak photo by Gertjan Hofman
Author photo by Lisa Gerard

Printed and bound in Canada

LIBRARY AND ARCHIVES CANADA CATALOGUING IN PUBLICATION

Kimantas, John
     The wild coast: a kayaking, hiking and recreation guide for north and
west Vancouver Island / John Kimantas.

Includes index.
ISBN 1-55285-648-8

     1. Kayaking—British Columbia—Vancouver Island—Guidebooks.
2. Hiking—British Columbia—Vancouver Island—Guidebooks. 3. Outdoor
recreation—British Columbia—Vancouver Island—Guidebooks. 4. Trails—
British Columbia—Vancouver Island—Guidebooks. 5. Vancouver Island (B.C.)—
Guidebooks. I. Title.

GV776.15.B7K55 2005   797.122'4'097112   C2005-900154-2

The publisher acknowledges the financial support of the Government of Canada through
the Book Publishing Industry Development Program for our publishing activities.

Contents

Acknowledgments

I would like to acknowledge the following for their invaluable assistance in the production of this book:

- B.C. Ministry of Water, Land and Air Protection

- B.C. Ministry of Energy and Mines

- B.C. Parks

- B.C. Ministry of Sustainable Resource Management
  Base Mapping and Geomatic Services Branch
  Resource Management Division
  Coastal and Marine Planning, Projects and Marine Initiatives

- Canadian Nature Federation

Also, a tip of the hat to ethnologists such as Philip Drucker, without whom so much would have been lost forever on the coast.

Thanks also to my father, Frank, for his unwavering support, and Sandy Arcand for her unwavering faith. To Matthew Gerard for surviving the dreadful August long weekend in Clayoquot, to Pennie Baumel for being there when needed, and to Damien McCrossin for our early paddling adventures and misadventures together that set the stage for this book.

Lastly, a thank you to the many wonderful people on the coast—those strangers who shared campfires, food and stories. There are no warmer people than those on a cold, wet coast.

Introduction

THE WEST COAST OF VANCOUVER ISLAND IS A MAGICAL MIXTURE: WAVE-pounded rocks, foaming water, miles of white sand beach, majestic fjords twisting deep into mountain passes and a parade of wildlife—from playful sea otters munching on crabs to gray whales arcing as they surface.

It takes only a visit to become hooked. Getting to know the coast well can take a lifetime.

This book is designed for those who want to get to know the coast better—whether by kayak, boat, foot or RV (though the emphasis on kayaking will be obvious). The outer coast from Port Hardy in the north to Esquimalt in the south is divided into 11 sections. Each chapter offers background on the attractions, history and ecology of the region, as well as launching and camping options. Detailed maps show the locations of all the major points of interest—from campsites to the best places to view wildlife.

Vancouver Island stretches 500 km (300 miles) end to end. But between Cape Sutil in the north and Rocky Point to the south, there are thousands of miles of coastline, thanks to five distinct major sounds. Three of those sounds have become internationally popular travel destinations. The southernmost, Barkley Sound, is liberally sprinkled with islands and protected as a national park. It has grown to become one of the top kayaking and tourism destinations in North America. Each year thousands are drawn to the protected channels, the sea caves, the beaches and the abundant wildlife.

To the north is Clayoquot Sound, an area that became the focal point for an international logging demonstration in 1993. The protests were destined to become the nation's largest case of civil disobedience. Hundreds would be arrested in a bid to protect Clayoquot's old-growth forests. The attempt would eventually fail, but public outcry would lead to two significant events for the sound: first, an appeasement to protect virtually all of Clayoquot Sound's

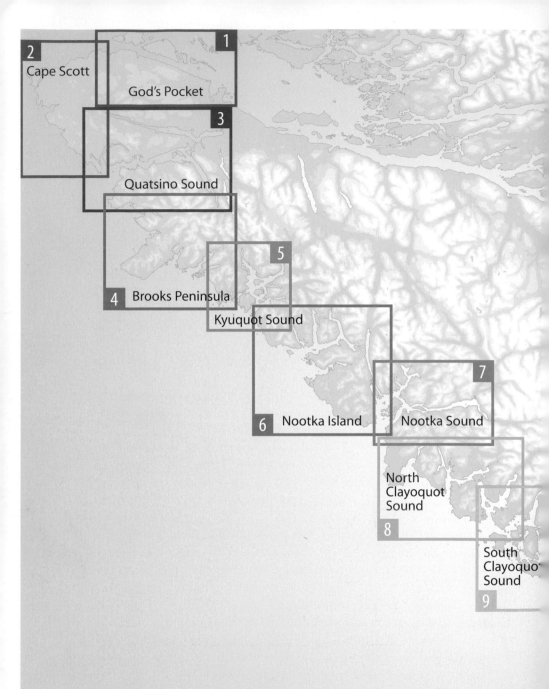

1

2
Cape Scott

God's Pocket

3

Quatsino Sound

5

4
Brooks Peninsula

Kyuquot Sound

7

6
Nootka Island

Nootka Sound

North
Clayoquot
Sound

8

South
Clayoquo'
Sound

9

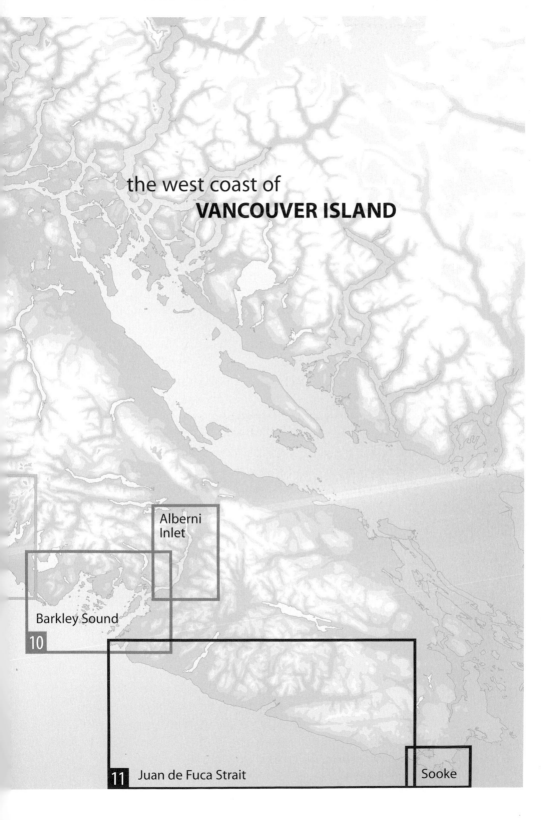

the west coast of
VANCOUVER ISLAND

Alberni
Inlet

Barkley Sound

10

11 Juan de Fuca Strait

Sooke

outer coast, then the creation of a scientific panel to review all logging and commercial use of the sound.

A network of provincial parks now stretches along most of Vancouver Island's southwestern coastline, from Hesquiat Peninsula in the north to Juan de Fuca Provincial Park.

North of Clayoquot Sound is Nootka Sound. The recreational focal point is Bligh Island Provincial Marine Park. Growing popular with kayakers seeking an alternative to the more crowded Broken Island Group in Barkley Sound, Bligh Island offers protected waters and channels to explore. It's also a gateway to some of Vancouver Island's most intriguing history, including the historic native village of Yuquot on Nootka Island.

Nootka Island is the most geographically imposing of the islands along the coast. Tucked in against Vancouver Island are numerous sheltered passages: Tahsis, Esperanza, Zeballos and Espinosa inlets, to name a few. But the best attractions are toward the open ocean: the wild and exposed Nuchatlitz and Catala provincial marine parks. Here kayakers can enjoy sheltered waters or explore wave-pounded reefs in one of the most inspiring wilderness settings on the coast.

Farther north, travellers will find the route less ventured. Brooks Peninsula is a massive physical barrier, with little land access and even less shelter. Many of the most rare and exotic birds along British Columbia's coast nest there. Tucked in around the peninsula are islands and waterways to explore, including Kyuquot Sound and the off-lying Mission Group Islands. To the north lie the Bunsby Islands, which have many attractions of the more popular archipelagos without the crowds.

The northernmost of the sounds is Quatsino, with its long passages and rolling hillsides. Here can be found features from the unique character of Kwakiult-Lawn Point Provincial Park to the six-gill sharks of Drake Island.

Perhaps the most exotic location, though, is the very northern tip of Vancouver Island. Remote to the point of being desolate, visitors will find miles upon miles of uninhabited white sand beach and more wildlife per square foot than anywhere else on Vancouver Island. Too wild and distant to be considered a destination by most people, it's still surprisingly accessible—from the white sands and sea stacks of San Josef Bay to the serenity of God's Pocket Provincial Park and the myriad of islands just north of Port Hardy.

Morning fog burns off as it blows over the mouth of Hisnit Inlet in Nootka Sound.

No two areas of Vancouver Island's wild coast are the same. And no matter which part of the island you choose to visit, be sure it will change the way you view the great outdoors.

HIKING THE COAST

In the several centuries since Europeans began their explorations of the North American continent, visitors to the outer coast of Vancouver Island have largely been limited to fishermen, loggers and a few recreational mariners and hardy hikers. That's changing today, with better public access, more parkland, a growing awareness of the coast's attractions and new modes of transportation, particularly sea kayaks. Kayaks allow travel to remote areas that are off-limits to recreational boat traffic.

Hiking is also growing ever more popular, but trail development hasn't kept pace. The West Coast Trail between Port Renfrew and Bamfield has become one of the most prestigious hikes in the world, a popularity that has forced park officials to limit the number of hikers per day through a reservation system. A proposal has been in the works for years to create a North Coast Trail from Port Hardy to San Josef Bay (see page 86).

The result is very few trails along the coast, considering the size of the area. The main exceptions are the following.

- *Cape Scott Trail:* This popular but often muddy hike leads 17 km (11 miles) from San Josef to the north coast and many of Vancouver Island's best and least-visited beaches. Numerous historic remnants can also be viewed (see page 83).

- *Nootka Trail:* Skirting the shore of outer Nootka Island, the trail runs from Louie Bay to Yuquot. It's an often difficult three to four days, with a great deal of beach walking interspersed with trails over rocky headlands. It's accessible only by water or air; hikers often arrange to be dropped off by plane at Louie Bay and picked up at Yuquot by water taxi (see page 204).

- *Hesquiat Peninsula Trail:* Leading from Boat Basin, a rough and rarely used trail follows the peninsula's shore to Escalante Point. It's a rugged, little-travelled and difficult wilderness hiking experience (see page 238).

- *Wild Side Trail:* A fairly challenging trail leads from Ahousat to Cow Bay, then to the top of Mount Flores on Flores Island in Clayoquot Sound. Access is marine only (see pages 250, 252).

- *Juan de Fuca Marine Trail:* This trail runs through Juan de Fuca Provincial Park from Port Renfrew to China Beach. It's a challenge equal in many ways to the West Coast Trail, but it's more accessible (see page 348).

Hikers walk the beach on the Nootka Trail, an heir to the West Coast Trail for the most challenging hike on the Vancouver Island coast.

There are regrettably few shorter trails that dot the coastline. For hikers seeking the ultimate challenge, the Bedwell Valley Trail runs from Bedwell Sound in South Clayoquot deep into Strathcona Provincial Park, or even right across Vancouver Island (see page 269).

CAMPING ON THE COAST

This book is intended to provide as many of the best camping options along the Vancouver Island coastline as possible. Those vary greatly from region to region. For instance, there are numerous headlands along the north coast with sandy stretches that aren't worth mentioning, since sprawling possibilities such as Shuttleworth Bight are located nearby. On the other hand, a small, flat headland behind a fish farm with a noisy generator in Hecate Channel is listed simply because there are no suitable nearby alternatives. You may also pass by beautiful crushed-shell beaches that look perfect for a campsite but aren't listed in this book. Beware of these—exits from pocket beaches can become blocked by boulders at lower tides. Another thing to watch for is disappearing beaches. What looks inviting at dinner time may be covered by water come midnight.

With about 2,000 km (1,200 miles) of coast it's impossible to mention every nook and cranny, but the intent is to list most practical options. If no options are listed along long stretches, such as Juan de Fuca Strait, it's because the shore is either completely rocky or beaches are too exposed to recommend. Be sure to read the description for each region and each camping area before setting out, and plan your trip around camping locations with contingency plans in mind. Camping locations aren't all equally good, and facing an unexpected wall of surf at the end of your paddling day is a surprise best avoided.

Campers should be aware of their own rights and also the rights of landowners. The vast majority of Vancouver Island is Crown (public) land. Crown land is available for recreational use such as camping. First Nation land is private property. Reserves were created in the 1880s around existing communities. The vast majority—in fact, all but a few—are now deserted. The reason they were picked for settlement was generally because they offered protected, easily accessible shoreline. This makes them ideal for camping by kayak, and a few even have established wilderness campsites. While some visitors may want to take the chance and pitch a tent on reserve land, be warned that in some areas campers will be escorted off the land. Other First Nation groups allow access with permission, and wherever possible, contact numbers have been provided in individual listings. All reserves are marked on the maps in this book in red with "IR".

Private property, indicated on the maps in grey, really doesn't become a factor, outside of a few pockets, until south of Juan de Fuca Provincial Park. There public land becomes the exception. During a circumnavigation of the outer coast in 2003, the area around Sooke proved to be the most difficult for finding camping locations. During foul weather I was forced to pitch a tent one night below a bluff capped by a mansion. The next night was spent in the spare room of a family in Sooke that adopted me until the storm passed. Had the weather been better, I probably would have used a beach in East Sooke Regional Park—not a recommended use, but the only real option east of Jordan River.

A common complaint against kayakers is they will camp anywhere—ignoring private property rights—when they feel justified, either by weather, fatigue or lesser circumstance. The mobility of kayaks is offset by a responsibility to not abuse the privilege. That means no-trace camping as a minimum. Having said that, the evolution of fine camping areas is a wondrous thing. The best wilderness campsites are beautiful beyond any park campground, where roots, trees, driftwood and other natural features combine to make wonderful living spaces that take advantage of the natural beauty of the area, enhancing it instead of destroying it. Ross Islets in Barkley Sound's Deer Group come to mind.

PADDLING THE COAST

The problem points

Any area along the exposed coast can be a problem, but there are certain areas I refer to as problem points. They're generally characterized by shallow ocean shelves that lead to steeper swell. They also involve the meeting of two or possibly more currents or weather conditions, typically the tidal outflows of inlets meeting the exposed waters of the Pacific Ocean. This can result in a confusing jumble of waves as currents compete. And to make matters worse, any number of rocks and reefs may lie submerged near the surface.

A mystique exists about the danger of kayaking the open coast, but when conditions are right it's an incredible place to be. The author relaxes on the sand beach at San Josef Bay near Cape Scott.

These characteristics make the following problem points particularly dangerous. Working down the coast from Port Hardy to Victoria, they're Tatnall Reefs and Nahwitti Bar (see pages 58–59), Cape Scott (see page 73), Cape Russell (see page 80), Brooks Peninsula (see page 134), Tatchu Point (see page 179), Ferrer Point (see page 201), Maquinna Point (see page 203), Hesquiat Peninsula (see page 231), Cape Beale (see page 332) and Race Rocks (see page 354).

Keep in mind problems aren't limited to these locations; any portion of the coast can be dangerous.

There are simple safety measures for rounding these areas. Listen to weather forecasts and don't attempt a crossing if winds are forecast to be high, or even moderate depending on your expertise. Leave early in the morning to round the difficult point at the calmest part of the day. And finally, time your crossing at or near slack tide. Follow these rules and chances are you'll have a safe journey; break any one of these rules and you're endangering your life and those of the people with you.

Managing open water

There are generally two types of paddlers—flatwater paddlers who prefer leisurely jaunts in protected water and those who have graduated to open water. Paddlers who make the leap won't look back. The open coast holds the greatest attractions: the best beaches, the best landscapes, the greatest wildlife and the most secluded areas. The fun begins with the swell, but unfortunately many paddlers will dart for cover when they reach it.

The truth is ocean kayaks are made for the ocean, and are perfectly suited for the vast majority of conditions in open water. There are five main concerns: swell, wind, wind waves, currents and reefs. Reefs are defined as submerged or semi-submerged rocks.

Despite the initial discomfort, swell isn't a great impediment to kayaking. Kayaks tend to stay upright in swell, reducing the rocking effect experienced by boats. As long as the swell isn't steep, it doesn't affect current or travel speed. The kayaker will simply rise and fall. Only when swell becomes steep—steep enough to threaten to break under its weight—does it become a problem.

Wind waves are a bigger danger. These tend to be shorter (1 to 2 feet/30 to 60 cm) and sharper. They can build up a current as well, and their sharpness can seriously affect a kayak's abilities. Combined with swell they become a double concern, as wind waves don't necessarily travel in the same direction as swell. When crossing one another, they can cancel each other out or they can double up to create momentarily large waves. This can be particularly hazardous when the wind and swell are at right angles to one another. Extremely sharp, pyramid-shaped waves can be followed by exceptionally deep troughs.

Wind is the third consideration, because it can rise quickly in the most exposed areas of the coast, from calm to storm conditions in less than an hour. Strong winds can build up enough current to potentially out-muscle a kayaker, driving a paddler toward rocks or shoreline.

The greatest danger is from reefs, especially when combined with swell. A 2- to 3-metre (6- to 10-foot) swell can obscure your view, because even when you're on the crest you cannot see into the troughs ahead. If you're paddling toward an unseen reef, the waves crossing the reef may not be particularly different from the rest—until a large wave passes. If it's large enough, it can break on the unseen rocks. If you're nearby, it can be deadly.

But the risk can be eliminated. The first truth is that the wind is usually calm in the morning and rises in the early afternoon. A must for open water is a VHF radio that monitors the marine forecasts. Generally speaking, while sun and rain predications can be off, their wind predictions hold true. Use them as a guide to plan your day.

Smart paddlers will rise early, be on the water at 6 or 7 a.m. and be off the water by noon, before the wind and swell rise. Not-so-smart paddlers will have a leisurely morning and start at noon.

The rule of higher wind in the afternoon applies to sheltered water as well. In fact, the secluded inner channels preferred by flat-water paddlers can often be worse than open water as the wind funnels between the mountains.

Managing the risks

A large wave crashing on an unseen reef is an image that will scare the bejesus out of novice paddlers. And rightly so. It should also scare veteran paddlers because it can kill. But there are ways to avoid this danger.

The first step for safety is to scan the horizon constantly. Look in all directions for white water. Usually you'll get to see the evidence of a rock long before you're near. It will be a white speck—the foaming water as waves break on the rock. Respect this clue and plan to avoid it. It sounds simple, but it's easy to get lulled into carelessness and miss the clues.

Another hint is foam residue. If you see a patch of foam on otherwise clear water, beware. This indicates that water was breaking somewhere nearby. It may have washed away from breaking waves near shore, but this usually leaves a trail. If it's an isolated patch, be extra careful. A hidden rock may be nearby—the worst kind of rock. The kind of rock where only the occasional large waves break on it. If you're next to such a rock when a big wave comes, you're in extreme danger.

Lastly, read the swell. If it gets steeper and taller, that means the ocean floor is getting shallower. This can mean you're on a wide and shallow shelf near shore, a hint you may want to get to deeper water. It may also mean you're in a localized area of shallow water, with a very distinct possibility of a reef nearby. In those instances turn to deeper water until the swell returns to the usual size and shape.

When reefs are all around, the general rule of thumb is to go outside them. You'll usually find that even in the worst reef-strewn waters, the line of reefs doesn't extend more than 1.5 km (a mile) outward. This isn't a great distance to travel to avoid danger.

The worst thing to do is travel between reefs in fairly close proximity. Terrible things happen to water when rocks are around. When you're near just one reef you're subject to rebound waves—that is, crashing water bouncing back off the rocks toward you. When there are two reefs, there are two possible sets of rebound waves to consider. Worse yet, the water being channelled through the passage causes turbulence. In otherwise manageable swell you may find yourself amid swell steepened by the shallow water, wind waves, two sets of rebound waves and turbulence from the current. Take the time to go around.

(Note that in calm water, kayaking in and around reefs and exposed shorelines can be the most rewarding part of a trip.)

The greatest rule is to never go where you're uncomfortable. If you don't like the waves, head back. And have contingencies for heading back—including the time to do so. Most problems happen when kayakers risk poor conditions to meet a deadline (such as returning to work on Monday). Plan for foul weather. Build in the time allowances. In the best case—perfect weather—this simply allows you more time to enjoy your trip.

Managing surf

The greatest feature of the open coast is the number of incredible beaches to be enjoyed. There are hundreds of kilometres of beach that attract just handfuls of visitors during the summer. If you want your own sprawling paradise, you'll have to be prepared for the possibility of landing or launching through surf. There's only one way to prepare for it: practice. Don't decide to land in the midst of a trip in

The sheltered waters of Barkley Sound's Broken Group are a popular destination for kayakers seeking scenery and serenity.

a loaded kayak because you think you can. You'll likely go over, even in low surf. Here are some tips to prepare you for the worst.

Launching

Launching is far simpler than landing. Generally you can launch into moderate surf with no more danger than getting wet. That's because most kayaks are made to slice into waves. Here's a technique that should work. Place your kayak where the highest wave will create about 20 to 30 cm (4 to 6 inches) of water. Sit in your kayak and do up your spray skirt. Hopefully you can do this before a wave comes that will wash you away; if not, jam your paddle into the sand to avoid being sucked into the surf. If you're sucked in too early, step out and pick a higher spot. If you're stranded, try and push forward with your hands and paddle or set yourself up again a little farther out.

Not all waves are created equal, so once you're in your kayak, your spray skirt is done up, your paddle is in your hands and you're floating on water but still inside the break line, be patient. Play in the shallow surf as you bide your time. Wait for the biggest wave to pass. Once it does, be sure it's not followed by a second large wave and then paddle like mad. You'll want to go as fast as possible. The worst place to find yourself is right before a breaking wave. If you do, the trick is to keep your nose directly into the wave. As long as you take it straight on you're likely to remain upright. Vary a fraction of a degree and you'll be in trouble. The wave will use that angle to push you sideways, and water has a lot of force. You can turn sideways almost instantly, and then you'll be rolled.

Landing

Landing is difficult because you'll be hit from behind by waves. Since most kayaks are fish-form, that is, slightly bulbous forward of the middle, they aren't as adept at slicing through waves coming from behind.

Here's the best way to approach a landing. Park yourself outside the break line and watch. For a long time. Look for big waves. Note where the largest begin to break. That's where you'll want to position yourself when you go in.

Once a big wave passes, one of two things will happen. You'll get a long line of smaller waves for a much safer entry, or a second large wave will follow. They often come in pairs, so watch for this possibility. Generally you can tell by the size of the approaching swell.

Once you believe you see the large wave coming, position yourself slightly behind where it will break. Ideally, it will break just before your kayak and your nose will rest on the foam, and you can simply follow it in. This isn't likely to happen, as the wave will probably be faster than your ability to paddle. If another wave is approaching from behind, my strategy is to actually paddle back into the wave. This means your kayak will slice into the wave instead of being pulled along with it.

If you find yourself pulled forward as if you're surfing, get out of the pull. Some people advocate plunging your paddle deep into the white water and using this as a brace to stay upright while surfing in. More power to them. This is good to use if you're pulled sideways and all other hope is lost. But often it works like this: the wave hits your stern and turns you. You plunge your paddle into the water to brace yourself. The wave hits you broadside. Over you go. How many times you want to practice this before you're successful is up to you.

So if you feel yourself being propelled forward, simply paddle backwards to fall out of the pull. Then follow the wave in.

If you're turned over, the good news is the water is usually shallow (that's why it's breaking). If it's not, the surf is almost certain to direct you, your kayak and your paddle toward shore. The best strategy is to swim up to your kayak, right it and hang onto the stern, riding it in like a surfboard.

Avoiding surf

The best first strategy is to avoid surf completely. Look for areas of beach behind rocky headlands or the extreme ends of a crescent beach. Here the protection will reduce or even eliminate crashing waves. In fact, it's possible to travel the outer coast of Vancouver Island and avoid moderate to high surf landings altogether.

Preparing for an expedition

A full lesson on provisioning for an extended trip by kayak is beyond the scope of this book, but a few general safety rules apply. Here's the minimum a traveller should take in terms of safety equipment when heading into the open water.

- *A VHF radio for monitoring weather reports.* Many come with a case for AA batteries as a backup when the Ni-Cd battery expires. Another option is a solar-powered battery charger. They're available at many hardware stores, and are small, affordable and reliable. Many VHF radio manufacturers state the radios are waterproof, but don't trust the claim (the same goes for a GPS). Keep the radio in

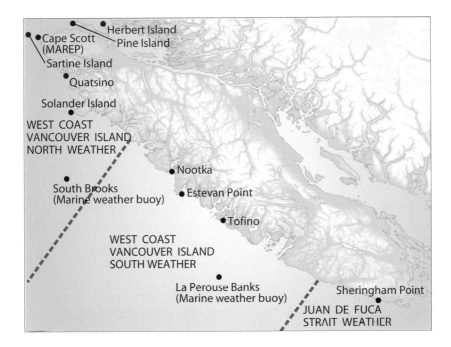

Herbert Island
Cape Scott
(MAREP)
Pine Island
Sartine Island
Quatsino
Solander Island
WEST COAST
VANCOUVER ISLAND
NORTH WEATHER
Nootka
South Brooks
(Marine weather buoy)
Estevan Point
Tofino
WEST COAST
VANCOUVER ISLAND
SOUTH WEATHER
La Perouse Banks
(Marine weather buoy)
Sheringham Point
JUAN DE FUCA
STRAIT WEATHER

a waterproof case. I've lost both a GPS and a VHF radio to salt-water. Both were marketed as submersible.

- *A tide guide for the coast.* An important point to remember about tide guides is the times are listed in standard time. You'll have to adjust for daylight savings time.

- *A GPS is recommended,* though I travelled down the coast without one. The advantage is the ability to know where you've been even if you don't know where you're going. With most you can pre-program waypoints; if you do this in advance using a chart, on the water you can tell how far you are from a location without ever having been there. Books are available listing waypoint locations. A GPS can also tell you your speed—a huge consideration when wind or current is affecting your travel. Often the effect can go unnoticed when you're paddling in open water. It's an important wakeup call if you're making progress at a mile an hour against the wind and your campsite is still eight miles away. Lastly, it's a safety item in fog. The few hundred dollars one will cost is a worthwhile investment.

- *Duct tape.* Buy the best waterproof variety you can find (not the bargain-basement variety; it won't be waterproof). The good stuff will allow you to tape your kayak back together if it snaps in two.

- *Charts.* See the chart information below.

- *Flares, a PFD, a pump, a paddle float, rope and all the other essentials.*

- *A water jug suitable for at least four or five days.* Water sources diminish as the summer progresses. Many, particularly at Cape Scott, are rich in minerals and rust-coloured. Waterfalls that are picturesque in June will be trickles in August. Water may need to be treated. Many islands have no freshwater sources at all.

- *A spare water bottle.* You never know when the first one will float away or spring a leak.

ABOUT CHARTS

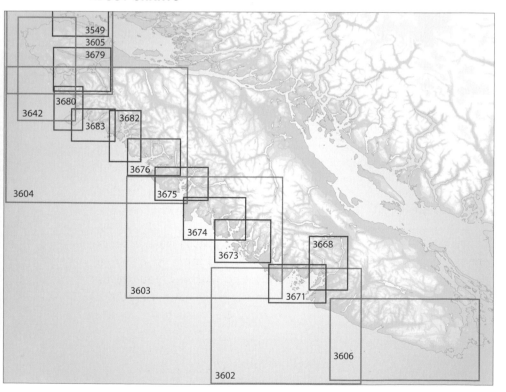

You'll need about a dozen charts to make your way down the entire coast; a few additional ones are recommended. The small-scale charts

are in orange in the accompanying illustration; charts 1:40,000 or larger are in purple. Note that small-scale charts cover a larger area and contain less detail than large-scale charts. Using just the small-scale charts, you could travel the coast covered here with just five, but at the cost of detail. In certain areas you won't have any choice, as large-scale charts aren't available. These are the north island from Shuttleworth Bight to Cape Russell; the outermost portion of Nootka Island; and Juan de Fuca Strait.

During a trip down the coast I decided not to bother with the portion of Nootka Island omitted between charts 3676 and 3675. The coast is straight and without reefs, so the chart really wasn't necessary. There's also a stretch between Cape Beale and Tsusiat Point in Juan de Fuca Strait that's off the chart unless you bring along chart 3602, which is mostly ocean. I made the choice early on to not bother with this chart, then was horrified that it wasn't there when it came time to use it. This portion of the coast is a long stretch with few landmarks, so careful tracking of the creeks is necessary to keep your bearing. I didn't have that information, so I wasn't sure exactly where I was until I reached Tsusiat Falls. For peace of mind, the extra chart would have been worth it. You can also cut down the size of charts to minimize overlaps and wasted space (such as almost all of chart 3602).

During my trip down the coast I travelled with two chart covers. The charts I needed that day were kept on the cockpit floor in front of my seat. The other chart case with the extra charts was laid flat in the bottom of the rear kayak hatch, taking up almost no space.

ABOUT WILDLIFE

The west coast is black bear country. The good news is black bears eat berries, not people. Even so, people live in fear of them. After dozens of close bear encounters, I've found most go like this: you see the bear, the bear sees you. You stare at one another for a moment in shock. You turn to get the bear spray; the bear turns and runs into the forest, never to be seen again.

I've had a few exceptions. One was at Nels Bight near Cape Scott in the summer of 2004. A bear there had claimed the water supply and was acting aggressively, not letting campers fill their bottles. Bear bangers weren't working. Another was at Hesquiat Peninsula. I was lying against a log reading. A bear wandered along the beach quite

A black bear is interrupted from his feeding near the shore of Clanninick Creek.

near me before we saw each other. We locked stares, but this time the bear didn't turn and run. It kept coming—well into my comfort zone—before turning off the beach (maybe 3 metres/10 feet away). I was told the next day by a native fisherman that it was an aggressive one and didn't tolerate humans too kindly.

Those were the worst cases. The best have been paddling past a family of bears, cubs and all, oblivious to our presence on the water. Many times I've peacefully shared beaches with bears. At Jepther Point outside Port Hardy I once waited in my kayak a half hour as a bear fed exactly where I wanted to pitch a tent. The next morning it was farther down the beach, feeding once again. We got along well, and I'm sure the same bear was there when I visited again next year, this time with a cub.

Bears are everywhere. At French Creek Provincial Park I paddled along watching a couple walk with a bear about 50 metres (175 feet) behind them, ambling along in the same direction. This went on for a humorously long time. They never noticed the bear; it turned off into the bushes before the couple began their walk back.

Conflicts only tend to occur when black bears learn to associate people with food. That's why it's important to cache your supplies. In remote areas far from busy campsites, the need isn't quite so urgent; bears leave humans well enough alone. In most wilderness sites I'll simply put the food inside the kayak for the night. Some would recommend against that, but if a bear is willing to rip apart a kayak to get food, better the kayak than me. I've never heard of this happening. String a food bag up in a tree, however, and it can be sport for a raccoon. And his family. And his cousins. And his cousins' cousins. If you've ever hosted a 3 a.m. free-for-all for raccoons, you'll never want to do it again. Raccoons, like bears, tend to associate humans with food in more popular camping areas. In most instances you'll never notice them.

Cougars are even more reclusive than bears. They live all over Vancouver Island but are rarely seen. Doug DeJarlais has lived in the most remote portion of the north island for years, at San Josef, and has seen cougars just a few times. The risk is truly minimal. To minimize the risk further, be loud and be big. If you see one, act aggressive. Bells on a backpack are another good trick, for cougars and bears. Put one on your dog if you have a pet hiking with you.

Lastly, there are also wolves. Many of the wolves in Clayoquot live side by side with humans, and the relationship isn't always good (see page 267). In wolf country, particularly Vargas and Flores islands in Clayoquot Sound, it's essential to cache your food and your belongings. Never tempt wildlife by offering food.

The wildlife that should concern you most are mice and crows. Mice will rummage through packs left outside tents, even chewing into dry bags and backpacks. Most crows won't bother you, but those that live near campsites can be evil. The worst offenders I've met were at Toquart Bay in Barkley Sound. These creatures would land on the kayak as soon as I turned my back. It made loading the kayak a very stressful venture—going to the car to get another load of equipment, only to have to run back swinging the paddle to chase away six crows picking apart the dry bags. It simply wasn't safe to leave a bag outside a hatch.

Wildlife is most often considered a danger to humans, but usually the reverse is true. Kayakers can be particularly obtrusive. They're low, fast and difficult to see, making it easy to sneak up on sea mammals and birds. For seals with pups or nesting birds, this can be devastating. The rarity of your appearance is no benefit. Studies have shown that remote locations are the most susceptible to disturbance by humans. Many unthinking kayakers (and boaters) haul out onto remote islets oblivious to the nesting birds and the rare and sensitive mosses, grasses, lichens and wildflowers that grow on a thin layer of soil over rocks—rocks that in just one trampling can be denuded of precious soil that took thousands of years to accumulate.

Kayakers have to take a new attitude to these remote areas. No-trace camping—"take only pictures, leave only footprints"—is no longer good enough. A healthy, distant respect for nature is equally crucial.

FIRST NATIONS HISTORY

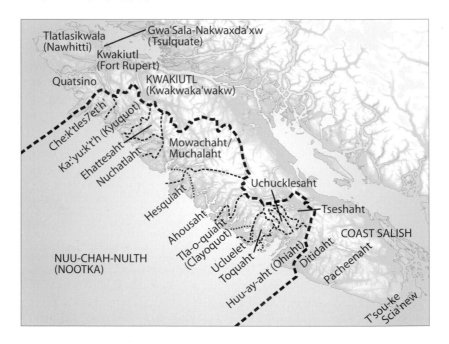

No journey to the west coast of Vancouver Island should be made without consideration for the native culture that thrived here for thousands of years before European contact. Places such as Yuquot on Nootka Island were once home to thousands of occupants. Now most village sites are overgrown. Some evidence remains in middens, or the occasional relic such as a housepost, but most villages have returned to the forest from which they came.

The Nuu-chah-nulth population was estimated to have been about 30,000 in 1788. It fell to below 4,000 by the late 19th century and to about 2,000 in the 1920s and 1930s. The fur trade and the introduction of alcohol would introduce economic subjugation, while the final insult would come in the 1880s when the Indian Reserve Commissioner parcelled off remaining native territories into small reserves. Now, more than a century later, the government is working toward treaty negotiations. The outcome will inevitably change the face of the West Coast. For instance, the Nuu-chah-nulth Tribal Council inked an agreement in principle on March 10, 2001, that includes up to 550 square km (212 square miles) of land, $241 million in a cash settlement, a share in the commercial fishery and forestry, plus a trust for Meares Island.

While the future appears brighter for Vancouver Island First Nations, much of their culture has vanished. A few early European pioneers would sketch the only written records of native life on the coast: Jesuit A. J. Brabant, John Jewitt who was captured and served as a slave for Chief Maquinna for several years, Capt. James Cook and John Meares. Their writings are among very few that provide glimpses of pre-contact native culture. In the late 1800s men like George Blenkinsop, W. E. Banfield, Edward Sapir, Gilbert Sproat, Philip Drucker and James Swan would attempt to chronicle what remained.

Interpretations of a language without writing has led to constant revisions. The Ohiaht, for instance, are the Huu-ay-aht today. Through the years they have also been documented as Huu'ii''atH, Huu'iia, Ohyaht, Ohiet, O.heh.ahts, Hoaiut, Ho?ai'ath and Huu7ii7aht. Names like Ho?ai'ath are probably the most accurate, accounting for sounds, such as a glottal stop, not included in the English alphabet.

In this book, historic references are used whenever possible—that is, the interpretations from the people who were the first to document the coast (though modern spellings are substituted for bands still in existence today). Credit must be given to George Dawson and his 1885 publication *Notes and Observations of the Kwakiool People of the Northern Part of Vancouver Island and Adjacent Coasts*. His references

A thriving native community, Refuge Cove is set on the coast at Hot Springs Cove.

helped locate and name villages from Quatsino Sound north. Philip Drucker's work *Northern and Central Nootkan Tribes*, first published by the Bureau of American Ethnology and reprinted in 1951, was used for naming and locating village sites throughout the central coast. The 1991 *Cultural Heritage Background Study, Clayoquot Sound* was used extensively for naming locations in that region. And lastly, the 1991 Canadian Museum of Civilization publication *Between Ports Alberni and Renfrew: Notes on West Coast Peoples* was used for naming and locating villages in Barkley Sound. These are all excellent resources for understanding the history of the coast. These, as well as other sources, are cited in the bibliography.

The native people of Vancouver Island comprise three separate linguistic groups. The Kwakwaka'wakw, more commonly known by the outdated name of Kwakiult, lived on the northeastern side of Vancouver Island and the outlying islands across to the British Columbia mainland. Their territory, as covered in this book, extends from Port Hardy and Hope Island off Vancouver Island's north shore across to Quatsino Sound. Brooks Peninsula served as the division between the Kwakwaka'wakw and the Nuu-chah-nulth. The Nuu-chah-nulth territory extended south to Point No Point in Juan de Fuca Strait, where the Coast Salish territory began.

The Nuu-chah-nulth existed along most of the shoreline covered in this book. While sharing a common language and ethnology, they were composed of groups with very distinct identities. The modern-day Nuu-chah-nulth is made up of 14 confederations (now referred to as First Nations), and each of those was composed of a variety of local groups.

The Nuu-chah-nulth were hunter-gatherers skilled in making canoes, fishing, hunting sea mammals and, most particularly, whaling. Elaborate social rituals, such as potlatches—gift-giving ceremonies— marked significant occasions or changes in rank. Wolf Rituals were a coming-of-age rite for males. These gatherings lasted for days, with dance and ceremony. Artistically, the Nuu-chah-nulth expressed themselves through totems, rock art, masks and carvings.

The very periphery of the coast covered in this book is Coast Salish land, which extended as far as Sooke Harbour and encompassed the Victoria region. Overall, their influence extended as far as Campbell River on the east coast of Vancouver Island, the Gulf Islands and along much of the coast of mainland British Columbia. Their traditional territories around Victoria and Vancouver have been prone to urban development. Confederations within the area covered by this book include Scia'new (also Beecher Bay) and T'sou-ke (formerly Sooke).

More about the ethnology of all these groups is touched upon in the description of coastal locations. Note that native sites mentioned in this book aren't an indication there will be visible remnants. Care must be taken when visiting historically sensitive areas. The sanctity of private property, archaeological remains and burial sites must be respected. It's against the law to disturb historic artifacts.

MAP SYMBOLS

Bird habitat: Areas of significant bird habitat or high concentrations of birds. Seabird nesting habitat is indicated by the following icon.

Bird nesting area: Seabird nesting locations.

Sea otter viewing area: Designates a few of the most prominent areas for viewing sea otters. While the otters' range now extends from God's Pocket to Clayoquot, higher concentrations of rafts (groups of otters) are likely to be seen in the areas noted.

Whale watching area: Highly subjective, this icon shows a few of the areas I've noticed that tend to attract a high number of whales during the summer. Experiences will vary. Spring and fall are the best times to see gray whales during their annual migration.

Rest area: A few locations along the coast are suitable for breaks, but camping isn't allowed. This icon designates those areas.

Food/supplies: There are only a few locations to get supplies in the North Island. This icon indicates some availability. See the accompanying text for more details.

Campsite: This symbol is used interchangably for wilderness, designated, undesignated or commercial camping locations. See the text for details.

Sea lion haulout: These symbols mark the most prominent year-round locations for seeing sea lions resting upon rocks (haulout locations).

Key fish area: This icon shows some of the most prominent fish locations on the coast. This isn't a fishing guide, however, and these icons are general indications only.

Killer whale viewing area: While transient orcas may travel the entire outer coast, a few areas are visited regularly by the resident populations. These icons indicate a few choice locations where the chances of seeing killer whales are above average.

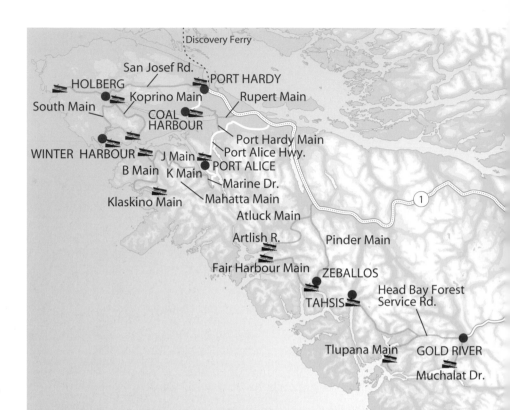

Discovery Ferry

San Josef Rd.

HOLBERG

PORT HARDY

Koprino Main

Rupert Main

South Main

COAL
HARBOUR

Port Hardy Main

Port Alice Hwy.

WINTER HARBOUR

J Main

PORT ALICE

B Main K Main

Marine Dr.

Klaskino Main

Mahatta Main

Atluck Main

Artlish R.

Pinder Main

Fair Harbour Main

ZEBALLOS

Head Bay Forest
Service Rd.

TAHSIS

Tlupana Main

GOLD RIVER

Muchalat Dr.

1

TOFINO

MAJOR TRANSPORTATION ROUTES

There are remarkably few roads that lead to Vancouver Island's west coast, with correspondingly few launch options. Each sound can be reached by vehicle, but conditions on logging roads can be rough. The only paved routes are to Coal Harbour, Port Alice, Gold River, Tofino, Ucluelet and Port Renfrew. Logging roads, such as those to Fair Harbour, can be poorly marked and confusing. Active logging spurs can appear better used than the main line, leading visitors astray. Watch roadsides for small markers; often these are your only clues. Backroad maps are recommended. A compass or GPS can also reduce the odds of being led astray. For more detailed descriptions of the various routes leading to the coast, see the entry "Getting Here" at the beginning of each chapter.

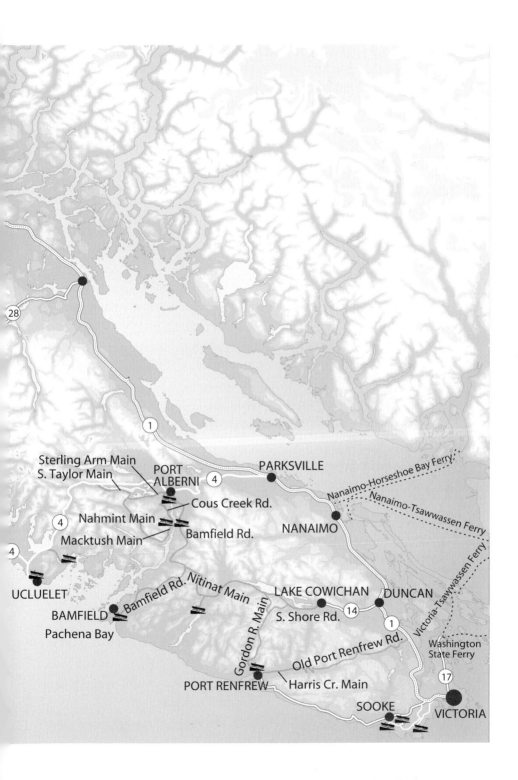

28

Sterling Arm Main
S. Taylor Main

PORT ALBERNI

4

Cous Creek Rd.

Nahmint Main

1

PARKSVILLE

Nanaimo-Horseshoe Bay Ferry

Nanaimo-Tsawwassen Ferry

4

Macktush Main

Bamfield Rd.

NANAIMO

4

UCLUELET

Bamfield Rd.

Nitinat Main

LAKE COWICHAN

DUNCAN

Victoria-Tsawwassen Ferry

BAMFIELD

Pachena Bay

Gordon R. Main

S. Shore Rd.

14

1

Washington
State Ferry

Old Port Renfrew Rd.

PORT RENFREW

Harris Cr. Main

17

SOOKE

VICTORIA

Anchorage: This icon is used to indicate the location of recognized all-weather anchorages. It's not comprehensive, as this guide isn't intended to replace cruising guides. These icons generally indicate the most popular locations and provincial boat havens.

Native heritage site: This icon indicates former village or camping sites, and doesn't indicate visible remnants. Respect private property rights and the sanctity of heritage items.

Launch site: This icon indicates locations suitable for launching small boats or kayaks.

Small boat launch site: This symbol indicates a launch specifically for kayaks or for launch sites suitable only for kayaks and other small rooftop-carried boats.

Lighthouse: This symbol is used for all lighthouse locations down the coast. It's not used to indicate lighted buoys or navigation beacons.

Marina: This icon shows locations where docks are provided, either privately or by the government.

Trail: The purple dotted lines indicate recognized hiking routes. They may or may not be maintained. Unmaintained routes can be overgrown. See the text for details.

Indian Reserve: The pink on maps indicates First Nations (Indian) land, as allotted in the 1880s. It's likely that within the next decade the amount of land will increase greatly as land settlements are reached. Reserve land should be treated as private property.

Parkland: Orange land indicates provincial parks or ecological reserves. Marine areas that are protected are indicated by a hatched orange line. The main maps for each chapter indicate parks with an orange hatched line only.

Private property: Grey areas on maps indicate privately owned land. Private property rights must be respected at these locations.

Municipalities: Grey areas (private property) outlined in purple indicate municipalities (towns, villages or cities).

Italicized text: Text in italics on maps indicates salt water place names.

Map numbers: The numbers in the boxes of full-page maps refer to pages with more detailed area maps.

God's Pocket

BACK IN 1995, THE NATURE OF VANCOUVER ISLAND WOULD FUNDAMENTALLY change. The reason was the creation of numerous new parks out of the Vancouver Island Land Use Plan. One of them had the fanciful name God's Pocket. It lay off the remote north coast of Vancouver Island, and it took several years before I made it up to Port Hardy to investigate what was behind this intriguing area—a jumble of islands that earned almost no mention in guidebooks anywhere, though fishermen and divers have known about them for years.

To my surprise, I found a paradise. God's Pocket, its associated islands, Goletas Channel—they're all perfectly suited to paddling. On a visit I had been out about eight days and had seen only one other paddling group, a tour based out of God's Pocket Resort. One morning I woke up at my camp alongside Bate Passage and heard a familiar sound—the exhalation of water from a blowhole. I took my morning tea and a seat alongside the passage as a pod of killer whales worked its way down the coast. One breached twice (jumped clear of the water, to land on its back) in a spectacular display, and I felt myself wondering— as I did many times over that week—why I was alone out here.

There are reasons. Port Hardy is a considerable trek up the coast. And the weather tends to be far more harsh than areas like the sunny Gulf Islands of southern Vancouver Island. But the real reason is it's undiscovered.

I've been back several times since. On the last visit I paddled with orcas in Hardy Bay, with gray whales off Mexicana Point and with sea lions and birds everywhere. I caught remarkable sunsets on picture-perfect beaches. I even had sunshine. And yet I saw no other kayakers. Novice to veteran paddlers will find reason to enjoy these shores—if they're among the few to take the time.

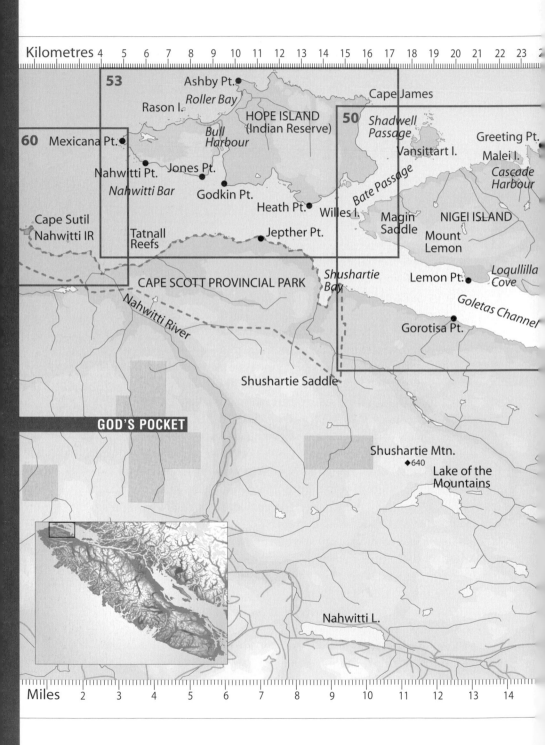

Kilometres 4 5 6 7 8 9 10 11 12 13 14 15 16 17 18 19 20 21 22 23 2

53

Ashby Pt.

Roller Bay

Rason I.

Cape James

HOPE ISLAND
(Indian Reserve)

50 *Shadwell
Passage*

*Bull
Harbour*

60 Mexicana Pt.

Vansittart I.

Greeting Pt.

Malei I.

*Cascade
Harbour*

Nahwitti Pt.

Jones Pt.

Nahwitti Bar

Godkin Pt.

Heath Pt.

Willes I.

Magin
Saddle

Bate Passage

NIGEI ISLAND

Mount
Lemon

Cape Sutil
Nahwitti IR

Tatnall
Reefs

Jepther Pt.

CAPE SCOTT PROVINCIAL PARK

*Shushartie
Bay*

Lemon Pt.

*Loqullilla
Cove*

Nahwitti River

Gorotisa Pt.

Goletas Channel

Shushartie Saddle

GOD'S POCKET

Shushartie Mtn.
◆640

Lake of the
Mountains

Nahwitti L.

Miles 2 3 4 5 6 7 8 9 10 11 12 13 14

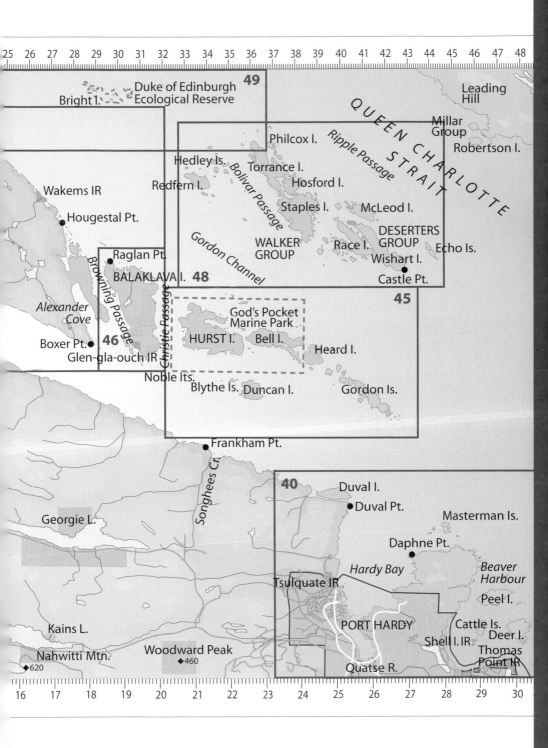

25 26 27 28 29 30 31 32 33 34 35 36 37 38 39 40 41 42 43 44 45 46 47 48

49

Duke of Edinburgh
Ecological Reserve

Bright I.

Leading
Hill

QUEEN CHARLOTTE

Millar
Group

Robertson I.

Philcox I.

Ripple Passage

STRAIT

Hedley Is.

Torrance I.

Redfern I.

Bolivar Passage

Hosford I.

Wakems IR

Hougestal Pt.

Staples I.

McLeod I.

DESERTERS
GROUP

Echo Is.

Raglan Pt.

Gordon Channel

WALKER
GROUP

Race I.

Wishart I.

Castle Pt.

BALAKLAVA I. **48**

Browning passage

45

Alexander
Cove

Christie Passage

God's Pocket
Marine Park

HURST I.   Bell I.

Heard I.

Boxer Pt.

46

Glen-gla-ouch IR

Noble Its.

Blythe Is.   Duncan I.

Gordon Is.

Frankham Pt.

Songhees Cr.

40

Duval I.

Duval Pt.

Masterman Is.

Georgie L.

Daphne Pt.

Hardy Bay

Beaver
Harbour

Tsulquate IR

Peel I.

Kains L.

PORT HARDY

Cattle Is.

Shell I. IR

Deer I.

Nahwitti Mtn.

Woodward Peak

Thomas
Point IR

◆620

◆460

Quatse R.

16 17 18 19 20 21 22 23 24 25 26 27 28 29 30

GETTING HERE

Port Hardy is located at the north end of the Island Highway that stretches from Victoria, 500 km (310 miles) away. Expect about a 7-hour drive plus breaks, or 5 hours from Nanaimo (390 km/ 240 miles). Two locations at Port Hardy provide access to the water covered in this chapter: Hardy Bay and Beaver Harbour. When the North Coast Trail (see page 86) is complete, a new access point may be added at Shushartie Bay. Until then, most trips into this region will originate from the Port Hardy area.

EXPLORING BY KAYAK

With so many options for exploring these islands, it's hard to go wrong. All the islands have their own beauty. The best places to camp are Bell Island, Balaklava Island or Cape Sutil, but the beaches near the estuaries on Vancouver Island have their own charm as well. There's aquaculture near God's Pocket Marine Park, but otherwise the shoreline is mostly pristine.

Recommended trips

- *If you have a day:* Beaver Harbour is a preferable day trip to Hardy Bay, though paddling to God's Pocket Marine Park and returning in a day is possible.

- *If you have a weekend:* Overnighting at God's Pocket Marine Park or Balaklava Island is highly recommended.

- *If you have three days:* As above, visit God's Pocket or Balaklava, but spend the extra day exploring the nearby islands. A trip to the Walker or Deserters group is an ambitious way to spend the middle day.

- *If you have five days:* You can leisurely explore the islands around God's Pocket, or, if you're more adventurous, circumnavigate Nigei Island.

- *If you have a week:* Any exploration of this length should include a visit to Cape Sutil and some exploration of the north island. You'll find the wildlife is plentiful, the beaches incredible and the seclusion complete. This trip means crossing Tatnall Reefs, but the wait for slack tide will be worth it. A visit to Bull Harbour and a walk to Roller Bay are also recommended. If you go this far northwest, consider circumnavigating Nigei Island or even Hope Island. The outer shoreline is worth seeing.

THE BASICS

Geology and ecology

The shallow waters and high currents in this area provide the two necessary ingredients for a rich marine environment: energy and nutrients. It's ideal for canopy kelp beds, which in turn provide habitat for fish and invertebrates. The main species of plant life are giant kelp, bull kelp and eelgrass. Eelgrass beds are rooted in fine sand and most commonly found in protected waters and intertidal shallows at the heads of inlets, such as Hardy Bay. Eelgrass provides

A natural bonsai-like tree ekes out a living on a rocky perch on Balaklava Island near Nolan Point.

habitat for a variety of species, including geese, swans and ducks, crab, herring and juvenile salmon. Clam beaches are common in this region, especially along the north side of Nigei and Hope islands and the Walker Group. Sea cucumber is another common resident. The giant red California sea cucumber, the largest and the only variety commercially harvested by divers, is found from the intertidal zone to about 250 m (800 feet) below the water's surface. The Deserters and Walker groups provide the complex ocean floor necessary for fish such as ling cod, halibut, rock cod and sole.

Sea mammals to be found in this region include the minke whale and Dall's and harbour porpoises. Harbour porpoises frequent water less than 20 m (65 feet) near bays, harbours and estuaries. Dall's porpoises prefer deeper ocean waters. A number of seal haulouts are located in the Deserters and Walker groups. Hardy Bay is a good place to see gray whales, while killer whales, humpback whales and northern sea lions can be found throughout the region.

Parks Canada, in its quest to protect portions of every ecosystem in Canada, is eyeing this area. The Queen Charlotte Strait proposal would protect approximately 1,500 square km (580 square miles) of this ecosystem, an area extending from Hardy Bay across the Queen Charlotte Strait to Cape Caution and Queen Charlotte Sound.

Weather

Northern Vancouver Island is among the island's wettest regions. Bull Harbour has the distinction of receiving about 2,200 mm (86 inches) of precipitation per year. Port Hardy receives slightly less at 1,800 mm (70 inches). Fog can be a factor in the summer. Winds are another concern. In Queen Charlotte Strait northwesterlies are predominant. Weather systems in the north island tend to be quite different from the rest of Vancouver Island, and it's not uncommon to find yourself in rain and cloud when the south island is enjoying sun.

Native overview

The north island is the land of the Kwakwaka'wakw, often referred to as the Kwakiutl linguistic group, one of the most diverse and interesting cultures to be found on the British Columbia coast. The cultural practices ranged from cannibalism to binding the heads of infants for shaping the foreheads of women. In this region the Nawhitti, now called the Tlatlasikwala, was the dominant group, though its fortunes would reach a low ebb following European contact. After amalgamating with the Nakumgilisala of the Cape Scott area, the last surviving members settled at Humtaspi at Bull Harbour on Hope Island. A century later government services were moved to Alert Bay, where most members live today, though some have recently moved back to Bull Harbour, giving life to an old native village.

THE SHORELINES

HARDY BAY

Dominated by the community of Port Hardy, Hardy Bay is well-used both commercially and recreationally. The bay has two marinas, three public wharves, a commercial wharf, four fuel storage facilities, significant residential development, a residential reserve, the city of Port Hardy and four log handling storage areas along its shores. This is probably the least secluded area in north Vancouver Island to explore, but the good news is it's localized. Outside the bay, development becomes increasingly rare.

The bay around the Quatse River Estuary is significant for migratory waterfowl and shorebirds, including scoters, American widgeon, green-winged teal, mallard, trumpeter swans, phalaropes and dabbling ducks. During the fall and winter months Canada geese,

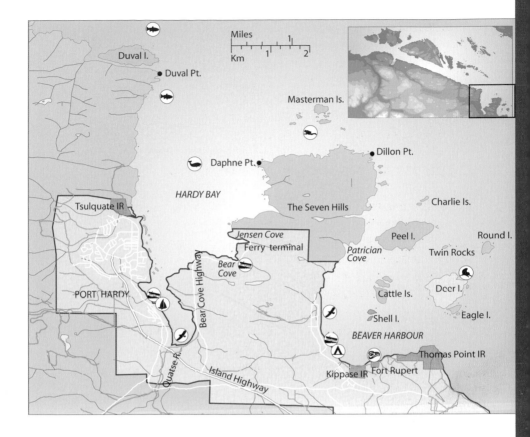

buffleheads and mergansers are also common. The Quatse River is a salmon spawning area; returning salmon attract other wildlife, such as eagles. Hardy Bay is also an excellent place to see gray whales, as they bottom feed in the bay's soft sediment. I also had the pleasure of paddling with a pod of killer whales once in the bay. Masterman Islands is a popular scuba diving destination.

Duval Island marks the western end of Hardy Bay and features a small channel next to Vancouver Island that can become impassable at lower tides. The area north of Duval Island is one of the most popular recreational fishing locations in north Vancouver Island, and a fishing resort and camp is located in the sheltered cove to the west of Duval Island.

Port Hardy

Port Hardy is a full-service community with boat launch ramps, an airport, hotels, a hospital and stores. A beach along much of the city's waterfront is backed by public green space, making for a pleasant

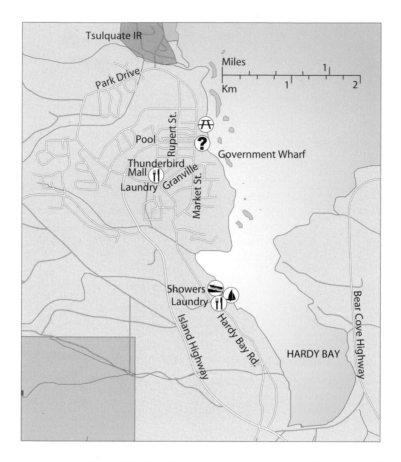

downtown. Port Hardy's deep-sea port accommodates large ships. It's the southern terminus for B.C. ferries to Prince Rupert, with connections to Bella Coola, the Queen Charlotte Islands and Alaska (call **250-386-3431** or visit **www.bcferries.com**).

Kayakers can rent equipment and/or learn how to use it here. Odyssey Kayaking offers rentals and tours (**1-888-792-3366** or **www.island.net/~odyssey**); Outdoor Experience offers rentals, tours and lessons (**1-866-902-0444** or **www.outdoorexperience.ca**); Port Hardy Adventure Centre/North Island Kayak offers tours and rentals. See **www.island.net/~trips**.

Launches: There are two main launches. Fisherman's Wharf boat launch is located just south of the downtown area. The launch is a paved boat ramp with no beach. Parking is available in a nearby parking lot for a daily fee plus a municipal fee for launching. Nearby amenities include water, the Quarterdeck Inn, IV's Pub, washrooms, showers and laundry. A free launch with free parking at Bear Cove has two boat ramps. One is older and in relative disrepair, but a rough beach is usable for loading and launching kayaks. A wooden dock is located alongside the newer ramp.

Camping: Commercial camping facilities are available near Port Hardy, but none are kayak-accessible. Campgrounds include Quatse River Regional Campground (**1-866-949-2395** or **www.quatsecamp-ground.com**); Riverside RV (**1-800-663-8744**); Wildwood Campsite (**250-949-6753**); and Sunny Sanctuary Campground (**250-949-8111** or **www.island.net/~sunnycam/**).

Place names: Port Hardy and Hardy Bay are named after Vice Admiral Sir Thomas Masterman Hardy, 1769–1939, Lord Nelson's captain in the *Victory* at the Battle of Trafalgar.

Beaver Harbour

Located east of Hardy Bay, Beaver Harbour makes for an interesting alternative to the more developed shoreline of Hardy Bay. The harbour is home to a significant number of waterfowl and migratory birds, including scaups, scoters, buffleheads, harlequin ducks, Canada geese and gulls. There are four known bald eagle nesting sites here, and Round Island is a popular seal haulout. All of Deer Island is privately owned. A trail runs along the shore of Beaver Harbour from Patrician Cove to Dillon Point.

Place names: Beaver Harbour was originally called Puerto de Guemes in 1792 by Spanish explorers Galiano and Valdes after the Viceroy of Mexico. It was later named Daedalus Harbour on an 1850 sketch, and was first labelled Beaver Harbour on an 1851 plan of the harbour. Evidently it was named after the paddle steamer *Beaver*, the first steam vessel on the northwest coast. Capts. Richards and Pender used the *Beaver* for their surveys of the British Columbia coast. She was sold in 1874 to be used as a freighter and towboat. In July 1888 she was wrecked when she ran aground at Prospect Point off Stanley Park near Vancouver Harbour.

Launches: Beaver Harbour Park, located on the northwest side of Beaver Harbour, provides free waterfront access, parking and a sheltered beach. Launching from here will allow you to bypass the busier stretches of Hardy Bay. Amenities include washrooms and picnic tables at pretty campsites lining the waterfront east of the parking area.

Fort Rupert

The fort was established in 1849 by the Hudson's Bay Company as a coal-mining centre, but it didn't last long, as better coal deposits were discovered in Nanaimo. The fort had two bastions, four large log houses, officers' quarters of 27 by 12 m (90 by 40 feet) and four cannons. A stockade surrounded the development, which protected about 100 people in 1850. By 1852, the population was 35. In 1889 the fort burned down, leaving just the chimney standing as it remains today. It's now a First Nations community. Several Kwakiutl tribes moved here to form Sa-kish, a village surrounding the fort at Fort Rupert, though archeological evidence indicates the area was first inhabited about 8,000 years ago. There are sandstone petroglyphs on the shore near the old fort site, but they may be difficult to find.

Place names: Fort Rupert was named after Prince Rupert, the Duke of Bavaria, Duke of Cumberland and Earl of Holderness.

A killer whale surfaces in Hardy Bay near the Mastermon Islands.

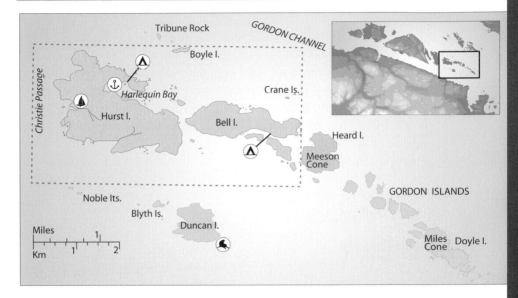

This marine park takes its whimsical name from a small cove on Hurst Island facing Christie Passage. The park comprises Hurst, Bell, Boyle and Crane islands and a multitude of other islets. It's considered one of the premier scuba diving areas on the Pacific coast. For kayakers, Harlequin Bay and the waters between the islands south of Bell Island make for wonderful protected paddling. Unfortunately, two fish farms are on the periphery of the marine park—one facing north at Duncan Island and another between Bell and Heard islands. Sea urchins are common on the southeastern end of Hurst Island around Meeson Cone and Boyle Island. These areas and the north end of Balaklava Island are considered the best sea urchin habitat in northern Vancouver Island. Commercial fishing takes place southeast of Doyle Island.

The name God's Pocket comes from an old native saying. All-weather shelters were few and far between for those making a canoe journey from the north, and those who managed to reach this area were said to be in "God's pocket."

A Sasquatch-like creature is said to live on the south side of Hurst Island. This entire group of islands is thought to be haunted.

God's Pocket Resort is located on the west side of Hurst Island. The resort predated the marine park. It offers cabins and is the base for a kayak tour company during early summer and a diving tour operation in later summer. It has a rustic and friendly atmosphere. Call **1-888-534-8322** or visit **www.godspocket.com**.

Camping: There are two unofficial but established wilderness campsites on Bell and Hurst islands. On the south side of Bell Island a site is set on a small headland near two outlying islands. Access is via a small crushed-shell beach. Campsites are on a level area up a fairly steep shell midden. It's a very pretty site. The Hurst Island site is in a mossy forest clearing above a steep embankment on the north side of Harlequin Bay. Access is by a crushed-shell beach. Many sites on the mossy embankment face a popular anchorage (which means less privacy), and the embankment is considerably steeper and much higher than at Bell Island. An alternative with a far wider selection is at south Balaklava Island to the west.

Gordon Islands

Located southeast of God's Pocket Marine Park and just 4 km (2.5 miles) across Goletas Channel from the Vancouver Island shore, the Gordon Islands are an interesting array of small islands and reefs dominated by Miles Cone on Doyle Island. This dominant geographic feature is known in the Kwakwaka'wakw tongue as Kel-skil-tim or 'high head.' The name refers to the Koskimo practice of binding the heads of women to create tall foreheads.

All the islands have steep, rocky shorelines and are inaccessible to casual visitors. Breeding sites for glaucous-winged gulls can be found along portions of these islands. Heard Island is privately owned and logged. There's commercial groundfishing on the southeast of Doyle Island, and fish farms are located near Doyle Island and at Heard Island next to Bell Island.

Place names: The Gordon Islands are named after Commander George Thomas Gordon, who died in 1887. His ship, the six-gun *Cormorant*, was the first steam naval vessel at Fort Victoria from 1846 to 1850.

Balaklava Island

Though not part of God's Pocket Marine Park, Balaklava is a recreational adjunct to the park, with many of the most popular camping sites and a plethora of exploration opportunities. Some areas have been logged, but much old growth remains, especially near the south end. The most popular diving area here is in Browning Passage, once rated by Jacques Cousteau as one of the best cold water diving destinations in the world.

Over a dozen eagle nests can be found along Balaklava, and sea urchins are common off the island's north end. Much of the centre of the island, particularly on the eastern shore, is privately owned, though currently undeveloped. A selection of small islands, islets and reefs lies off the southwestern shore of Balaklava Island near Nolan Point. The islands shelter numerous pocket coves and beaches along the south shore of Balaklava, which provide access to both the campsites here and the old-growth forests behind them.

The Scarlett Point Lighthouse began operating on April 12, 1905. A drying mud cove is located just south of Scarlett Point.

Caution: Currents can run as high as three knots in Christie Passage and Browning Passage. This can create far-reaching unstable waters and rips into Goletas Channel or Gordon Channel. Novice paddlers are advised to pass between islands at or near slack tide.

God's Pocket Marine Park: God's Pocket Marine Park was born out of the Vancouver Island Land Use Plan in 1995, which dramatically increased the number of protected park areas on Vancouver Island. God's Pocket is an undeveloped park, with no official amenities or trails. Harlequin Bay on Hurst Island is a popular anchorage with diving, boating and wildlife viewing. The park remains one of Vancouver Island's best-kept secrets. Bald eagles, whales, porpoises and a variety of seabirds are among the popular wildlife attractions.

The campsite on Bell Island faces a quiet cove.

Place names: Scarlett Point was named after Sir James York Scarlett, born in 1799 and a general in the British Army. He led a cavalry charge at Balaklava in the Crimean War, a fact leading to the island's name.

Camping: A wilderness campsite on Balaklava Island is midway along Browning Passage on a grassy clearing above a pleasant beach. Camping is possible anywhere but privacy is correspondingly limited. The land was left vacant for recreational use after it was logged many years ago. Remarkably, it has remained clear. The other site is at Nolan Point. To the west of the point are many pocket coves with gravel beaches. Above the beach are many level, mossy sites separated by trees. The choices are varied and extensive enough to allow considerable privacy. It pays to walk the waterfront from Nolan Point toward the reserve land, as some exceptionally pretty spots may be found that aren't immediately evident.

DESERTERS AND WALKER GROUPS

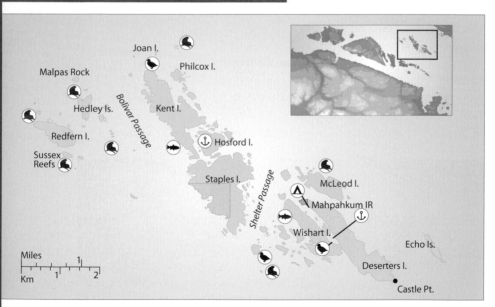

Located across a 4-km (2.5-mile) stretch of open water from God's Pocket Marine Park, both groups offer a maze of islands, waterways and reefs to explore. The islands have high seabird, sea lion and seal populations and are being considered for marine park status. They're most popular among recreational users for their safe anchorages and for scuba diving. Most of the shoreline is rocky, steep and overgrown, so the islands themselves have limited recreational value. The exceptions are the channel between Deserters and Wishart islands and the south cove of Kent Island, which have sand/mud beaches at lower tides. A lack of established camping areas means the islands are best enjoyed as a day trip from God's Pocket Marine Park.

Orcas, humpback whales and gray whales can be found here. Dall's and harbour porpoises also inhabit the area. The waters are used for salmon trolling, gillnetting, seine fishing, plus hook and line and longline ground fisheries.

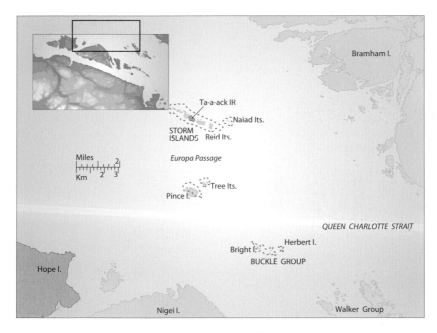

Duke of Edinburgh Ecological Reserve: The Duke of Edinburgh Ecological Reserve is composed of six islands grouped in three clusters, plus 535 hectares (1,320 acres) of marine environment. It's not a likely location to venture by kayak or even boat due to its isolation. The reserve was established in 1988 to protect the largest seabird nesting colony in Queen Charlotte Strait and the second-largest seabird nesting site on the west coast of Canada (the Scott Islands off the northern tip of Vancouver Island is the largest). Here you'll find the largest colony of rhinoceros auklets in Canada and the largest colonies of Leach's storm-petrels and fork-tailed storm-petrels in B.C. Some 161,600 pairs of rhinoceros auklets nest on Pine and Storm islands—about one-quarter of the global population. There are also about 276,000 pairs of Leach's storm petrels—about 3 percent of the global population but half the western Canadian population. Expect to see Cassin's auklets, black oystercatchers, pigeon guillemots, glaucous-winged gulls and bald eagles. The waters around these islands are also important for migrating red-necked phalaropes. In July and August thousands feed at the tide lines. This is also an important area for Dall's porpoises and Pacific white-sided dolphins. A permit is required to land here.

Camping: Beaches exist on Wishart Island and at Kent Island near the anchorages, but little of these beaches remains above the water at high tide. At Deserters Island a cabin has been built near shore facing a nice beach. It's located in the protected waters facing Wishart Island. The cabin is clean and dry and user-maintained. A logbook chronicles numerous visits over the years.

NIGEI ISLAND

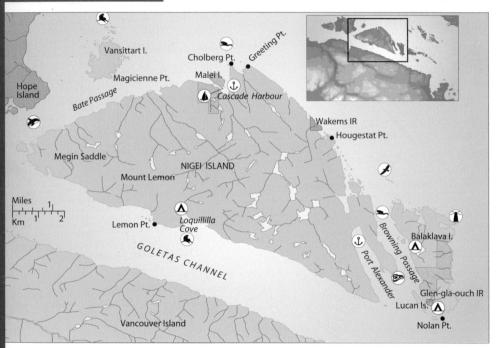

Nigei Island isn't a park but it's not likely to be commercially developed soon. Only a small area of the island has suitable timber for logging, and that's mostly immature (though some recent logging has taken place around Megin Saddle). The result is pleasant paddling in a relatively pristine and undeveloped setting. Massive cliffs face Goletas Channel, while the outer island features interesting reef-strewn waters and a number of coves.

Caution: Currents are a factor all around Nigei Island, and can run as high as 3 knots in Browning Passage and up to 5 knots in Bate Passage. The interesting thing about Bate Passage is that it runs in the opposite direction of Goletas Channel, so you're likely to find the tide running in a favourable direction somewhere no matter the time of day.

Place names: Nigei is the hereditary name for the principal chief of the Tlatlasikwala First Nation. The island was named Galiano Island up to 1900, earning that name from the explorers Galiano and Valdes in 1792. It was changed by the Geographic Board of Canada in 1900 to avoid confusion with the other Galiano Island in the Strait of Georgia.

Port Alexander
This popular anchorage is deep and sheltered with a pleasant beach at the head of the inlet. One of the old fortified villages of the Tlatlasikwala was located on the point at the east entrance to Port Alexander. There was another village on the islet in the centre of the harbour and several houses under the overhanging cliff on the east side of the harbour's head.

Cascade Harbour
Malei Island shelters Cascade Harbour, which is often used as an anchorage. The southern shore of the harbour and Malei Island are privately owned and partially developed. The Malei Island Resort has a lodge and water taxi, and offers scuba diving, fishing, kayaking and wildlife viewing. There's a telephone here. Call **250-949-8006** or email **malei@mail.north.island.net**.

Loquillilla Cove
The cove is a pleasant change in the otherwise unbroken shoreline along Goletas Channel. At the head of the cove is a nice beach. Numerous islets flank the cove's outside edge.

Camping: The beach at the head of Loquillilla Cove has no established campsites and no access to the forest behind, limiting camping to the beach above the high tide line. This site may lack the charm of Balaklava Island and God's Pocket Marine Park, but it's worth knowing about in the event travel along Goletas Channel turns sour.

Vansittart Island
Located north of Nigei Island, Vansittart is a gem. Numerous reefs, islets and coves surround it, and some old-growth forest and several nice beaches can be found on the island. Groundfish are commerically fished northeast of Vansittart Island.

Camping: There are no established campsites here yet, but the potential exists. Two beaches, one on the southeast corner of the island and

Jepther Point offers magnificent views along Goletas channel toward Nigei Island.

another to the northeast, offer access to grassy areas. The latter beach is set within an old-growth forest with numerous monster-sized trees. Unfortunately, the ground isn't particularly flat, as the grass grows in large tufts. It will take time for a suitable camp to evolve. This island would make a beautiful marine park one day.

Place names: Vansittart Island is named after Capt. Nicholas Vansittart whose frigate *Magicienne* served in the Baltic harassing the Russian coast during the Russian War of 1854–55.

HOPE ISLAND

This huge island is most popular for recreational boaters visiting Bull Harbour on trips around Vancouver Island. The entire island is a Tlatlasikwala reserve. For kayakers, Hope Island offers sandy beaches, dramatic shorelines and the challenge of paddling exposed water. There are numerous seal and sea lion haulouts. Ashby Point, a remote, wind-beaten spot located on the north end of Hope Island, is a haulout for the endangered northern sea lion.

The south side of Hope Island facing Vancouver Island has significant populations of waterfowl and marine birds, including phalaropes, rhinoceros auklets, marbled murrelets, gulls, murres, scoters and Pacific loons. Geoduck beds are found on the northeast side of Hope Island. Herring concentrate in outer Bull Harbour. A

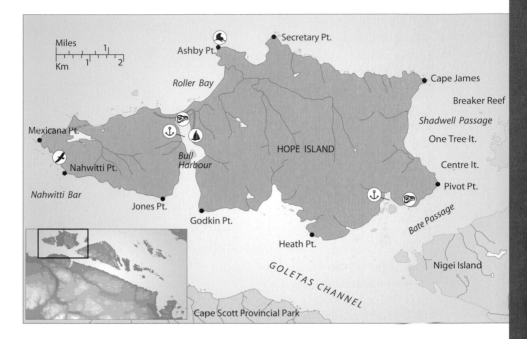

survey has identified 91 kelp beds around Hope Island covering 895 hectares (2,212 acres). Cape James, meanwhile, is a good place to find the endangered tiny white black-spotted chiton *Hanleyella oldroydi*. The waters around Hope Island are used for commercial salmon gillnet, seine, hook and line and longline fisheries.

South of Cape James facing Vansittart Island is a large, relatively sheltered and very pretty sand and gravel beach that extends most of the way to Pivot Point. Note that, as inviting as it is for camping, it's reserve land.

Hope Island, or Xwamdasbe, is one of the Tlatlasikwala First Nation's six reserves. Formerly the Nawhitti band, the name was changed in 1985. The Tlatlasikwala in the past shared the Cape Scott region with two other groups, the Yutlinuk and Nakumgilisala.

Place Names: Hope Island is named after Vice Admiral Sir James Hope, the commander of the North America and West Indies station from 1864 to 1867. His most famous action was a bungled attempt to clear the Peiho in China where he lost three boats and 11 others were severely damaged.

Bull Harbour

The harbour is a fitting end to an exploration of the islands north of Port Hardy. A government dock is the focus of waterfront activity. A trail leads from the dock to Roller Bay. Be sure to watch for interesting rock formations at the west side of the entrance to Bull Harbour and the rock pillar on the island inside the harbour.

Bull Harbour is the site of Humtaspi, a historic native village established in 1850 after the destruction of the village at Cape Sutil. Recent residential development has seen life return to the island, and the current population is estimated at about 40. In the 1880s Ned Frigon opened a

A rock pillar resembles a noble native at the entrance to Bull Harbour.

fur-trading post here to service local natives and passing sealing and whaling ships. Frigon was a French-Canadian who came to the coast and married a native known as Long-headed Lucy. In 1889 he operated a store, hotel and saloon near the village of Quatsino in Koprino Harbour. Islands in Quatsino Sound's Neroutsos Inlet near Port Alice bear his name.

Sir George Simpson mentions his visit to the harbour and the sea lions here in his 1841 book *Journey Round the World, Vol. I.* Bull Harbour was named after the sea lion bulls.

Kalect Island

On the southeast side of Hope Island, Kalect helps protect a cove popular as an anchorage. A sand and gravel beach to the east is topped by a grassy ridge. Although it's an inviting camping spot, this is reserve land. The Kwakiutl village Mel'-oopa once sat atop the grass ridge. Nearly all the residents were killed in a raid by the Bella-Bella.

Nolan Point offers views clear along the south end of God's Pocket Marine Park.

GOLETAS CHANNEL

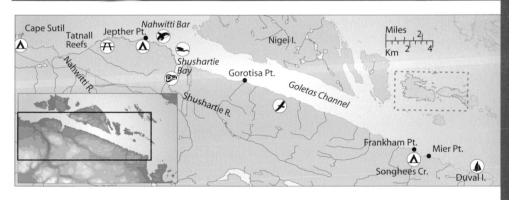

Goletas Channel runs 37 km (23 miles) between Duval Point and the far end of Hope Island, and encompasses a number of major watersheds on Vancouver Island as well as numerous cobble beaches. Low, rocky shoreline characterizes most of the Vancouver Island shore along Goletas Channel. The westernmost portion is protected as the recent Nahwitti-Shushartie addition to Cape Scott Provincial Park. Currents are strong in the channel and crossings at its western terminus can be difficult. Winds can funnel down the steep shorelines of Goletas Channel. Conditions may be turbulent where Goletas meets Christie, Browning and, in particular, Bates passages.

Pocket beaches can be found on the headlands around Cape Sutil.

Place names: Galiano and Valdes sailed through here during their exploration of Vancouver Island in 1792 in the schooners (called "goletas") *Sutil* and *Mexicana*. The entrance to the channel is named after both vessels—Mexicana Point on Hope Island and Cape Sutil on Vancouver Island.

Songhees Creek

This creek is bordered by two scenic cobble beaches. It's the first major respite west of Hardy Bay along an otherwise unbroken rock shoreline.

Camping: Casual wilderness camping is possible on the beach at Songhees Creek above the high tide line. Good pebble beaches are located on both sides of the creek, but the best and largest beach is to the west. Flat stretches of sand can be found above the high tide line, with the best near the headland. Another option closer to Duval Island is a small east-facing beach tucked into a tiny cove. It offers good protection from westerly gales.

Shushartie Bay

This bay is set within the Cape Scott Provincial Park Nahwitti-Shushartie Addition boundaries. The head of the bay is dominated by an expansive drying gravel and mud estuary. Ruins of docks can be found on both sides of the bay, as well as other relics of past development. Some work is more recent, such as a road bulldozed to the shoreline just east of the bay. Nonetheless, the Shushartie valley bottom has had minimal logging and contains a substantial old-growth spruce forest. The lower Shushartie River is significant fish habitat, plus a deer and elk wintering range. It also provides coastal waterfowl habitat.

As well as two fish farm licences, Shushartie Bay will likely become a site where local First Nations harvest marine plants for use in fertilizer and food products. There's log handling and storage in Shushartie Bay and ships often anchor here as well. Much of the land around Sushartie Bay was recently owned by Weyerhaeuser, and there were two forest licences to Richmond Plywood and Interfor. Those interests were recently purchased for parkland in 2004. Note that the bay isn't suited for camping, and seemingly inviting areas may be below the high tide line. This will likely change as the North Coast Trail is constructed (see page 86). Expect vehicle access, a trail-head and a campground in close proximity to Shushartie Bay in the near future.

The native village Khatis, located at the head of Shushartie Bay, was valued for its clam and crab beach. By 1800 Shushartie Bay had grown to be the primary trading centre for sea otters on Vancouver Island. Sea otters were eliminated on the coast by 1830, and by 1836 Shushartie Bay had drifted into insignificance. In the late 1800s, the bay became a landing point for Cape Scott settlers, primarily because it was one of the few safe harbours along this stretch of coast, and a wharf, post office, hotel, store and salmon cannery were located here. Today the only remnant of the community is the wharf. Near the eastern shore of the bay are two graves: one for a man named Edward who died on a whale hunt on March 8, 1844; the other for John Thompson who died May 8, 1844, of an unknown cause.

Place names: Shushartie Bay is a variation on the Kwakiutl name Zu-zada, meaning 'a place possessing cockles.' Galiano first named it Puerto Gorostiso in 1792.

Jepther Point

Jepther Point is unique along this stretch of Vancouver Island for its expansive pebble beach that rounds both sides of the point. It's also one of very few known whale rubbing beaches on Vancouver Island. These rare beaches have pebbles that are attractive to orcas; the whales come alongside the shore and rub themselves on the pebbles. A similar beach at Robson Bight Ecological Reserve, farther south on Vancouver Island, is now an ecological reserve where public access is

Daylight fades on Goletas Channel. This view is from Jepther Point looking over Nahwitti Bar toward Mexicana Point.

banned. No ban yet exists at Jepther Point. Note that seeing killer whales using the beach will be the exception, not the rule. This area is also remarkable bald eagle habitat: 25 occupied nests are located between Nissen Bight (see page 70) and Shushartie Bay.

Nahwitti Bar

Located between Tatnall Reefs and Nahwitti Point just west of Bull Harbour, this submerged sandbar rises to about 10 m (33 feet) below sea level. Where the deep water of Queen Charlotte Strait meets this shallow ledge is particularly troublesome given the strong tidal currents through Goletas Channel. When the tidal current opposes swells, which have thousands of miles to build up in Queen Charlotte Sound, the water can literally back up. The current can run as high as 5 knots and if ebb tide meets northwest winds, the result can be breaking waves of over 2 m (7 feet) in height. These waters can be extremely dangerous. Cross at or near slack tide.

Gold was mined briefly at Dakota Creek and at Gold Beach, opposite Nahwitti Bar. Skinner Creek, which runs into the ocean at the midpoint of Tatnall Reefs, is one of the few remaining places to see the Dominion Government Telegraph line built across the north island in the late 1800s. The remains are near an old homestead on a ridge to the west of the creek. The other place to see the remnants of the line is at the Stranby River.

Tatnall Reefs

Rather than crossing Nahwitti Bar, most kayakers are likely to attempt Tatnall Reefs, which run alongside Vancouver Island. Water can be as shallow as 3 m (10 feet) over portions of the reef. Fortunately, the depth is greater closer to shore, so it's possible to hug the coast and miss the worst of the reefs. Strong currents back up as they cross the reefs, creating choppy, confused waters. Cross at or near slack tide. To wait out the tide, just east of the reefs are several pocket cobble beaches well protected from surf and wind by neighbouring rocks. The Nahwitti River estuary offers shelter on the west side. Several beaches fronting Tatnall Reefs look inviting but are exposed to moderate to high surf.

Nahwitti River

Just west of Tatnall Reefs is Nahwitti River. The estuary can be navigated for a short distance. Intensive logging and booming in the early 1990s caused slides and floods. The result is that the lower river's holding pools have been eliminated and the original course of the river altered. The lower river now meanders over a broad flood plain.

A wagon route was meant to link Cape Scott through the Nahwitti to Shushartie Bay as a transportation corridor for the Cape Scott settlement. It was never completed. Instead, a narrow track was built along an existing telegraph route as far as the Stranby River. It was later extended to Fisherman Bay, allowing goods to be transported to the Cape Scott settlement.

A pleasant beach just east of Tatnall Reefs provides an ideal resting spot for anyone waiting for slack tide.

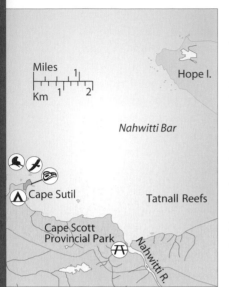

Cape Sutil

Cape Sutil, the most northerly point on Vancouver Island, is a hint (if you're approaching from Port Hardy) of the stunning beauty in store along northern Vancouver Island. Cape Sutil is shaped like a hook and protects a crescent of white sand beach beautiful enough to be the envy of most tropical resorts. The cape itself is a rock bluff surrounded by reefs popular with bald eagles and other bird life. The north end of the cape is an unoccupied reserve. A petroglyph located on the rocks at Cape Sutil is evidence of the long history of human occupation here.

During the first half of the 19th century, the fortified village of Nahwitti occupied the east side of Cape Sutil. Its demise was spawned by the June 1850 desertion of three sailors from the Hudson's Bay Company ship *Norman Morrison*. Within days all three deserters had been killed, possibly in the mistaken belief by the Nawhitti that they were runaway slaves. Either way, the British navy retaliated by sending the corvette *Daedalus* in October to find the murderers. In their attempt to capture the culprits the village was burned. The following summer HMS *Daphne* was sent to attack the same village, which had since been rebuilt. Five Englishmen and six Nawhitti were reportedly killed before the Nawhitti presented the English with the bodies of three men they claimed to be the murderers, ending the conflict. In 1879 the cape was designated Indian Reserve, which has since remained uninhabited as the residents moved to Bull Harbour after the attack.

Camping: Cape Sutil shelters one of the prettiest and least visited beaches on Vancouver Island. The beach is fine white sand with minimal to moderate surf. The lowest surf is to the north near the cape. Camping is possible along an almost unlimited sandy stretch above the high tide line.

Place Names: The cape was named Cape Sutil on the charts of Galiano and Valdes in 1792 after their exploring schooner *Sutil* (meaning "subtle"). Capt. Vancouver referred to *Sutil* as "the most ill calculated and unfit vessel that could be imagined for such an

The headland at Cape Sutil was once a fortified native village site.

expedition." The cape was renamed Cape Commerell in 1860 when it was surveyed by Capt. Richards, but the original Spanish name was restored by the Geographic Board of Canada in 1906. The original name, Nahwitti (which has a variety of spellings including Nawitti and Newitty) was the name of a Kwakiutl chief. By the mid-1800s, the word Nahwitti had been expanded to describe the three tribes and their village.

One of the oddest features of Cape Scott Provincial Park is the unique desert tombolo, complete with sand dunes and its own peculiar ecosystem.

Cape Scott

I HAD NO IDEA WHAT TO EXPECT THE FIRST TIME I VISITED THE NORTH shore of Vancouver Island. I pictured a barren, dangerous stretch of ocean with reefs, rocky shorelines and little respite from the harsh weather. The reefs and rocky headlands were there, of course, but when I set foot on Shuttleworth Bight it was hard to believe I was the only person on such a grand beach. Of course, few others could even hope to get here. With no road access or trails, only kayaks or small boats could visit.

I've made the trip back many times since, the last in 2004. There's a sense of accomplishment in rounding Cape Sutil and leaving civilization behind. The swell breaking on reefs can be intimidating, but the stretches of open water between the bights are fairly short. The rewards are seclusion, unbelievable wildlife and unforgettable scenery. If you make it as far as Nels Bight, you can also hike to intriguing pioneer remnants and to the lighthouse at Cape Scott.

There can be a downside. I've spent days huddled in a tent waiting out storms at Guise Bay and Lowrie Bay. I've been pummelled by waves and weather at Cape Scott and Cape Russell. This can be a dangerous and forbidding stretch, but it's certainly nothing like the image I conjured up. It may be that very intimidating mystique keeps others away. Personally, I won't complain.

GETTING HERE

Road entries are few and far between on the north coast. None exist within the Cape Scott Park boundaries, though that will likely change when the North Coast Trail is complete (see page 86). Until that time, explorers have really only a few access points to the

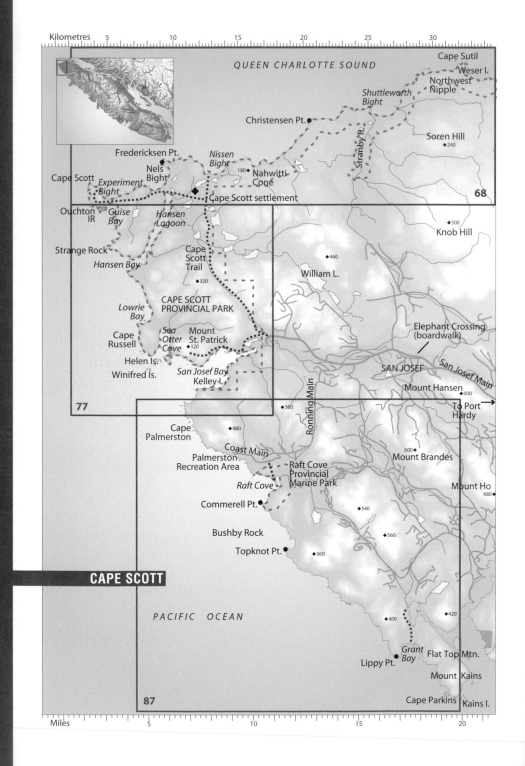

Kilometres

QUEEN CHARLOTTE SOUND

Cape Sutil
Weser I.
Northwest Nipple
Shuttleworth Bight
Christensen Pt.
Stranby R.
Soren Hill
◆240

Fredericksen Pt.
Nissen Bight
Nels Bight
Cape Scott
Experiment Bight
180◆ Nahwitti Cone
Cape Scott settlement

68

Ouchton IR
Guise Bay
Hansen Lagoon
Knob Hill
◆500

Strange Rock
Cape Scott Trail
William L.
◆460

Hansen Bay
◆320

Lowrie Bay
CAPE SCOTT PROVINCIAL PARK
Elephant Crossing (boardwalk)

Cape Russell
Sea Otter Cove
Mount St. Patrick
◆320
SAN JOSEF
San Josef Main

Helen Is.
San Josef Bay
Mount Hansen
◆600

Winifred Is.
Kelley I.
To Port Hardy

77
◆360
Ronning Main

Cape Palmerston
◆480
Mount Brandes
600◆

Coast Main
Palmerston Recreation Area
Raft Cove Provincial Marine Park
Mount Ho
680◆

Raft Cove
Commerell Pt.
◆540

Bushby Rock
◆560

Topknot Pt.
◆360

PACIFIC OCEAN
◆400
◆420

Grant Bay
Flat Top Mtn.
Lippy Pt.
Mount Kains

87
Cape Parkins
Kains I.

Miles

CAPE SCOTT

water—Port Hardy (see chapter 1), San Josef Bay on the island's west coast or Quatsino Sound (see chapter 3). To launch at San Josef Bay, turn left onto the gravel San Josef Road as you enter Port Hardy; another hour or so will get you to the two launch options at San Josef. San Josef Road is quite well marked and in good shape. Cape Palmerston Recreation Site is also accessible by vehicle. To get there, take San Josef Road west from Port Hardy and turn south on the Ronning Main. Signs will point the way to Raft Cove. To get to Cape Palmerston, continue past the Raft Cove parking area by staying on the Ronning Main. After a few miles you'll have an option of a left-hand turn onto Coast Main. Coast Main will lead to the recreation area. Veteran paddlers might want to try a launch from Cape Palmerston, though it's not recommended.

EXPLORING BY KAYAK

The waters around Cape Scott attract only a handful of kayakers each year. Getting here can be the difficult part. The most remote sections involve multi-day expeditions through exposed waters, with Cape Scott potentially the most dangerous. Any trip to the outer waters should build in an allowance for foul weather days.

Recommended trips

- *If you have a day:* San Josef Bay is the only practical day trip, as there are so few launch sites in this region. Kayaking here will expose you to everything—beautiful beaches, sea caves, rugged shorelines and even the windswept Winnifred Islands, if you choose to venture that far.

- *If you have a weekend:* Since San Josef Bay is the only realistic launch site for this stretch of coast, your options are limited. Consider paddling to Lowrie Bay or even Guise Bay the first day and returning the next, though the possibility of foul weather could make for an unplanned long weekend. Rounding Cape Russell, a stretch of open water you must cross to get to these points, can be difficult. Otherwise, overnighting on the beach at San Josef Bay would not be unpleasant.

- *If you have three days:* Paddle to Guise Bay. On the second day either hike the trails of Cape Scott Provincial Park to see the historic attractions or nose around the cape by paddle (weather and conditions permitting).

- *If you have five days:* The extra time allows for many more options. You can launch from Hardy Bay and jump to Jepther Point (see chapter 1), Cape Sutil and Shuttleworth Bight and then return by the same route. This trip is highly recommended, though the time frame is short. This would bring you to the most remote coast on Vancouver Island. The other option is a launch from San Josef Bay and a trip around Cape Scott. A possible itinerary would be Guise Bay, Nissen Bight, Shuttleworth Bight and back, with an allowance for foul weather.

- *If you have a week:* Launch from either Hardy Bay or San Josef Bay and work your way toward (or around) Cape Scott as time, weather and inclination allow. There are various secluded beaches to stay on either way. Once either at Guise Bay or Nels Bight you can safely explore by foot, if you desire, taking in the main attractions of the Cape Scott Trail. Several days lolling on perfect beaches is highly recommended.

- *The ideal trip:* Launch from Port Hardy and end the trip at San Josef Bay or even Winter Harbour in Quatsino Sound. Transportation is the only hurdle, but the effort will be worth it. You'll have the pleasure of rounding the whole north coast including Cape Scott, passing all the most magnificent beaches, viewing the most secluded stretches of shore and seeing wildlife at its best. A short itinerary could be Port Hardy, Jepther Point, Cape Sutil, Nissen Bight, Guise Bay and San Josef Bay. To extend the trip, consider adding Raft Cove, then Winter Harbour. Building in foul weather days is a must.

A rock outcropping reduces surf on the west side of Nissen Bight.

THE BASICS

Geology and ecology

The north island is a mix of sedimentary and volcanic rock and is geologically more similar to the Queen Charlotte Islands than Vancouver Island. Recently in geological terms (during the Pleistocene epoch, as little as 11,000 years ago), glacial ice moved south and southwest across the Queen Charlotte Strait, scouring the Cape Scott area. Remnants of that glacial wash form upland pockets among otherwise boggy lowlands. An interesting geological anomaly is a tombolo with sand dunes connecting Cape Scott to Vancouver Island, plus blowholes, black gravel beaches and sea stacks.

Sitka spruce is the most common tree cover. Mammal residents include killer whales, gray whales, sea lions, seals, harbour porpoises, gray wolves, cougars, beaver, river otters, minks, raccoons, Roosevelt elk and black bears.

Weather

Cape Scott is situated in the wettest climate of Vancouver Island, with annual precipitation reaching as high as 5,000 mm (200 inches). The prevailing summer wind is northwesterly, exposing most of the north-facing beaches to the weather. Temperatures rarely reach into the 20's C (70's F); the average temperate in August is 16°C (60°F). July and August are the driest months, with about 100 mm (4 inches) of rain each month (compared to 355 mm/14 inches in November). Wind is another common feature; hurricane-force winds as high as 190 km/h (120 mph) have been recorded.

Native overview

North Vancouver Island is the home of the Kwakiutl linguistic group, referred to today as the Kwakwaka'wakw. One band, the Tlatlasikwala, formerly known as the Nahwitti, lived along the coast from Shushartie Bay to Cape Scott, leaving 12 identified archaeological sites including burial grounds, middens, fish trap remnants, petroglyphs and the disappearing remains of a fortified village. Historic village sites were located at Hansen Bay, Fisherman Bay, Hanna Point, the mouth of San Josef Creek, Shuttleworth Bight and Shushartie Bay. The main village site was at Ouchton. The story of a fortified village at Cape Sutil is described in chapter 1 (see page 60).

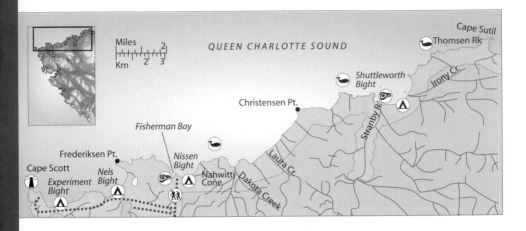

THE SHORELINES

THE NORTH COAST

The north coast has some of the longest beaches on Vancouver Island, separated by impenetrable rocky headlands, and the waters are often pocked by rocky reefs. While the terrain is varied, you won't find mountains; most of the park is low rolling hills under 300 m (1,000 feet).

Shuttleworth Bight

The bight, a 180-degree arc of beach broken only by the Stranby River, isn't accessible by foot. Of Cape Scott Provincial Park's five major river systems, the Stranby River is the most intact. Although it has been logged, old-growth timber can still be found at the bottom of the valley, particularly to the east toward Irony Creek. There's also an unaltered spruce flood plain ecosystem in the lower watershed. Roosevelt elk use the Stranby River valley.

Shuttleworth Bight was home to an old village site called Go'saa, and was used as a main fishing station. In the late 1800s the Dominion Government Telegraph built a telegraph network through the area. Portions of the line can still be seen near the Stranby River and near an old homestead on a ridge top just west of Skinner Creek. In the early 1900s, five families settled near Cache Creek, now called the Stranby River. The Shuttleworths were early settlers. By 1915 a store, church, post office and one-room school were located at the river's mouth. The harsh climate, poor transportation routes and limited natural resources resulted in most settlers abandoning the area by the 1920s.

Until 2004, the mouth of the river was privately owned and a house is located there. That and two large holdings by Shuttleworth Bight Holdings Company Ltd., along the west and east sides of the bight, are now parkland.

East of the bight toward Cape Sutil is a less inviting shoreline of rocky headlands and reefs, with a few pocket beaches. Numerous reefs dot this area, making for hazardous travel near the shore when there's swell.

Christensen Point

East toward Shuttleworth Bight, there are numerous reefs, while to the west of the point is a long, exposed beach. Black bear trails line the shore between Laura Creek and Christensen Point. Bears will often forage along the beaches for food. The north coast forest is prone to blowdown due to high winds, lack of shelter and wet soil. The area between Laura Creek and Christensen Point bears evidence of that, but this same stretch is also home to Sitka and hemlock that have survived over 250 years. The trees, measuring as high as 37 m (120 feet), can be found between Laura Creek and the area 2 km (1.2 miles) east of Christensen Point.

Travel notes: During a summer trip around the outer coast I had up-close experiences with about 48 whales. Most were seen in just four areas, one of which was between Cape Sutil and Nissen Bight. The other areas were Brooks Peninsula, Flores Island in Clayoquot Sound and along the coast of Pacific Rim National Park.

Gray whales can regularly be seen feeding on the ocean floor between Cape Sutil and Cape Scott.

Nissen Bight

The fine, white sand beach here is about 1.6 km long (a mile). It's accessible by foot via the Cape Scott Trail and is a popular camping destination for hikers. A North Coast Trail is in the works that will link Nissen Bight with Shushartie Bay, completing a trail from one side of the coast to the other (see page 86). The beach at Nissen Bight is exposed to the surf that rolls in from Queen Charlotte Sound. The best protection is to the west behind a headland shared with Fisherman Bay.

In the Kwakwaka'wakw tongue, Nissen Bight was known as Kechegwis, which means 'wood drifted on beach.'

Camping: All of Nissen Bight is open to camping. Many wind baffles have been constructed using driftwood. Water is available from a river east of the beach, while a pit toilet and bear cache are to the west.

Fisherman Bay

This bay is separated from Nissen Bight by a rocky headland with a steep gravel beach. A barge used as a breakwater washed ashore in 1946 and broke apart on the beach. The remains can still be seen. Fisherman Bay can be explored by crossing the headland from Nissen Bight or via a short path from the trail leading to Nissen Bight.

Sand dunes line the neck between Guise Bay and Experiment Bight.

Fisherman Bay was the site of an early Nakumgilisala village. The native name, Beka, means 'meeting of the spirits.' Ships used Fisherman Bay as the primary supply spot for the Cape Scott colony. A store and post office were built here in the late 1800s. Unfortunately, high winds meant a dock couldn't be built, so goods had to be brought ashore by skiff. A sawmill was moved piece by piece the 5 km (3 miles) from the bay to Hansen Lagoon.

Nels Bight

Nels Bight is a popular destination for hikers completing the Cape Scott Trail. At 2.5 km (1.5 miles), it's among the longest beaches on Vancouver Island. A blowhole can be found at Frederiksen Point on the northeast side of Nels Bight. The ocean swell funnels into an opening and shoots up through the blowhole in a display similar to a geyser. In Kwakwaka'wakw the name for Nels Bight is Tsewunchas, meaning 'winter place.'

Experiment Bight

Experiment Bight is accessible by foot from the Cape Scott Trail, though it's rarely visited. A wide sand neck separates Experiment Bight from Guise Bay to the south. This sand neck, or "blow out," and its dunes are remarkable for a variety of reasons. Very few plants can survive in the harsh dune environment, but this neck has developed its own ecosystem with plant species introduced by Danish settlers hoping to stabilize the sand.

Experiment Bight was previously home to a native fishing village called Gwegwakawalis, meaning 'whales on the beach.' Some shells and bones on the beach are from the village's midden. A large depression resembling a footprint found its way into Kwakwaka'wakw mythology. It's said to be the footprint of Kanekelac, who could step from Cape Scott to Triangle Island in a single bound.

Camping: Of the four main beaches accessible by the Cape Scott Trail, Experiment Bight is the least used by hikers. It's off the main trail and there's no fresh water. The best shelter is on the west side. It's ideal for kayakers overnighting before rounding Cape Scott.

Place names: Experiment Bight is named after the vessel *Experiment*. Both it and *Captain Cook* were piloted by James Stuart Strange of the East India Trading Company. *Experiment* arrived in Nootka Sound in 1786.

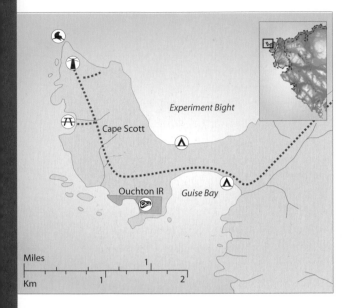

Cape Scott Provincial Park: Cape Scott became a provincial park in 1973, protecting 15,070 hectares (37,240 acres) along the north-westernmost section of Vancouver Island. Another 6,779-hectare (16,750-acre) section, known as the Nahwitti-Shushartie Addition, a stretch of coast from Dakota Creek to Shushartie Bay, was added in July 1995. Another portion was added in 2004.

CAPE SCOTT

Known as the Graveyard of the Pacific (one of several along this exposed coast), Cape Scott raises a frightening image of storms, high winds and raging seas. While that can indeed be the case, it can also be a remarkable journey and rounding the cape is a badge of honour among both kayakers and mariners. Extreme caution is necessary, but for those who dare the rewards can be substantial.

In Kwakwaka'wakw this area was known as Tsekume, 'trail on the surface.' The sand neck is believed to be the location of a major Indian battle and is a recognized First Nation burial site. Two early attempts were made to settle this area by Danish immigrants, and the area would spring to life again in 1942 when Canada moved to improve its coastal defences during World War Two. Cape Scott was strategic for a combined military and air force base, and a radar station was constructed. The station was demolished after the war, but remnants remain, including the wooden roadway that's part of the Cape Scott Trail from Guise Bay to the lighthouse.

The Cape Scott Trail ends at the lighthouse, built in 1960. Most kayakers and marine travellers skirting close to shore will only get to see the foghorn, which is situated on the most northwesterly point of Vancouver Island. The rest will be hidden atop the hill. The lighthouse is still manned, and the grounds are accessible to the public. Here you can purchase chocolate or a cold drink and sign the guest

The lighthouse at Cape Scott provides views towards Cox Island.

book. What you can no longer do is walk to the tip of Vancouver Island. A boardwalk and suspension bridge that used to allow hikers to walk across to an outlying rock became unstable and were removed. The stairs from the lighthouse to the bridge have also been closed due to deterioration and there are no plans to replace them.

Caution: Cape Scott is one of the most dangerous areas on Vancouver Island. Tidal currents run up to 3 knots, which can lead to rips, standing waves and confused waters. Winds are notorious for rising quickly, from calm to 45 knots in less than an hour.

Place names: Cape Scott was named in honour of David Scott, a Bombay merchant and one of the principal financiers of the trading voyage of James Strange with Capts. Guise and Lowrie in 1786. Strange would claim the area for King George III. He was seeking sea otter pelts.

Tips on rounding Cape Scott: Extreme caution is necessary when rounding the cape. Most of the necessary safety measures are common sense. Be sure to time your trip at slack tide, which is listed in its own section of the tide guide. Note that slack tide is very short. Opposing the current is very difficult, so your best bet is to time your trip with the tide turning in your favour. If you're rounding the cape and the tide turns to oppose you, you could be in for a very difficult fight, as the tidal current tends to be quite strong all down the cape to Guise Bay. It's also advisable to round the cape in the morning before the winds and swell have a chance to build. There's a multitude of reefs on the western side of the cape, so be sure to give them plenty of room.

Travel notes: On one visit I was lucky enough to pass the cape in absolutely calm conditions. There was barely a ripple as I passed between the foghorn and the first offshore rock. However, I soon saw the first tell-tale rips—the current was beginning to strengthen. I looked at my watch. It was 6:53 a.m.; slack tide was listed as 6:50. Minutes later I was in the middle of a major fight. A southerly had picked up and I was headed right into it. Combined with the current and choppy, six-foot waves my progress was often cut to zero, despite hard paddling. It was a lesson to time the trip in the direction of the new tide.

SCOTT ISLANDS

Five islands lying 10 to 46 km (6 to 28 miles) off Cape Scott constitute this remote provincial park. From east to west they're Cox, Lanz, Beresford, Sartine and Triangle islands. Lanz and Cox are the largest, at 764 hectares (1,888 acres) and 978 hectares (2,416 acres) each, while Beresford is the smallest measuring just 14.5 hectares (36 acres). The provincial park was formed out of the Vancouver Island Land Use Plan in 1995 to protect the bird habitat. The park also incorporates three ecological reserves established in 1971—Anne Vallée (Triangle Island), Beresford Island and Sartine Island.

The Scott Islands are the most important breeding grounds for seabirds in British Columbia. The three outer islands are home to over 2 million breeding birds, or just over 38 percent of the breeding

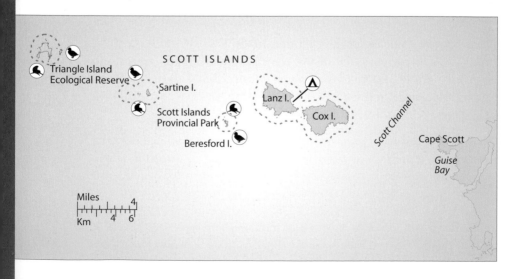

Miles of unspoiled beaches along the north island allow kayakers and hikers to camp just about anywhere. Simply choose your personal paradise and pitch a tent.

seabird population of B.C. The islands are also extremely important for Cassin's auklets, supporting an estimated 58 percent of the world population. Triangle Island supports most of the breeding common murres and tufted puffins in B.C., and is the only breeding site for the thick-billed murre in B.C. The Scott Islands are also important breeding habitat for pelagic cormorants, Leach's storm petrels, fork-tailed storm petrels, black oystercatchers, glaucous-winged gulls, common murres, thick-billed murres, pigeon guillemots, Cassin's auklets, rhinoceros auklets and tufted puffins. Other species associated with the islands include northern fulmar, bald eagle, peregrine falcon, marbled murrelet and horned puffin. Unfortunately, mink and raccoon were introduced to the island in the 1930s, and are believed to be responsible for reducing the historic seabird population.

The rocky shores and islets of Triangle, Sartine and Beresford islands are used as haulouts, breeding grounds and rookeries by northern sea lions, also known as steller sea lions, considered rare both provincially and globally. The colony on these islands is the largest in British Columbia. A federal policy to eradicate sea lions was in place from 1915 to 1965 to protect the commercial fishery. Other marine mammals to be found on or near these islands include the sea otter, minke whale, humpback whale, gray whale, sperm whale and killer whale.

Groundfish and squid thrive along these shorelines, while geoduck and sea urchin beds can be found around Lanz and Cox islands.

The Scott Islands were historically home to the Yutlinuk, a tribe now extinct. Evidence suggests they used the islands to gather seabird eggs. Archeological information is currently very limited; on Triangle Island four sites have been identified—three shell middens and a village site. The middens suggest a lengthy occupation.

European occupancy was short-lived. One of the most unsuccessful lighthouses on the B.C. coast was constructed on Triangle Island in 1909–10. The lighthouse beam could be seen as far as 80 km (50 miles) away, but only on a clear day. For the nine years of its operation the lighthouse keepers were dogged by wind, rain and fog. Conditions were so bad the keepers were unable to have sheep and chickens, as they kept blowing away. In the end the lighthouse proved to be too exposed to the elements and too high to be seen in cloud cover, and after nine years it was dismantled. The lantern is now at home in the Canadian Coast Guard base in Victoria. The base of the lighthouse and two other foundations are still visible on the peak of the island. In a bay on the northeast side of the island are the remnants of a tramway used to hoist supplies up the steep cliff face from the beach to the lighthouse.

Cox and Lanz islands

Cox Island is the easternmost and largest of the group at about 4 by 2.5 km in size (2.5 by 1.5 miles). The rugged island features bays, beaches, cliffs, gorges, pinnacles and steep ridges. The island rises to 312 m (1,023 feet). Lanz Island is separated from Cox Island by a channel about 1 km (.6 mile) wide. Like its larger neighbour, it features a rugged, rocky shore with cliffs and crevices and many small bays and cobble beaches. The tallest slope reaches 212 m (695 feet).

Caution: Reaching Cox or Lanz island, at 10 km (6 miles) off the coast of Cape Scott, is an ambitious but achievable kayaking goal for veteran kayakers. The other islands in this group, however, are more exposed and more rugged, and it would be dangerous to attempt the crossing. Beresford, Sartine and Triangle islands aren't open to the public. The best approach to Cox and Lanz islands is from San Josef Bay, overnighting at Guise Bay and completing the run the next morning before winds can build—if conditions are acceptable.

Camping: While any of the small bays and beaches of Lanz and Cox islands could serve as home for a night, the most desirable location is the sand beach on the east side of Lanz Island.

Triangle Island

Triangle Island (Anne Vallée Ecological Reserve) is 46 km (28.5 miles) off Cape Scott, and is the most westward reach of the southern B.C. coast. The southwest peninsula, known as Puffin Rock, drops dramatically into the sea, as do many of the offshore rocks. The maximum elevation is 194 m (636 feet). Treeless offshore pinnacles are located off Triangle Island. A permit is required to visit the island, and access is restricted to scientific research and monitoring. The same applies to Beresford and Sartine islands. Distance would make them impractical kayaking destinations anyway.

Place names: In 1982, Triangle Island Ecological Reserve was renamed Anne Vallée Ecological Reserve as a tribute to the biologist, who died from a fall while studying puffins on the island.

WEST CAPE SCOTT PROVINCIAL PARK

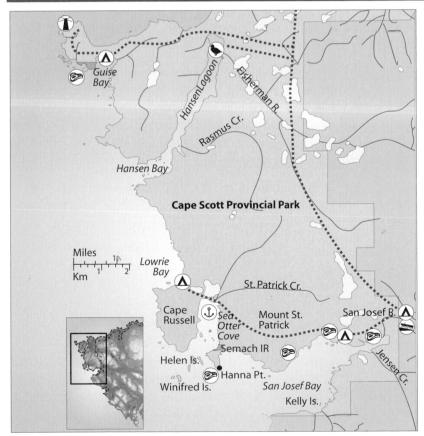

This is the most accessible portion of Cape Scott Provincial Park, thanks to launches at San Josef Bay. Highlights include the beautiful white sands of Lowrie Bay and San Josef Bay. The reef-strewn coastline of Cape Russell can be forbidding.

Guise Bay

Guise Bay is the south-facing beach of the sand neck that links Cape Scott to the rest of Vancouver Island (see page 71 for more details). In Kwakwaka'wakw, Guise Bay is known as 'where canoes run ashore in heavy swell.' Just west of Guise Bay is the Ouchton Indian Reserve, a site of mythical importance, where a major Nakumgilisala village was located.

Numerous historic remnants of the early Danish settlement can be seen at Guise Bay, including farm implements. Portions of old fences made of driftwood are still visible on the meadow behind the beach. N. P. Jensen's gravesite, outlined by a small picket fence, is set at the forest edge. Just northeast of Guise Bay on a side trail are several partially collapsed buildings associated with the World War Two radar station.

Camping: Wilderness camping is possible above the high tide line at Guise Bay. Surf is lighter to the west, though the best beach for camping is to the east. Rusty water is available from a difficult-to-reach stream to the east. Tents can also be pitched on the meadow behind the beach. Strong southerlies (to be expected during storms) can make conditions here miserable.

Caution: The entrance to Guise Bay is rimmed by a multitude of semi-submerged or submerged reefs. During some tides the west entrance to the bay can become a wall of breaking waves. Be sure to keep a good distance.

Hansen Lagoon

Hansen Lagoon extends north from Hansen Bay for 5 km (3 miles) to end in a saltwater marsh and tidal mudflats. It was this lagoon that captured the imagination of N. P. Jensen, who saw the potential of the fishing and natural hay meadow and settled here in 1893. Other Danish settlers would join him, and their handiwork, from an impressive dyke to rusting machinery, remains today.

The lagoon was known to the Nakumgilisala as Wachlalis, meaning 'river on the beach in bay.' An early village was located here.

Remnants of the corduroy trail created for the World War Two radar station make up the final stretch of the Cape Scott Trail.

The mixture of fresh water and salt water creates one of the most varied environments on the north coast. There are geoducks and a variety of clams. The tidal flats are also home to a great number of crabs, including the hairy hermit crab, helmet crab and Dungeness crab. Winged residents include sandhill cranes and common snipes at the head of the lagoon and spotted sandpipers, semipalmated plovers and killdeers on the mud flats. Migratory birds that use the sheltered waters include great blue herons, Canada geese and trumpeter swans. The abundant food and shelter in the lagoon makes it one of the best areas to find migrating birds on the northwest coast of Vancouver Island.

Camping: While there are a variety of beaches in Hansen Lagoon suitable for wilderness camping, the best location is probably due east of the entrance to Hansen Bay. Camping farther up the lagoon isn't necessarily possible or even desirable, since it's a drying mudflat. In addition, the neighbouring meadow is ditched,

The Cape Scott Settlement: Danish settlers made two attempts to settle at Hansen Lagoon, the first in 1897 and the second in 1910. The second was the most successful, and the cape had a population of 1,000 at its peak in 1914, with a church, post office, school and community hall. The early pioneers recognized the farming potential and built a dyke across the lagoon. One dyke was completed in 1900, but on the very night they celebrated its completion it was washed away by a storm. They also attempted to stabilize the sand dunes at Guise Bay. Difficult transportation, however, proved to be the community's un-doing. By 1918 only five families remained.

making it extremely difficult to get from the lagoon to the meadow. The ditches may be covered by thick grass, making a broken leg a real possibility.

Lowrie Bay

Lowrie Bay is another sweeping white sand beach within Cape Scott Park. Long breakers could make a surf landing difficult, though the southwest portion is protected by a small islet attached to the beach at low tide. The bay offers good shelter from southerlies, and is preferable to Guise Bay for waiting out a storm.

Hiking: A fairly easy 2-km (1.3-mile) trail leads from Lowrie Bay to Sea Otter Cove, allowing people to hike from the San Josef trailhead to Lowrie Bay. Not many make the trip. The hike to Sea Otter Cove from San Josef Bay is a 10-km (6-mile), five-hour journey for expert hikers only. One option is to boat from the launch at San Josef River, moor at the trailhead in Sea Otter Cove, then hike into Lowrie Bay.

Camping: Camping is wilderness above the high tide line. There's a pit toilet along a short trail west of the beach. Slightly farther along the trail is a cabin. The cabin is dry, has two bunks, a wood stove, a table and other amenities. It's user-maintained. Be sure to read the guest book and one young girl's delightful interpretation of her arduous journey.

Cape Russell

Any trip up or down this coast will mean crossing Cape Russell. At the best of times it's an interesting trip past numerous rocks off a rocky coastline. At the worst it's one of the most exposed and moody stretches of coast. Wind waves, swell and currents can combine to make conditions miserable. There are many reefs well offshore, requiring a close watch for rogue waves breaking on unseen rocks.

Travel notes: I've paddled Cape Russell three times. The first time I was surprised by the number of reefs. A clear path was difficult to find. The second time was uneventful, and made me wonder what had troubled me the first time. The third time was part of a trip down the entire outer coast of Vancouver Island. The distance between Lowrie Bay and Sea Otter Cove turned out to be the most difficult three miles of the entire journey, even after waiting a day at Lowrie Bay for better weather. Be sure to give this cape the respect it deserves. While it can be a pleasant area, it can also be the worst of the worst.

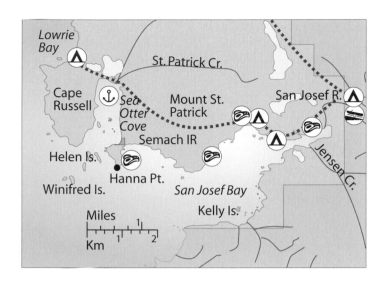

Sea Otter Cove

Sea Otter Cove offers protected waters when San Josef Bay cannot. It's one of the few sheltered areas between Quatsino Sound and Bull Harbour and is most popular as an anchorage. The islands, reefs and shore outside the cove are exceptionally pretty, though the cove isn't especially remarkable. Trees grow to the high tide mark, making camping very difficult. It lacks nice beaches or any sort of interesting rock formations, though St. Patrick Creek is pretty.

Caution: You may be tempted to pass north of Helen Islands and out through the west channel of Sea Otter Cove. Few mariners will go this route, instead using the narrower passage next to Hanna Point. Why? The west entrance can be blocked by breaking waves. It's possible to paddle through the more westerly entrance without difficulty, but be sure of the conditions before attempting it.

Place names: The *Sea Otter* was a vessel commanded by Capt. James Hanna. It visited this area in 1786.

San Josef Bay

San Josef Bay offers an interesting array of geological features and a pretty white sand beach. Within the headland that separates two beaches at the head of the bay are several sea stacks and caves. Other interesting rock features are located all around the cove, which makes for especially scenic paddling.

San Josef Bay was an adjunct to the Cape Scott settlement. Henry Ohlsen's store, an Anglican church and several homesteads were located here. Some rotting planks and rusting relics are all that remain. In 1904 Ohlsen was told he had six months or less to live unless he moved to a dry climate. Instead, he moved to the wettest possible place to live, San Josef Bay. He was buried in 1944.

The mouth of San Josef River was the site of an early Nakumgilisala village.

Place names: Called St. Patrick's Bay by Capt. Hanna in 1786, Spanish officer Lt. Francisco Eliza renamed it San Josef Bay in 1791.

Camping: Wilderness camping is possible anywhere along the two main beaches at the head of the bay. Amenities include pit toilets and bear caches. Hikers often choose to stay near the mouth of the San Josef River. Paddlers can stay at smaller pocket beaches along the north shore of the bay. The beach is open to surf that varies from low to high. The best protection is generally to the north.

Two campgrounds offer vehicle access near the launch sites. One of them, San Josef Heritage Park and Campground, has been privately operated by Doug DesJarlais since 1990. The campground has numerous tent and RV sites with varying degrees of shelter and privacy near the San Josef River. Amenities include fire pits, pit toilets,

The pretty beach at Cape Palmerston is one of the few areas on the northwest coast of Vancouver Island easily accessible with a vehicle.

a few wooden picnic shelters and Doug's unique north island hospitality. He is also working on building a hostel. Donations are accepted for camping and use of firewood. Slightly upriver is the San Josef Recreation Site, which is maintained by Western Forest Products. Here you'll find numerous pretty and private camping sites set in an old-growth forest next to the San Josef River. Amenities are picnic tables, fire pits and pit toilets. Camping is free. Mosquitoes can be numerous at both sites.

Launches: There are two locations for launching, and both are a mile or so (1.6 km) up the San Josef River. Both are prone to the same difficulties: at lower tides, portions of the river can become too shallow to pass without a portage and fighting the flow can be difficult along the shallower portions. These difficulties are greatly reduced at higher tides. However, the main obstacle is where the river meets San Josef Bay. The river current can clash with incoming swell, causing a series of standing breaking waves. The surf can be moderate or even high. Again, the best condition is at higher tides, when even small boats can navigate the river. The launch at San Josef Heritage Park and Campground is rough and steep. A donation is requested of $5 per day to park. At San Josef Recreation Site, a good dirt ramp leads to the river. The parking is free.

Hiking: San Josef Bay is a fairly simple 2.5-km (1.5-mile) hike from the Cape Scott trailhead. Parking at the trailhead is provided by Western Forest Products. Another trail continues from the bay up Mount St. Patrick. Here hikers will find a bog at the peak with stunted trees and open or sphagnum moss-covered pools. The reward is a panoramic view over the inland park and the beach. An extremely rough trail continues on past Mount St. Patrick to Sea Otter Cove, with another leg leading to Lowrie Bay. This route is recommended for experienced and hardy hikers only. The 12-km (7.5-mile) trip takes about six hours to complete, and the route through Sea Otter Cove is passable only at lower tides.

Hiking the Cape Scott Trail: Once considered the muddiest, wettest and most miserable trail on the West Coast, Cape Scott Trail has undergone numerous improvements. The addition of boardwalks has greatly reduced the difficulty. Even so, hikers should be equipped for wet, muddy weather. Expect muddy conditions year-round at the head of Sea Otter Cove, San Josef River estuary, Eric Lake, St. Mary Creek, Rasmus Creek and upper Hansen Lagoon. Good hiking boots are recommended and gaiters are advised for keeping out mud and grit. Good grips on the boots are necessary for walking on slippery boardwalks.

Points of Interest

Here are some of the features to be found within Cape Scott Provincial Park. For simplicity, the numbers match the BC Parks brochure.

1. **Henry Ohlsen's home, store and post office**, 1908 to 1944. A few planks and rusty relics can still be seen. Follow the trail to San Josef Bay.

2. **Sea stacks.** You can find these wave-eroded rocks between the first and second beaches at San Josef Bay. They're accessible by foot at low tide.

3. **Sea caves.** Located near the sea stacks between the first and second beaches at San Josef Bay, they're accessible only at low tide.

4. **Corduroy Road.** A road was built here in 1908 to connect the south end of Eric Lake to the San Josef store and post office.

5. **Wharf.** This served as a transportation link for the Cape Scott community during its peak years until a trail was built around Eric Lake. It's located on the lake's south end.

6. **Giant Sitka Spruce.** It measures 7.2 m (23.6 feet) in circumference. It can be found about a 20-minute hike north of the Eric Lake camping area.

7. **Telegraph line.** The line was built to Cape Scott in 1913. Remnants of it can be found along the trail.

8. **Farm fence posts.** These vestiges of an agricultural adventure lost can be found running alongside the trail in two areas and perpendicular to the trail at an open bog.

9. **Breakwater.** An old sailing vessel was sunk here to act as a breakwater, but storms soon drove it ashore, where it remains today.

10. **Wooden cart.** Alfred Spencer farmed here until 1956. The cart can be found off the north end of the trail.

11. **Caterpillar tractor.** This was the first motorized machine used at Cape Scott. It can be found between two trees on the north side of the trail.

12. **Collapsed tool shed.** An interpretive sign is located trailside.

13. **Second dyke.** It's visible as raised shoreline along the northwest shore of Hansen Lagoon. The dyke was meant to make the area suitable for a pasture. It was built in 1905.

14. **First dyke.** In 1899 residents built a large mound of rocks that runs 720 m (2,360 feet) along Hansen Lagoon's shore.

15. **Boiler.** This machine was used by N. P. Jensen for his sawmill circa 1898. It's now lodged in the riverbank on Fisherman River.

16. **Plank road.** It was constructed for hauling goods between World War Two buildings in 1942.

17. **Building ruins.** About 50 m (160 feet) before Guise Bay a small trail leads away from the main trail. Here you can find a long rectangular building believed to have been a store during the Second World War.

18. **Building ruins.** A small trail at Guise Bay leads to two World War Two cabins.

19. **Driftwood fence posts.** A driftwood fence was built behind Guise Bay by N. P. Jensen in 1910 to stabilize the sand dunes for use as a pasture.

20. **A-frame structure.** This was used as a cougar trap by the Jensen children at the sand neck. A cougar was apparently captured and held for about 10 minutes—much to the children's surprise.

21. **Native fishing site.** This was located at the west end of Experiment Bight. Shells and bones mark the location.

22. **Plank road.** This route was used to carry goods to the light station.

23. **Sea stacks.** A side trail to the lighthouse leads to a gravel beach. Seven sea stacks can be found at the beach's north end.

24. **Cape Scott Lighthouse.** It was built in 1960.

25. **Christiansen grave.** The grave is the burial place of the adopted son of the local school teacher, 12-year-old William Christiansen, who died of an infected cut on his foot in 1906. The inscription on the pink granite gravestone reads, "The sun went down while it was yet day." More graves are located off a side trail across from this one. N. P. Jensen's gravesite is near the sand neck by the forest's edge.

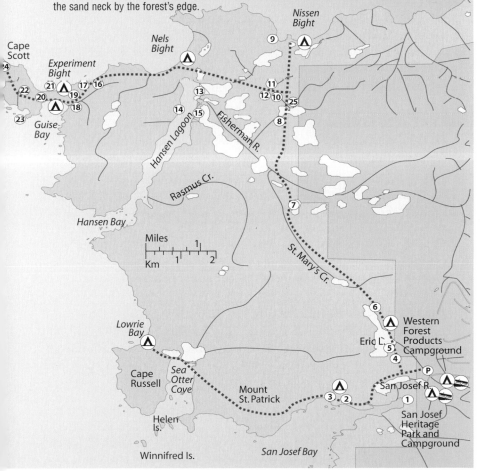

The trail to Nissen Bight is 15 km (9 miles), or between five and six hours of hiking. Another option is turning west through the old Cape Scott settlement to Nels Bight, a 16.8-km (10.4-mile) hike. Experiment Bight is 18.9 km (11.7 miles), while Guise Bay is 20.7 km (12.8 miles). The full distance to the Cape Scott Lighthouse is 23.6 km (14.6 miles). Side trails lead off to San Josef Bay, Sea Otter Cove and Lowrie Bay. Details of those routes are covered under individual entries.

Kayakers landing at Guise Bay, Nels Bight, Nissen Bight or Experiment Bight will have access to the trail system. Kayakers are expected to pay the fee for camping. The park warden patrols the various beaches, enforcing the payment. A payment box is located at the trailhead.

The community of Port Hardy is leading the charge to extend the Cape Scott Trail to create a North Coast Trail from Nels Bight to Shushartie Bay. A local group, the Northern Vancouver Island Trail Society, has been raising government and private funds to build the trail, which will include about 14 bridges along its length. When complete, it will link Shushartie Bay to San Josef Bay, a hike rivalling and perhaps even surpassing the famous West Coast Trail. A trail once existed in the late 1800s and was used by the Cape Scott settlers to transport goods from Shushartie Bay, but it's almost completely overgrown. The trail starts about .5 km (.3 mile) from the east end of the beach at Nels Bight. From there a good push may get you in about 1 km (.6 mile). It was once possible to reach the remains of a 340-m (1,115-foot) bridge over a lake, but not with the current trail condition.

Historic remnants should not be disturbed. Many of the old buildings are unstable. Travel along many beach routes is dangerous or even impossible at higher tides. Both bear and cougar inhabit the area. Food should be cached at night.

CAPE PALMERSTON

The outer coast of Vancouver Island south of San Josef Bay to Quatsino Sound is exceptionally rugged and beautiful. Unfortunately, there are very few sheltered landing spots along the 26-km (16-mile) stretch. The best choice for a break is Raft Cove, a pretty, white sand beach south of Cape Palmerston.

Caution: Kayakers must be experienced and familiar with conditions on the open coast. Once in open water between San Josef Bay and Quatsino Sound there are no all-weather spots to stop.

Cape Palmerston Recreation Site

Located on the south end of Cape Palmerston, this site offers camping and beach access by vehicle. A narrow cobble beach is surrounded by rocky headlands and offshore rocks. If you drive here, a short path leads to the shore.

Camping: Five wooden tent pads are located in the mature forest behind the beach. Two overlook the beach; the other three are set back a short distance in the woods. The pads aren't vehicle-accessible and the walk is several hundred metres. If you're arriving by kayak,

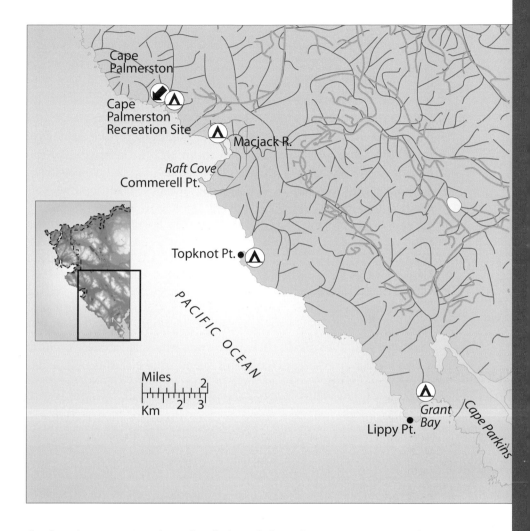

the beach access is relatively sheltered, but there are many rocks, some submerged, that require careful navigation. If conditions are normal there should be no breakers on the beach, but the swell will break on the outlying rocks. Numerous other pocket beaches along this stretch can also serve as campsites.

Launches: In a pinch, the beach at Cape Palmerston can be used as a launch site, though it requires a fairly lengthy walk from the parking lot. A launch through the rocks near the beach can also be tricky. This would be recommended only for confident, veteran paddlers. The nearest alternatives are at San Josef Bay or Winter Harbour.

Raft Cove

Raft Cove is a provincial park protecting a forested upland, a huge white sand beach, a sand spit and the associated estuary of the Macjack River. Kayaking is possible for a distance up the Macjack, though surf at the mouth can be a problem. The park is accessible by a rough logging road, then a difficult 45-minute trail. If conditions have been wet, it will be a muddy 45 minutes. A rare geological formation can be found toward the south end of the cove near the mouth of the Macjack: a pyroclastic surge formation left over from earlier volcanic activity. A key salmon area lies offshore from Raft Cove to Topknot Point.

Raft Cove and the Macjack estuary were both once used by the Quatsino, but a formal archaeological inventory of sites has yet to be done. The Quatsino Band is claiming Raft Cove as its traditional territory in treaty negotiations.

There are remains here of early attempts to settle the Cape Scott area, including the cabin of Willie Hecht, a pioneer in the early 20th century. The cabin can be found to the south of the Macjack River.

Raft Cove Provincial Park was established to provide vehicle access to the northwest coast. This would make it the only road-accessible oceanside campground in a provincial park on northern Vancouver Island. Two road access routes have been proposed: Port Hardy to Holberg to Raft Cove; or Port Hardy to Coal Harbour to

If you're looking for somewhere where the sand can squish between your toes, Raft Cove has more than enough to spare.

Sea stacks line the shore at low tide at San Josef Bay.

Holberg to Raft Cove. A 40-unit campground with facilities such as pit toilets and a water system is planned, with an additional six to eight walk-in campsites in the forested area along the spit. Day hiking trails will be built into the upland area.

Camping: The most popular camping area is the beach facing out to the ocean. Clearings in the forest behind the beach provide an alternative to camping on the sand. Amenities are a pit toilet. If you're kayaking in, be warned that the surf can be high. One option is to find a way through the surf to the Macjack River and land in the shelter behind the spit. Navigating this region is for veteran kayakers only who are familiar with surf. In the event of a southerly, the best shelter for kayakers will be on the south side of the Macjack.

Grant Bay

Grant Bay has an interesting sand beach accessible by trail from Browning Inlet. Recent logging has brought new logging roads with closer access by car. Surf can be moderate on the beach. Up a short embankment from the beach is a pleasant grassy area.

Western Forest Products is studying the potential for developing a trail from Grant Bay to Raft Cove to connect the headlands and beaches for recreational use. Along with other plans, it would be possible to have a trail from Winter Harbour to Port Hardy. In the meantime, a Land Act notation is being sought to preserve Grant Bay for public recreation. That could mean a park in the future.

Raft Cove Provincial Park: The park, established in 1990, protects 640 hectares (1,600 acres) of land around a sandy bay at the mouth of the Macjack River. A trail leads from the logging road through old-growth hemlock, western red cedar and Sitka spruce to the beach. Here visitors will find pristine wooded areas, an expansive sandy beach and spit, an estuary, boggy areas and rugged rocky headlands. The centrepiece of the park, a long sandy spit, was formed by surf meeting the river runoff at the mouth of the Macjack. The pristine beach stretches for over 2 km (1.2 miles).

Raft Cove is a beautiful provincial park that may one day be the only drive-in coastal campground in the north island.

Quatsino Sound

CHAPTER THREE

THE NORTHERNMOST OF THE FIVE MAJOR SOUNDS OF VANCOUVER ISLAND, Quatsino Sound has over 120 km (75 miles) of channels and inlets to explore. Four major arms that branch off from the sound are dotted with five quaint communities, each with its own distinctive personality, from the historic waterfront boardwalk of Winter Harbour to contemporary Port Alice.

The inlets can offer tranquil, protected waters to explore, but they're long, the attractions are generally few and far between and man-made interference is high. The backdrop is a distracting patchwork of bald hills and fish farms. Other industry further erodes the scenic quality.

Varney Bay, Quatsino Narrows, Drake Island, Koprino Harbour and the striking open oceanfront toward Kwakiutl Point are worth visiting, however. Unusual wildlife such as six-gill sharks, ruins of old commercial ventures and a multitude of native heritage sites add to the appeal. The bottom line is some people could have a wonderful time here, while others will be disappointed that it failed to live up to the overwhelming beauty of the other more wild and mountainous sounds on Vancouver Island. The key is picking and choosing where to go in a way that will match expectations.

GETTING HERE

The Island Highway to Port Hardy is the gateway for all marine access points in Quatsino Sound. They're Coal Harbour, Port Alice, Rupert Inlet, Holberg, Winter Harbour, Spencer Cove Recreation Site and Mahatta River. Coal Harbour and Port Alice are blessed with paved routes leading directly from the highway. To reach Rupert Inlet, take

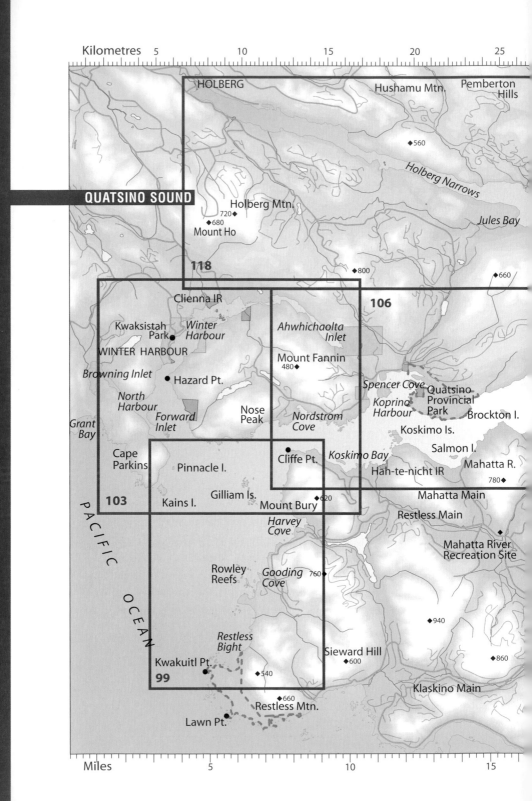

Kilometres

HOLBERG

Hushamu Mtn.

Pemberton Hills

◆560

Holberg Narrows

QUATSINO SOUND

Holberg Mtn.

Jules Bay

720◆

◆680

Mount Ho

◆800

◆660

118

Clienna IR

106

Kwaksistah Park

Winter Harbour

Ahwhichaolta Inlet

WINTER HARBOUR

Mount Fannin

480◆

Browning Inlet

Hazard Pt.

Spencer Cove

Quatsino Provincial Park

North Harbour

Koprino Harbour

Brockton I.

Forward Inlet

Nose Peak

Nordstrom Cove

Koskimo Is.

Grant Bay

Cape Parkins

Koskimo Bay

Salmon I.

Hah-te-nicht IR

Mahatta R.

Pinnacle I.

Cliffe Pt.

780◆

103

Kains I.

Gilliam Is.

620◆

Mahatta Main

Mount Bury

Restless Main

Harvey Cove

◆

Mahatta River Recreation Site

Rowley Reefs

Gooding Cove

760◆

◆940

P A C I F I C   O C E A N

Restless Bight

Sieward Hill

◆860

Kwakuitl Pt.

600◆

99

540◆

Klaskino Main

660◆

Restless Mtn.

Lawn Pt.

Miles

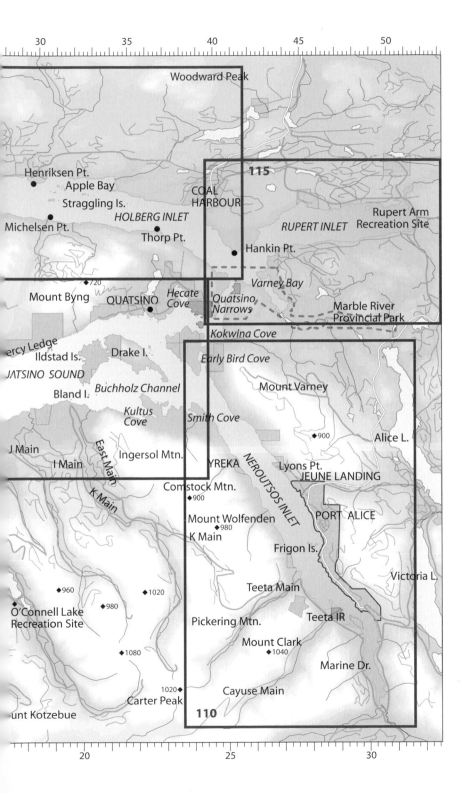

30   35   40   45   50

Woodward Peak

115

Henriksen Pt.

Apple Bay

Straggling Is.

HOLBERG INLET

COAL
HARBOUR

Michelsen Pt.

Thorp Pt.

Hankin Pt.

Rupert Arm
Recreation Site

RUPERT INLET

◆720

Mount Byng   QUATSINO   Hecate
Cove

*Quatsino
Narrows*

Varney Bay

Marble River
Provincial Park

Kokwina Cove

ercy Ledge

Ildstad Is.

Drake I.

Early Bird Cove

JATSINO SOUND

Bland I.

Buchholz Channel

Mount Varney

*Kultus
Cove*

Smith Cove

◆900

Alice L.

J Main

East Main

Ingersol Mtn.

YREKA

Lyons Pt.

JEUNE LANDING

I Main

K Main

Comstock Mtn.
◆900

NEROUTSOS INLET

PORT ALICE

Mount Wolfenden
◆980

K Main

Frigon Is.

Victoria L.

◆960

◆1020

◆980

O'Connell Lake
Recreation Site

Teeta Main

Teeta IR

Pickering Mtn.

◆1080

Mount Clark
◆1040

Marine Dr.

1020◆

Cayuse Main

Carter Peak

110

unt Kotzebue

20   25   30

Rupert Main off the Island Highway. It's the left turn immediately after the paved turn-off for Port Alice (maybe 100 m/330 feet distant). Rupert Main ends in a junction with the Port Hardy Main. Turn right (north), and you'll see the access points leading to the inlet almost immediately. An option a little farther down the inlet is a dock launch. From the Rupert Main junction, turn left, then make a quick right onto Varney Main. The dock is located at the end of the road. Note that this is a restricted logging road, and weekday access is likely to be prohibited.

For the closest accesses to inner Quatsino Sound, Winter Harbour or Spencer Cove are recommended launch sites. Unfortunately, just getting there can be a bit of an adventure, as the logging roads are rough and portions can be active. Both launches involve taking the San Josef Road west from Port Hardy past Holberg, a small town with its own launch site on the east side of the inlet.

To get to Spencer Cove (Koprino Harbour), take the South Main at Holberg. This route also leads to Winter Harbour, but in less than 3 km (2 miles) take the Southeast Main (essentially, stay straight). That will turn into Koprino Main, which will lead directly to the recreation site. For Winter Harbour, there are two ways to get there. You can take South Main at Holberg and stay on that all the way to Winter Harbour. Or you can follow San Josef Main west of Holberg for a couple of miles until you reach the major logging road heading south. It's well marked. This will eventually connect with South Main (in 7–8 km / 4–5 miles).

Lastly, Mahatta River is a popular option for launching into the inner sound. From Port Alice, follow Marine Drive south, then north again as it turns around the outside of Neroutsos Inlet. A few switchbacks will lead to Teeta Pass, then K Main, I Main and finally J Main. Finally, take Mahatta Main to the launch site. It sounds convoluted but is reasonably straightforward and well marked. Gooding Cove day use area is reached by the same route, but instead of taking Mahatta Main at the Mahatta River Campsite, take Restless Main west. It will eventually lead to Harvey Cove, then Gooding Cove. For logging conditions on the access roads, call the Juneau Western Forest Products operation at **250-284-3395** or email **info@western-forest.com.** The office provides free backroad maps.

Kwakiutl Point on the outer sound is a rugged area surrounded by islets and reefs.

EXPLORING BY KAYAK

Quatsino Sound features so much shoreline it could take weeks to see it all, but only a few areas are truly spectacular, reducing the length of time it will take to see all the good stuff. Those standouts include Varney Bay (and Marble River), Quatsino Narrows, Drake Island, Buchholz Channel, Koprino Harbour and the outer entrance to Quatsino Sound. The latter is certainly the most scenic, though flatwater paddlers will undoubtedly prefer Koprino, Drake Island and Varney Bay.

Recommended trips

- *If you have a day:* For a beautiful day trip, visit Varney Bay and Marble River. Launch out of Coal Harbour. If you have time and can make slack tide, a nose into Quatsino Narrows would be a bonus. Another nice day trip would be Koprino Harbour with a launch from Spencer Cove or Mahatta River. Some will find Forward Inlet with a launch from Winter Harbour rewarding. You may even want to tuck into Grant Bay. Finally Ahwhichaolto Inlet's seclusion and serene setting will appeal to many. Launch from Winter Harbour.

- *If you have a weekend:* For a nice overnight journey, launch from Coal Harbour, paddle through Quatsino Narrows and stay at Ildstad Islands. Circumnavigate Drake Island. The more adventurous can launch from Winter Harbour and overnight at either Grant Bay or Restless Bight. The latter entails a fairly lengthy open crossing.

- *If you have three days:* Take the weekend trip of your choice and take the extra day to explore areas more thoroughly, particularly if you're staying at Restless Bight (recommended).

- *If you have five days:* With this much time you can travel from Coal Harbour through Quatsino Narrows and get to Koprino Harbour with a stay at Spencer Cove. For more adventure, take a day trip to Gillam Islands or overnight the third night at Restless Bight. To avoid the narrows, launch at Port Alice.

- *If you have a week:* If you have this much time, a week spent here (while pleasant enough) won't introduce you to the features of the more spectacular spots of Vancouver Island. But if you must spend it here, add an exploration of the outer coast to the five-day journey mentioned above. Extend the trip by camping at Grant Bay, Gooding Cove or Restless Bight.

- *The ideal trip:* Quatsino Sound may be the least inviting sound on Vancouver Island for kayaking, but it's probably the most appealing for exploring by foot and RV. Marble River, Spencer Cove and Grant Bay are all pretty areas to visit, as are Mahatta River and Gooding Cove on the south shores. Families or casual hikers could spend a wonderful week here day-tripping. As for kayaking, the outer coast is definitely the highlight. A run from Coal Harbour and down the outer coast to end at Klaskish Inlet near Brooks Peninsula would be a splendid trip, if you can arrange the transportation.

THE BASICS

Geology and ecology

Quatsino shares features of both Vancouver Island and the Queen Charlotte Islands. It's characterized by glacially smoothed and fault-ridden bedrock hills, with a low-lying topography. The fjords, such as Quatsino Sound and Neroutsos Inlet, have formed along fault lines. The u-shape of the major valleys is just one indication that glaciers were instrumental in shaping this land. The glaciers over northern Vancouver Island are believed to have been no thicker than 750 m (2,461 feet), compared to a maximum of 2,000 m (6,562 feet) in the Strait of Georgia. Major glaciers 900 m (2,953 feet) thick are believed to have covered Neroutsos Inlet and Quatsino Sound.

Winter Harbour is a collection of homes scattered along the waterfront with the oldest portion joined by a historic boardwalk.

The hills here are generally covered in western hemlock, which can be found in stands with amabilis fir and western redcedar, along with Sitka spruce, yellow cedar, Douglas-fir, alder, shore pine and mountain hemlock. Animals such as black-tailed deer, cougars and black bears are common, as are bald eagles. Many at-risk species reside in this area: the Pacific water shrew, a resident of riparian areas and wetlands; Keen's long-eared myotis (bat), which inhabits caves and trees in coastal rainforests; the northern goshawk, which nests in mature forest stands; and the marbled murrelet.

Other notable species to watch for include ermine in thick riparian understorey, Vancouver Island wolverine (found at high elevations only), Roosevelt elk, great blue heron, peregrine falcon, white-tailed ptarmigan, western screech owl, northern pygmy owl, Huttin's vireo and sandhill crane.

Weather

Quatsino Sound's annual precipitation can be as high as 4,000 mm (157 inches) at Holberg—or about four times the amount experienced at Victoria to the south. The amount increases the farther one travels up the inlets. Pacific winds carrying moisture are forced to rise over Vancouver Island's mountains, and as the clouds cool they're less able to hold moisture.

Monthly average temperatures are just about identical at four weather stations in Quatsino Sound (Holberg, Port Alice, Coal Harbour and Quatsino). Temperatures average 3°C (37°F) in January and 15°C (59°F) in August. While that sounds cool, it's not dramatically different from Victoria, one of the warmest cities year-round in Canada.

The entrance to Quatsino Sound, Holberg and Rupert inlets, and to a lesser degree Neroutsos Inlet can be subject to strong winds. The channeling can create dangerous conditions in these inlets, so the inner waters are no guarantee of protection.

Native overview

This is the land of the Kwakiutl. Four bands historically made it their home: the Klaskino, Quatsino, Gopino and Koskimo. All four tribes were known to bandage the heads of infant females to produce an elongated, conical form. They were also celebrated among other tribes for producing good potatoes, which were grown in small patches on cleared spots, most particularly former village sites. Once a powerful tribe, the 1904 census listed the Koskimo population at just 18.

The name of the Quatsino is thought to be derived from Kowat-se, meaning 'west side' or 'people of the west.'

THE SHORELINES

QUATSINO ENTRANCE

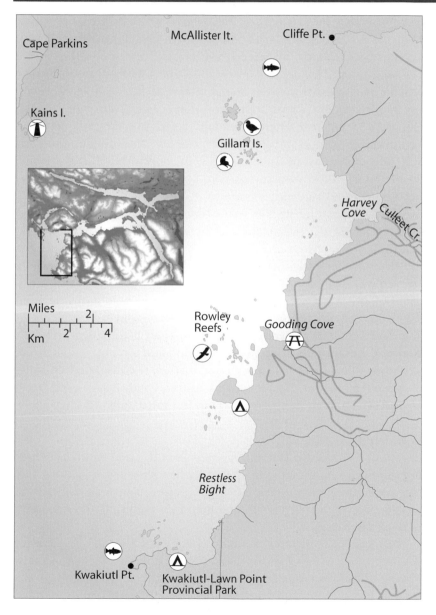

Holberg, Neroutsos and Rupert inlets tend to be lacking in scenic features and high in industrial use, but the outer coast is quite the opposite. Dramatic rocky headlands, wave-pummelled reefs, exposed islands rich in wildlife and sheltered coves with white sand beaches are common, and there's little sign of human development beyond distant logging. If you've debated the switch from flatwater kayaking to open water, here's incentive. The outer waters are the place to see many of the largest and most rare sea mammals in Quatsino Sound. Gray and humpback whales migrate through the sound during the fall and spring. Minke whales can be seen here. Transient killer whales can be seen all year round, while about 72 percent of the northern resident orca population have been observed in the Quatsino Sound area. Their appearance seems to correspond with the migration of salmon in the summer and fall. Note that commercial shipping passes east of Gillam Islands, while offshore gravel deposits are being eyed for their commercial potential. Offshore oil and gas development is also being examined.

The only marine reptile that occurs in Quatsino Sound is the leatherback turtle (*Dermochelys coriacea*), the largest living turtle. Leatherbacks captured accidentally by commercial fishing have been measured up to 2.4 m (7.8 feet) in length and 900 kg (2,000 pounds) in weight. Adult leatherbacks are migratory, and can travel more than 15,000 km (9,300 miles) in their annual migrations, making them the widest-ranging reptile species. They appear here between July and September, feeding on jellyfish. Their biggest threat is collision with motor vessels, accidental fishing and swallowing anything that looks like food. The Pacific population is considered critically endangered, and the Department of Fisheries and Oceans is planning a recovery strategy to help keep them in Canadian waters.

Cape Parkins

Located on the north side of Quatsino Sound, Cape Parkins shelters Forward Inlet. To the northwest is the white sand beach of Grant Bay (see page 90), while the shores of Cape Parkins have their own pocket beaches between rocky bluffs and behind a multitude of reefs. It's a very exposed area.

The Kains Island Lighthouse off the tip of Cape Parkins provides the weather readings for Quatsino on coast guard marine broadcasts. The lighthouse is located on the southeast end of Kain Island. It was established in 1909, and a fog alarm was added in 1923. It's manned but not open to the public.

Gillam Islands

Gillam Islands lie about 2 km (1.2 miles) off Vancouver Island in the mouth of Quatsino Sound. The shores are rocky and only the northernmost island is forested, with just dwarfed spruce on other islets. Salmonberry, currant, salal, elderberry and crabapple grow thickly on all but the low, rocky islets. There are no beaches or landing opportunities. The islands are important seabird habitat, home to the second-largest storm-petrel colony in B.C., with both fork-tailed and Leach's storm-petrels to be found here. The fork-tailed colony is about 1.7 percent of the global population and 22 percent of the Canadian population. Leach's storm-petrels, at 72,000 pairs, make up about 2.6 percent of the global population and 13 percent of the national population. Just over 1 percent of the nation's black oystercatcher population nests here, along with 2.6 percent of the glaucous-winged gull population. Other seabirds include pelagic cormorants and pigeon guillemots. They may not nest here, but tufted puffins can be seen here and in the waters at the entrance to Quatsino Sound. The islands are also a sea lion haulout. Gillam Islands will soon have protection under the Land Act for marine conservation and protection. As of 2004 they had no special status.

Gooding Cove

South of Cliffe Point the shoreline is largely unbroken cliffs with the occasional pocket beach. At Gooding Cove a flat portion of the shoreline opens up to a selection of beaches broken by rocky outcrops and strings of reefs. The major beach is Gooding Cove, which, unfortunately, is modified due to logging and a road leading along its eastern edge. Otherwise it's over a quarter mile of sand and gravel. Other beaches can be found along this stretch, though a multitude of reefs can make it hazardous to navigate. Many of the reefs can be submerged. Accessible by logging road, Gooding Cove Day Use Area provides foot access from vehicles to the beach. Rowley Reefs, just off the cove, provide overwintering habitat for storm petrels, gulls, cormorants, alcids and shore birds.

Restless Bight

This stretch of shoreline has numerous beaches broken by rock bluffs. The bight is almost completely enclosed by reefs, and navigating the reefs is the biggest hurdle for visitors. There are four main beaches at Restless Bight, with the two most significant at each end. The north

Restless Bight is characterized by rocks and reefs, with numerous white sand beaches to be found behind them.

beach is backed by Crown land and open to recreational use, including camping. It's well sheltered. The other significant beach to the south falls within Kwakiutl–Lawn Point Provincial Park.

Camping: Both the north and south beaches offer fine wilderness camping above the high tide line on beaches well protected from surf. The south beach tends to be most popular, as it's within the provincial park and is very scenic.

FORWARD INLET

Forward Inlet provides the first sheltered waters south of Cape Scott and gives access to north Vancouver Island's northwesternmost community, Winter Harbour. Forward Inlet is almost completely undeveloped. There are a few nice beaches, but most of the shoreline is steep and rocky. Picnic Beach is a popular sandy beach just south of Hazard Point. A scattering of pretty islands dot the inlet. Botel Park can be reached without a boat; a trail leads from Winter Harbour. North Harbour, hidden behind Matthews Island, is a popular anchorage.

Both Forward Inlet and Winter Harbour are major herring spawning grounds and important geoduck areas. A significant abalone ground is located at Flint Rock north of Matthews Island. The various inlets, lagoons and estuaries are used by a variety of seabirds including trumpeter swans, western grebes, marbled murrelets and surf scoters, as well as ducks, mergansers, eagles, loons and alcids. Sea otters and sea lions tend to congregate at Hazard Point.

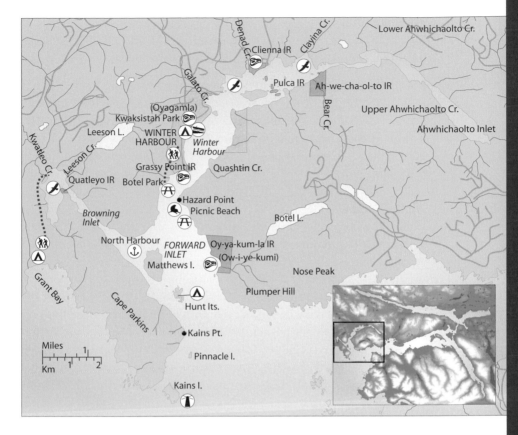

The principal village of the Kwatsino was Ow-i-ye-kumi. Set on the low neck of a small peninsula on Forward Inlet's east side, it had good beaches for canoes and a low cliff protected it inland. It was once high on the rocks above to the east, and was fortified. When peaceful times arrived, the village moved to the waterfront. An old Gopino village was located at Grassy Point, but the Kwatsino came down from San Josef Bay and drove the Gopino from Forward Inlet.

Camping: Wilderness camping is possible at any of the pocket beaches along Forward Inlet. In the middle of the two Hunt Islets facing east is a pleasant cobble beach, well protected from the weather and wonderfully private, though enclosed.

Place names: Forward Inlet is named after HMS *Forward*, a gunboat used on the Vancouver Island coast in the 1860s. It was later sold to the Mexican government, only to be seized by revolutionaries and burned.

Browning Inlet

This long, narrow waterway shoals up to a drying mudflat. Recent logging has dramatically affected the aesthetic appeal.

Hiking: A half-hour trail will take you from Browning Inlet to Grant Bay. If you're exploring by car, recent logging has extended the road access, allowing a shorter route by foot to Browning Inlet. The turnoff is prior to reaching Winter Harbour (there's a sign, but it's hard to see). Active logging means the road could be closed during the week.

Winter Harbour

Winter Harbour refers to both the waterway and the community. The permanent population of about 20 lives along the north shore and on a few of the nearby islands. Mud and gravel beaches are common in the harbour, especially on the east side. Inviting grassy banks along the inlet are intertidal and only a few provide shelter above the high tide line. The harbour becomes increasingly secluded the farther east you go, as few boats bother with the shallow, muddy water that extends into Ahwhichaolto Inlet. Winter Harbour features bed and breakfasts, a small store, a post office, an RV park and a regional campground. A trail leads to the beach of Botel Park. Winter Harbour, like many of B.C.'s early coastal towns, was built along the waterfront and connected by a boardwalk over the mud. The community is closer to China and Japan than any other North American settlement.

Winter Harbour was known as Oyagamla to local First Nations. By 1850, four Kwakiutl tribes—the Klaskino, Gopino, Quatsino and Koskimo—wintered here. A crab and clam cannery was built in 1904 by Jobe (Joseph) Lee Leeson, a miller who pre-empted the land in Winter Harbour (then called Queenstown) in 1891. He later established the J. Leeson and Son Trading Post to service whaling schooners and local natives. Botel House, Meyer House and the processing plant still stand.

Place names: Winter Harbour earned its current name first in the 1800s when it became popular as a sheltered harbour, although in 1890, when first surveyed, the community was called Queenstown. The name was officially changed to Leeson Harbour after the pioneer family in the 1930 *B.C. Gazetteer*, but the name would be changed again, in 1947, back to Winter Harbour after a request by residents.

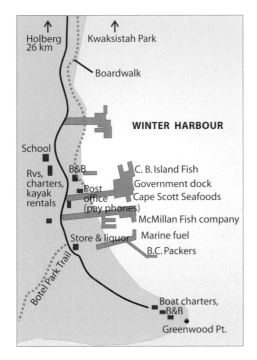

Camping: Kwakistah Park regional campground is located on the water at Winter Harbour. It's accessible by road. It features 12 small and disorganized campsites, picnic tables and two sheltered day-use areas. Seasonal fees are charged. An alternative for paddlers is wilderness camping on the cobble beach on Hunt Islets or the beautiful sand beach at Grant Bay.

Ahwhichaolto Inlet

This inlet makes an interesting side trip. Paddlers must navigate a muddy shoal near the entrance, after which the inlet meanders through a picturesque river-like setting. Finally it opens into the wider inlet, which has a pretty, steep shoreline with a number of cobble or rough beaches for a break. If you're adventurous, try and find the old steam donkey at the very far end of the inlet. The shallow inlet, frequently flushed by tides, provides a rich marine environment.

INNER QUATSINO SOUND

East of Forward Inlet, Quatsino Sound becomes a relatively straight channel with many bays and islands to explore. There are detractions —logging operations, fish farms and logged hillsides—but the charm of Koprino Harbour, Drake Island and Buchholz Channel compensates. Like many areas of Quatsino Sound, there are long paddles with few recreational opportunities. The only official camping is at Spencer Cove. A campsite is located at Ildstad Islands.

Important prawn grounds are located from Monday Rocks on the southwest of Koprino Harbour to Drake Island. At Cross Island and Ildstad Island the adjacent upland is habitat for the endangered common water shrew and ermine. Brockton Island to Ildstad Island is an important sea otter feeding and rafting area. Koskimo Islands are notable for their sea cucumber, crab, abalone and sea urchin.

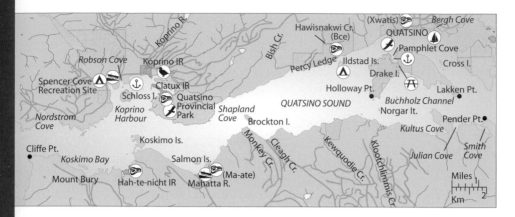

Four of the six finfish aquaculture operations in Quatsino Sound are located on the south shores between Cliffe Point and Brockton Island. The farms raise Atlantic salmon, which take 20 months to rear from smolt to market. The farms produce $9 million in fish each year and employ about 30 people.

A principal Koskimo village named Bce was located at Hawisnakwi Creek north of Ildstad Islands. Ildstad Islands were apparently used as a native burial site, and sepulchral boxes were found here in pioneer times.

Place names: Quatsino is supposedly derived from the word *Koskimo*, the name for the natives who lived here. The name of Quatsino Sound appeared on both Galiano's and Vancouver's charts of 1792. It was named Quatsinough Harbour in 1849. It was surveyed by *Plumper* and *Hecate* in 1860–62 by Capt. Richards. At that time it was given its current name.

Caution: Winds will channel along the sound, and tend to increase in the afternoon.

Camping: Ildstad Islands are a recognized camping area but have no official designation. Rough beaches exist around the larger of the two islands, and camping is wilderness above the high tide line.

Koprino Harbour

Koprino Harbour and the waterfront along Quatsino Provincial Park are some of the prettier sections of Quatsino Sound, with numerous islets, coves and estuaries to explore. The area behind Spencer Cove has a small marina, a log boom and crane, a recreational campground and some housing. To the east side is the Koprino River estuary and some small inlets. The entire inner harbour can become a shallow, drying mudflat at lower tides. Koprino Harbour is a popular anchorage, with spots at Spencer Cove, Robson Cove and behind Schloss Island.

Koprino Harbour is notable for valuable marbled murrelet habitat in the Koprino River area. It may yet be designated as a Wildlife Habitat Area or Old Growth Management Area to protect the nesting habitat. The harbour is also an important sea cucumber area and crab area.

The Kiaw-pino had a few rough homes on the east cove of Koprino Harbour used in the summer and the fall for salmon curing. A fur trading post was located here in 1889, and run by Ned Frigon (see pages 54, 108).

Camping: Eleven campsites are provided at Spencer Cove Recreation Site by Western Forest Products. Some nice waterfront sites are available, but many are taken over on a semi-permanent basis by trailers. Amenities are fire pits, picnic tables and pit toilets. There's no fee.

Launches: Spencer Cove Recreation Site has a disused boat launch that leads down to a rough beach. It's suitable for kayaks. A launch preferred by boaters is located at Robson Cove. The launch area isn't quite so rough as Spencer Cove, but parking is an issue along the narrow logging road. Kayakers might prefer leaving from the quieter recreation site.

Mahatta River

This stretch of shoreline is dominated by a major logging camp at Mahatta River. The Koskimo had a summer village here named Ma-ate. Wooden tombs were placed on the nearby islands and rocks.

Launches: Mahatta River is a popular access point for boats travelling Quatsino Sound. The launch is provided by Western Forest Products. Mahatta River Recreation Site, located farther up the logging road, offers seven campsites at no charge.

Drake Island

Drake Island is a large and beautiful island with numerous bays and associated reefs to explore. The most popular area is Pamphlet Cove, a well-used anchorage. Pamphlet Cove, while surrounded by undeveloped private property, is recognized as a provincial boat haven. The cove is important spring habitat for mergansers.

Six-gill sharks are abundant near Drake Island, one of the very few places they're found around Vancouver Island. Usually measuring

Quatsino Provincial Park: Quatsino Provincial Park is a 654-hectare (1,616-acre) undeveloped park that protects an old-growth forest, some small lakes and the eastern waterfront of Koprino Harbour. It's pure wilderness: there are no established campsites and very little potential for wilderness camping, and no trails. It does, however, have some interesting waterfront, including tall cliffs toward Shapland Cove on the park's east shoreline. The park protects the nesting and feeding habitat of a high concentration of bald eagles. It's also popular territory for black bears. Two uninhabited reserves are located on the park's boundaries. These shelter two narrow and shallow inlets best explored at higher tides.

An eagle departs from its roost high atop a tree overlooking Koprino Harbour. Quatsino Provincial Park is generally inaccessible except along the water, which is blessed with numerous coves and rocky bluffs to explore.

about 5 m (16 feet) in length, the six-gill shark has retained its more primitive sixth gill (most sharks have evolved to use five gills). The shark prefers deep water, and it's not quite known why it comes near the surface only in certain areas. Quatsino First Nation is applying for three deepwater shellfish tenures to test mussel and oyster productivity near Drake Island and Buchholz Channel.

Ned Frigon set up a fur-trading post at Koprino Harbour in 1889 (see pages 54, 107). When Quatsino began to thrive Frigon moved to Pamphlet Cove and, at the age of 66, built another store. His Central Hotel, a three-storey structure complete with a saloon, was built in 1909. It was located alongside a floating wharf. Historic remnants dot the area.

Buchholz Channel, south of Drake Island, is a particularly pretty area that's wonderful for casual exploration. An array of coves with numerous rough beaches are protected by islets and reefs. There are some log sorting operations here, but it's still remarkably pristine.

Place names: Drake Island is named for Sir Francis Drake. It's believed by some that his famous 1550 expedition involved contact with natives near here, a notion popularized in some media reports. The belief is discounted by most historians, who instead place his contact—the first on the Pacific coast of North America—somewhere south of San Francisco.

Quatsino village

Quatsino is a pioneer community of just under 100. The original church, school, customs house, hotel and store still stand. There's no road access to the rest of the island. The community has a dock and float at Bergh Cove. Schooling is available for students from kindergarten to Grade 6, after which they must travel to Port Hardy. The community is accessible by water taxi, a 15-minute trip from Coal Harbour.

Four Kwakiutl tribes abandoned the outlying villages to settle together here at a village called Xwatis. The village's totem poles were made famous through paintings by artist Emily Carr. Today the village is the Quattishe Indian Reserve. A group of Norwegians from North Dakota were the first Europeans to settle here in 1894, calling it Scandia. The 30 original homesteads were ringed around Hecate Cove and went as far west as due north of Pamphlet Cove. The original lots were 32 hectares (80 acres) each. About half have since changed over to timber leases. Some reverted back to Crown land. Most others were subdivided in 1995 into 98 lots.

Quatsino's first general store opened in 1895 when Thomas Norgar arrived with a load of goods. The store, a two-storey building with a false front, became the centre of the colony, and was expanded to include the first post office and the first government wharf. It was located where the Quatsino Lodge is today. By 1899 the community had a school and weekly mail by steamer. The residents included miners, ranchers, prospectors, farmers, merchants, a teacher and a "gentleman." A cannery was added by 1910, and by 1920 the population was about 500, with the cannery employing 128.

NEROUTSOS INLET

Neroutsos Inlet is almost 30 km (18.6 miles) long and is characterized by steep shorelines and few beaches. A scattering of islands, historic relics and a nice cove or beach here and there make it quite pretty. A drying mudflat lies at the inlet's head. The inlet is impressive for the peaks on its west side. The tallest and most rugged is Mount

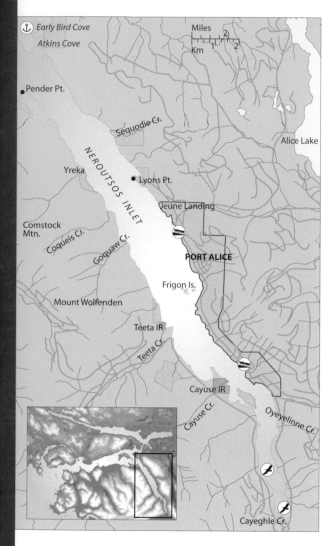

Wolfenden at 1,273 m (4,176 feet). North of it is Comstock Mountain at 1,106 m (3,628 feet). Both are free from logging, making for wonderful views to the west. Far different is the view to the east, where logging is active and many of the mountainsides have been denuded. Industrial activity at Jeune Landing, including a quarry, keeps the background noise of trucks prevalent along much of the inlet. Neroutsos Inlet and its estuaries are considered important prawn and crab areas.

Place names: Neroutsos is named after Capt. C. D. Neroutsos, once the manager of the B.C. Coast Steamships Line. The inlet was first named Alice Arm but was changed to avoid confusion with a mainland inlet.

Atkins Cove

This cove is a popular anchorage for one or two boats. A channel that runs shallow in low tides leads to picturesque and secluded Early Bird Cove. Be sure to watch for the rich intertidal life in the channel if you venture in.

Yreka Mine

Remnants of this failed mining operation can still be seen today, including the wharf, some building foundations, numerous rusting relics and the tram supports. Trails start from a rough beach next to the wharf.

Three early Scandinavian settlers staked claims here and in 1897 built a trail to the 400-m (1,300-foot) level to haul up machinery. The mineral rights were sold to a Montana company and in 1902 the mine opened. At the time it was said to have the finest floating dock on the west coast. The $300,000 spent on development included a sawmill, a blacksmith shop, bunkhouses, a cookhouse, the mining recorder's office and a post office. Two baby trams were built, one 270 m (885 feet) and the other 130 m (425 feet). The main aerial tram extended 1,200 m (3,940 feet) up Comstock Mountain. The supports are still visible. Large ore bunkers, each with a 2,500-ton capacity and trestles, were also built. The mine was an open quarry plus three tunnels, one reaching a depth of about 250 m (820 feet). But only three loads of ore would ever be mined. The first 100-ton load went to Crofton on east Vancouver Island. The other loads went to Tacoma, Washington. Dry conditions the following three years didn't allow enough water to work the machinery, and the mine never reopened.

Port Alice

Port Alice is a pleasant little community built to replace the original one a few miles farther up the inlet, making it Canada's first instant community. Today the population is about 1,000. Jeune Landing is a northern extension of the same community. Port Alice has a shopping centre, hotel, RV campsite, liquor store, hospital, library, laundromat and marina. The pulp mill at Port Alice, the town's major employer, was closed for an extended period in 2003, and many believed it would never reopen. Thanks to a restructuring of bankrupt parent company Doman Industries, it was purchased in June 2004 by U.S.-based LaPointe Partners. While Port Alice was stable in the 1970s and 1980s with a population of about 1,500, it declined to 1,100 in 2001. Since LaPointe has been on the scene the mill has been operating at full capacity, giving the community hope for the future.

Historically, the major link between Quatsino Sound and the rest of the world was passenger steamer. For about 30 years Port Alice was the end of the line for two famous steamers: *Princess Maquinna* and *Princess Norah*. The trip from Victoria took seven days. The ships would overnight in Quatsino Sound to load pulp at the Port Alice mill. Passengers would use the time to sightsee and buy fruit at Quatsino village orchards. The pulp mill began operation in 1920 when Whalen Pulp and Paper mills purchased the area in 1917. The mill at Port Alice is the oldest operating kraft mill in British Columbia.

Place names: Port Alice is named for Alice Whalen whose family operated the first company to have timber rights in the area. Their lease ran from 1901 to 1916, but was never used.

Launches: The main boat ramp is located in the town next to the marina. The ramp is nicely protected. At Jeune Landing, just to the north of a welcome sign and information kiosk, a rough road leads down to an equally rough launch. It's much quieter than the marina's launch, but is more open to swell if wind blows down the inlet.

QUATSINO NARROWS

All the tidal waters from Holberg Inlet and Rupert Inlet must pass through this narrow channel twice a day each way, making for dangerously strong currents. During slack tide, travellers can enjoy sheer cliffs in a waterway just a few hundred yards wide. Quatsino Narrows is prime sea otter habitat. About 500 sea otters, or 17 percent of the current population in B.C., are estimated to live in Quatsino Sound—near its carrying capacity. On the west shore of the narrows is a large cave once used as a burial site by the Koskimo. In pioneer times coffin boxes were found that were falling apart from age.

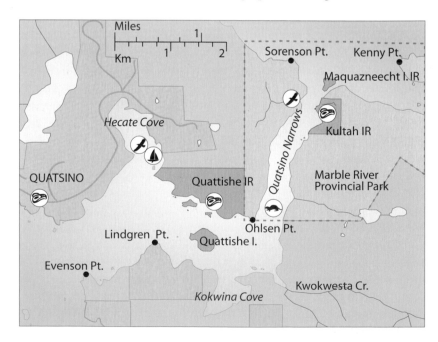

Caution: Currents in the narrows can run as high as 8 knots and the passage must be made at slack tide. Turbulence can be highest at Makwaziht Island on the northeast side of the narrows. The channel is about 3 km long (2 miles), or about 40 minutes of paddling time, so it's advisable for kayakers to travel in the direction of the changing tide. Tides can be waited out in Kokwina Cove or Varney Bay.

Kokwina Cove

If you're interested in getting near the narrows without entering it, Kokwina Cove and neighbouring Kokwina Creek both make interesting destinations. Stay alongside the shoreline and go behind the rocks and islets to avoid the worst of the current. Kokwina Cove has several rough beach areas for a break but isn't recommended for camping.

RUPERT INLET

Rupert Inlet is a 10-km (6-mile) stretch dominated by an abandoned copper mine. Varney Bay is the highlight; otherwise, the inlet is quite unremarkable. At the head of the inlet is a recreation area next to a private campground. The inlet contains some of the most important eelgrass and clam beds in Quatsino Sound. The estuaries of Coetkkwaus and Waukwass creeks provide key shelter for marine birds during large storms.

The mine, its associated buildings and the waterfront along the north end of the inlet are still here a decade after its closing. The huge open-pit mine was the third-largest copper mine in Canada. Owned by BHP Copper, it opened in 1971 and closed in 1995 after having produced 1.2 billion kg of copper, 31.4 million kg of molybdenum and over 330,000 kg of gold. The huge pit went to 402 m (1,300 feet) below sea level. It was the lowest open-air point on earth. It's now flooded and is a deep lake. The copper mine was allowed to dump its mine tailings into the inlet. The tailings weren't supposed to spread, but they did. Fortunately, the wildlife is recovering well, with the largest change a shift from a rocky to a sandy ocean bottom. More mining may be in the region's future. Significant limestone deposits adjacent to Rupert Inlet may be developed, and would require the building of a barging infrastructure.

Camping: The Rupert Arm Recreation Site is located at the head of the inlet south of Washlawlis Creek. The stretch along the waterfront

The coast at Restless Bight and Kwakiutl Point is surrounded by interesting rocks and reefs.

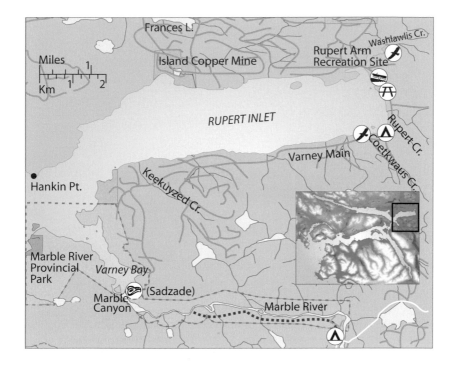

is disorganized; various dirt roads lead to clear areas that could be used as campsites, and often are, though Western Forest Products asks that there be no camping here. A few junky tarp and frame structures have been built in a forested area next to the waterfront. For those with vehicles, Marble River Recreation Site, while not accessible to the ocean, is a far prettier camping alternative.

Launches: The Rupert Arm Recreation Site has a boat launch at the end of a dirt road easily reached from Rupert Main, which leads directly from the Island Highway north of the Port Alice turnoff. Alternatively, Varney Main, the logging road that runs south of Rupert Inlet, will eventually lead to a dock and parking area. Launching can take place from the dock. Varney Main is active and access may be restricted due to logging.

Varney Bay

Varney Bay is an area of high production for marine life and migratory birds, including the imperilled surf scoter, dabbling and diving ducks, gulls, western grebes, marbled murrelets, alcids, eagles and herons. The estuary is also a productive sea urchin site and home to a steelhead run.

Bear Falls is one of the visual highlights of a jaunt along the trail in Marble River Provincial Park. It came by its name honestly—bears can be spotted here fishing for salmon during the annual runs.

Seals use it as a haulout and calving area. Western Forest Products has created a 120-hectare (300-acre) Varney Gene Pool Reserve to protect one of the most northerly Douglas-fir stands on Vancouver Island.

Marble River Provincial Park: This provincial park, established in 1995, includes Marble River Canyon and the estuary at Varney Bay and protects one of the most important salmon runs in Quatsino Sound. It's 1,512 hectares (3,740 acres) in size, with about 20 km (12 miles) of shore. It also preserves the unique coastal features of Quatsino Narrows. While there are no developed facilities in the park itself, the neighbouring Marble River Recreation Site offers camping, day use and access to the trail running alongside a portion of Marble River.

Marble River

Marble River runs from Alice Lake to Varney Bay. The most scenic section of the river, Marble Canyon, is navigable by kayak or small boat through Varney Bay. Interesting vegetation hangs over rocks that have been eroded into intricate caves and fissures. The Alice Lake side of the park is accessible by car from the Port Alice Highway. The upper river is a popular run for whitewater kayakers. The largest chinook run in Quatsino Sound is produced in Marble River, where chinook escapement averages 2,200 spawning fish.

A native village is believed to have been located at the mouth of the river—Sadzade, meaning 'having spring salmon.'

Camping: Western Forest Products has provided a picturesque recreation site at the entrance to Marble River Provincial Park. Several dozen quiet camping sites, some very private, are spread through a mature forest. Amenities include pit toilets, picnic tables, firewood and fire pits. Sites are suitable for both tents and RVs. There's no charge. A day area is located toward the highway entrance, with access to a boat ramp at Alice Lake. This site isn't accessible by marine travellers from Quatsino Sound. A downside, like many upland campsites, is the possibility of a high number of mosquitoes.

Varney Bay is a refuge for migratory birds including surf scoters, eagles, gulls and a wide assortment of ducks.

Hiking: A trail from the Marble River Recreation Site (not accessible from Quatsino Sound) leads to Bear Falls. An extension leads to a cobble shoreline farther down the river. An unofficial trail extends to Quatsino Narrows, but it's overgrown.

HOLBERG INLET

Holberg Inlet is 30 km (20 miles) long and in places only a few hundred metres (yards) wide. Two communities are set on the far ends of the inlet: Holberg to the west and Coal Harbour to the east. Logging has left a scenic buffer of just a few rows of trees along much of the shoreline, greatly diminishing the aesthetic appeal of the rolling hills, which are a patchwork of clear-cuts. Other industrial activity includes

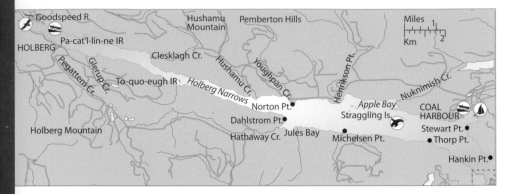

log booming and fish farming. A lack of campsites makes the inlet a long area to explore without a place to stay overnight. Major prawn grounds are located throughout Holberg Inlet.

Caution: Holberg Inlet is susceptible to the build-up of steep wind waves, particularly during southeast winds.

Camping: Many gravel bays and estuaries topped with grass look promising for wilderness camping, but the grass is generally intertidal and will be underwater at high tide. As a rule the tree line grows down to the high-water level. As a result there are very few appropriate areas to pitch a tent along the inlet.

Coal Harbour

This historic community occupies a sheltered cove backed by a rough beach. Homes line much of the cove. Several piers (one in ruins) and two beached vessels add to the character. A colourful monument is the jawbone of a blue whale at the entrance to the town. At 7 m (23 feet) it's believed to be the largest jawbone in the world. The harbour contains important clam beds.

Coal was found here in the 1850s by a geologist serving aboard the first steam-driven ship on the West Coast, the Hudson Bay Company's *Beaver*. The first claim on the property was in 1862. Unfortunately, the Coal Harbour seam only opened to about 45 cm (18 inches) at its thickest, and the mine was soon abandoned, especially since a much larger strike was found in Nanaimo. The community returned to life in 1894 as a Scandinavian settlement. The small town that developed included a bar, company offices and a coal pit surrounded by shacks.

During World War Two, Coal Harbour would become a seaplane and military base for the Royal Canadian Air Force. Today's community centre, store and shipyard are all former air force buildings. A whaling station operated at Coal Harbour from 1947 to 1967, making it the last one along the North American coast. The operation used plane hangars left by the RCAF World War Two base. The Western Whaling Corporation would kill over 4,000 whales and ship over 2 million pounds of meat to Japan, but it still managed to lose over a million dollars. The whaling station is now used as a shipyard.

Launches: Coal Harbour has a boat ramp that's ideally located for trips to Quatsino Narrows or Varney Bay.

Straggling Islands

Located just west of Coal Harbour, these islands are among the prettiest areas to visit in this inlet. Gravel and grass beaches are sprinkled liberally across the area. The Straggling Islands are known for their high biological diversity and productivity. They're home to a large seal population and are a transient killer whale feeding area.

Goodspeed River Estuary

Feeding into the head of Holberg Inlet, Goodspeed River is responsible for the fan-shaped delta at the inlet's head and a layer of fresh water over the salt water that runs about 3 m (10 feet) or more in depth. The combination of fresh and salt water attracts a variety of migratory birds, including gulls, swans, geese and both diving and dabbling ducks. The rich marine environment includes a salmon spawning and rearing area.

Holberg

Holberg is primarily a logging camp with about 130 permanent residents. It serves as a field office for Western Forest Products. A Canadian Armed Forces base to the northwest of Holberg was decommissioned in the 1980s. Once a thriving community, all traces of the base have been removed. Holberg has a gas station, post office, well-stocked store, motel with attached campground, medical clinic, school, pub and restaurant.

Holberg became famous in the late 1940s and early 1950s for having the largest floating camp in the world. It featured electricity, hot water, plank sidewalks and a population of over 250. By 1948 it was over a quarter of a mile long (.4 km) with over 50 buildings.

Place names: Baron Ludwig Holberg was a Danish historian and dramatist.

Launches: A boat ramp is located along the northeastern end of the inlet. It's accessible via a gravel road running alongside the inlet. The boat ramp is set in a sheltered nook behind a dock.

Camping: A commercial campground RV park, part of the Holberg Motel, serves as housing for Western Forest Product employees. It doesn't have a sign nor does it advertise. Inquiries can be made at the store just down the road.

Caution: If you're driving to Holberg or beyond it to Coal Harbour, be warned that these roads are among the most destructive for tires in the north Island. Locals joke about how many tires they have gone through. On one trip to Winter Harbour I got two flats, the second halfway between Winter Harbour and Holberg, and with only one spare you know what that means. Fortunately, the Holberg Motel fixes tires.

A rusting steam tractor lies in the bushes at Apple Bay in Holberg Inlet.

Brooks Peninsula

ALL KAYAKERS HAVE A STORY ABOUT THEIR MOST WONDERFUL EXPERIENCE on the water. Mine is Brooks Peninsula. From the moment I rounded the reefs to reach Kwakiult Point, I knew this area was magical. The trip around Brooks Peninsula was a crossing I was dreading. The peninsula juts 13 km (8 miles) into the open Pacific with little relief from the weather, and the area has a reputation for storms. But in the end, it was the most spectacular day of kayaking I've had. The sun was shining, the surf was low and the wildlife was a parade. The morning started with a humpback whale jumping in front of my kayak near Guilliams Island, and it only got better from there. Gray whales dotted the ocean between Cape Cook and Clerke Point. At one point two surfaced side-by-side so close to the front of my kayak I'm surprised I wasn't hit; you couldn't have shoehorned the one any tighter between my kayak and the other whale. The low swell that day allowed a thorough exploration of Solander Island, one of the most intriguing spots on the coast. Lunch was at Nordstrum Creek, and my only regret is not camping there to extend this incredible journey.

I was lucky; later that summer a group spent at least five days waiting for good weather to make the crossing around the peninsula. But from my perspective, it's worth the wait, and even if you can't make it, worth the try.

Equally magical are the Bunsby Islands and the Mission Group Islands. Most kayakers congregate around Spring Island, with only an adventurous few making it as far as Columbia Cove. The reason, of course, is to avoid the open coast. Yes, there are some risks, but they're minimal if the proper precautions are taken, and the rewards—well, what is the perfect day of paddling worth to you?

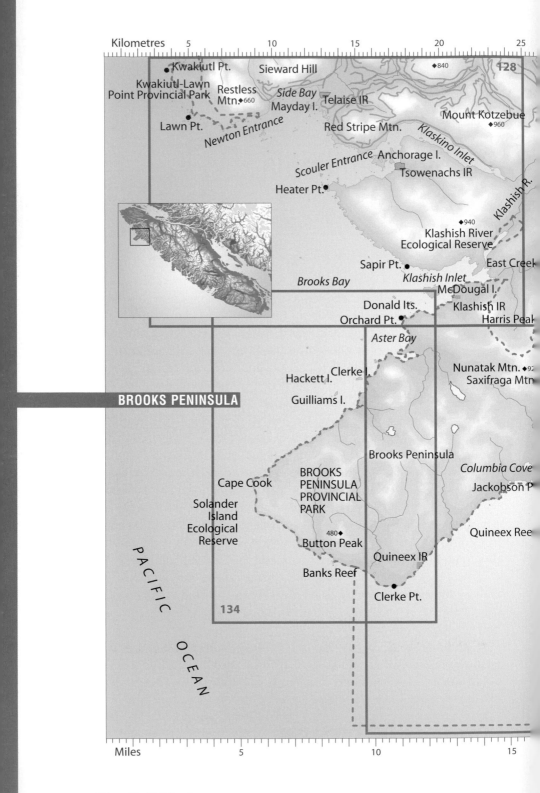

Kilometres   5   10   15   20   25

- Kwakiutl Pt.
Sieward Hill
◆840
128

Kwakiutl-Lawn
Point Provincial Park
Restless
Mtn.◆660
Side Bay
Mayday I.
Telaise IR

Lawn Pt.
Newton Entrance
Red Stripe Mtn.
Mount Kotzebue
◆960

Klaskino Inlet

Scouler Entrance
Anchorage I.
Tsowenachs IR

Heater Pt.

Klashish R.

◆940
Klashish River
Ecological Reserve

Sapir Pt.
East Creek
Brooks Bay
Klashish Inlet
McDougal I.

Donald Its.
Klashish IR
Orchard Pt.
Harris Peak

Aster Bay

Clerke I.
Nunatak Mtn. ◆9
Hackett I.
Saxifraga Mtn

BROOKS PENINSULA
Guilliams I.

Brooks Peninsula
Columbia Cove

Cape Cook
BROOKS
PENINSULA
PROVINCIAL
PARK
Jackobson P

Solander
Island
Ecological
Reserve
480◆
Quineex Ree

Button Peak
Quineex IR

Banks Reef
Clerke Pt.

P A C I F I C

134

O C E A N

Miles   5   10   15

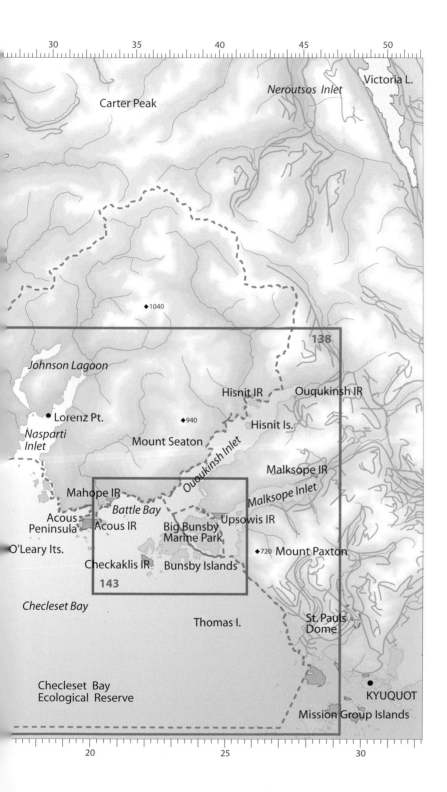

GETTING HERE

Brooks Peninsula is one of the least accessible areas on the Vancouver Island coast. Klaskino Inlet is the most direct entry point to northern Brooks Peninsula. It can be reached from Port Alice by taking Marine Drive then following logging roads. The most direct route is via Cayuse Main/Klaskish Main, but it's gated in two locations (Interfor gates) and isn't well marked. A longer route via Teeta Pass, K Main, I Main, J Main, then Klaskino Main is recommended. It's comparatively well marked. Once you get to the Mahatta River Campground you're in good shape. Klaskino Main leads south from the Mahatta Mainline at the campground. You may also want to consider launches from Quatsino Sound (see chapter 3). Access to south Brooks Peninsula must come from Kyuquot Sound (see chapter 5).

EXPLORING BY KAYAK

One of Brooks Peninsula's biggest barriers to exploration (right after wind and storms) is a lack of launch sites. The only access to south Brooks Peninsula is from Kyuquot Sound. It takes the best part of two days of paddling just to get to the Bunsby Islands. A growing alternative is water taxis equipped to transport kayaks. Otherwise a week or more is needed to explore the most remote areas.

Recommended short trips

- *If you have a day:* The only possible day trip in the waters around Brooks Peninsula would be an exploration of Klaskino Inlet from the inlet's launch. A lunch at Heater Point or Lawn Point would be ideal.

- *If you have a weekend:* Accessibility is still a problem on two-day trips. Consider a launch at Klaskino Inlet and overnighting at Heater Point, Lawn Point or Klaskish Inlet.

- *If you have three days:* A launch at Klaskino Inlet is still recommended. Camp at a central location, such as Heater Point, and explore Brooks Bay during the extra day. Venturing as far as Solander Island is a possibility, if the weather cooperates.

- *If you have five days:* This is the recommended minimum time to explore the Bunsby Islands. Launch from Fair Harbour, overnight the first night at Rugged Point or Spring Island (see chapter 5 for more on these locations), then continue on to the Bunsby Islands.

Return by the same route. The other option is a more thorough examination of Brooks Bay with a launch from Klaskino Inlet or Quatsino. Areas to explore would be Lawn Point, Klaskish Inlet and Solander Island, if possible.

- *If you have a week:* Brooks Peninsula remains a huge barrier between Brooks Bay and Checleset Bay. In a week a kayaker could leave Fair Harbour in Kyuquot Sound and explore to Clerke Point, or leave Quatsino and do the same. It's unlikely there would be time to explore both sides of the peninsula, unless....

- *The ideal trip:* By working out the transportation details for a launch at Quatsino or Klaskino Inlet and an arrival at Kyuquot Sound, kayakers would get to see all of Brooks Peninsula. Leave from Winter Harbour or Mahatta River, overnight the first night at Lawn Point, then continue on to Aster Bay. Weather permitting, round Brooks Peninsula and overnight at either Nordstrum Creek or Jackobson Point. Continue on to the Bunsby Islands and then the Mission Group, finally arriving at Fair Harbour. It could be accomplished in a week, but the possibility of being weathered in while trying to cross Brooks Peninsula could delay you for several days. Ideally plan for two weeks, and if you complete the trip with time to spare you can relax at Spring Island or Rugged Point for a few days, basking in your achievement on the beautiful beaches.

Just southwest of Jackobson Point are two wonderful beaches. Here a river winds its way through the white sand.

An intriguing sea stack in the Bunsby Islands goes by the appropriate name of Green Head.

THE BASICS

Geology and ecology

Brooks Peninsula dominates the surrounding coastline, jutting out 13 km (8 miles) into the open ocean at a width of 10 km (6 miles). A mountainous ridge with spurs forms the backbone of the peninsula, while lower, rolling hills skirt the mountains. Many geologists believe the peaks and ridges above 600 m (2,000 feet) likely escaped the ice age over the last 25,000 years, resulting in the existence of many rare and unique plants. A fault line, the Cape Cook Fault, runs from northeast of Cape Cook to Amos Creek. For evidence, look for thin slices of limestone and chert (a variety of silica) northwest of the creek. Also, sharp-angled fragments of gabbro, a coarse-grained igneous rock, can be found along the fault line, evidence of the underthrusting of the two plates of the fault. Another series of north-east faults extend across Vancouver Island, and are known as the Brooks Peninsula Fault Zone.

Much of the ecology of Brooks Peninsula is similar to other regions of the west coast of Vancouver Island, with lowland forests composed of western redcedar and western hemlock. Exposure to the weather results in poor forest with low-quality wood, dead tops and infection from dwarf mistletoe. The presence of yellow cedar and absence of amabilis fir is unusual for the coast. Near the shoreline salt-tolerant Sitka spruce is dominant. Brooks Bay is a significant bird area, in great part due to Solander Island, home to one of the major seabird colonies on the British Columbia coast. The islands in both Brooks and Checleset Bay are habitat for seabirds.

Weather

The cool, moist climate here is dominated by the westerly winds that prevail during summer from mid-May to mid-September. Winds tend to be far worse at Brooks Peninsula than in Brooks Bay or Checleset Bay due to the peninsula's exposure. It's not uncommon to see the cape capped in dramatic cloud cover in otherwise clear conditions, an indication of the different weather system surrounding the peninsula.

Native overview

Cape Cook marked the division between two very diverse cultures, the Kwakwaka'wakw (Kwakiutl) to the north and Nuu-chah-nulth (Nootka) to the south. Checleset Bay was the historic territory of the

Chicklesaht, a tribe that wintered at Acous Peninsula and summered at Upsowis. Remnants of other fishing stations and villages are scattered across the region. Only a handful of archaeological sites have been found along Brooks Peninsula. North of Brooks Peninsula the land was home to the Quatsino, who had villages in Side Bay, Klaskino Inlet and Klaskish Inlet.

THE SHORELINES

BROOKS BAY

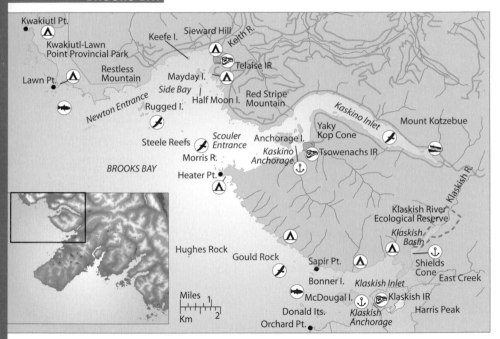

Connected to the huge body of water known as Brooks Bay are Side Bay, Klaskino Inlet and Klaskish Inlet. Open waters host numerous seabird colonies, wonderful beaches and a collection of exposed islands. The inlets are more secluded and protected, most notably Klaskish Basin. These waters are highly accessible thanks to the boat launch at the head of Klaskino Inlet, and camping choices abound. Gray whales, tufted puffins and sea lions will vastly outnumber the tourists. Brooks Bay falls within the Solander Island and Brooks Bay Important Bird Area, and is year-round habitat for gulls; shore birds; alcids, including the marbled murrelet; common murres; diving ducks, including surf scoters; grebes, loons, mergansers and cormorants. The islands and reefs are breeding grounds for glaucous-winged gulls, black oystercatchers and pigeon guillemots. The coastal waters within 500 m (1,640 feet) of the Brooks Bay shoreline are considered important feeding grounds for marbled murrelet. A survey in 1991 found 213 marbled murrelets along this 46-km (28-mile) stretch of coast.

Caution: The southern portion of Brooks Bay is prone to sudden and severe wind gusts during southeast gales due to the wind patterns surrounding Brooks Peninsula.

Lawn Point

Lawn Point offers one of the most unusual environments on the Vancouver Island coast. The long, thin neck of land is almost entirely flat and covered in grass. A short climb to two jutting, flat-topped promontories offers wonderful views of the surrounding bays. Lawn Point has beaches to both the northwest and southeast, though the northwest beach is an inaccessible jumble of rock at lower tides and is best avoided. The main beach to the southeast is well protected by a long line of reefs that may be submerged or semi-submerged in higher tides (see

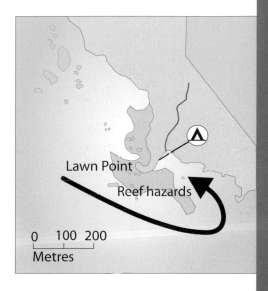

the inset map for the best route to the beach). The beach is beautiful white sand tucked into the shelter of Lawn Point with views across Brooks Bay to Brooks Peninsula.

Caution: The waters between Kwakiutl Point and Lawn Point are strewn with reefs and submerged rocks, which can make for dangerous conditions. Use caution, especially in heavy swell.

Camping: Camping is wilderness above the high tide line. Ruts and thick tufts of grass on the berm at the headland make it unsuitable for camping. The beach, however, is fine. The berm provides some protection from westerly winds. There are no facilities, except for fresh water from a stream at the north end of the beach. Surf is generally very low due to the shelter of the reefs and Lawn Point.

Side Bay

Side Bay is conveniently protected from the prevailing summer westerlies. The shore is a mix of gravel and sand beaches between rock bluffs. At Keith River a sprawling sand and cobble beach extends north. The nearby northern shoreline is pocked with sea caves and other interesting features. Rugged Islets, Mayday Island and a host of reefs dot the bay. Keith River is navigable for a fair distance through a pretty estuary. At the river's mouth, gravel shoals are covered by small breaking waves that hide a deeper channel meandering up the river. The channel will run shallow at low tide. While Restless Mountain has escaped the worst of the logging in this area, Red Stripe Mountain hasn't. Many of the other mountains here share the same fate.

Launches: A logging road to the north of Side Bay runs along the entire length of the bay. A launch from the logging road cuts into Side Bay, but it's not easy to find—I missed it completely. According to Western Forest Products, there's road access to a gravel beach at Side Bay, but there's no ramp from the high tide line to the water. If the surf is down, it may be possible to launch a very small boat from here.

Camping: Many of the gravel beaches in Side Bay are steep, with few flat areas above the high tide line. The largest beach is north of Keith River. While most of the beach is reserve land, the northern portion isn't. Or look for a small but inviting spot for one tent on the gravel bar immediately south of Keith River. The nicest beach, however—a white, crushed-shell beach—is located in a small indentation a short distance south of Keith River. All west-facing beaches can be moderately exposed to weather.

Rugged Island

Rugged Island is part of a string of islands and reefs that more or less form a line from Lawn Point to Heater Point. The shorelines are generally rocky and the islands inaccessible. Rugged Islands and the nearby islets and rocks are included in the Solander Island Important Bird Area, and a visit here will introduce you to a number of seabirds not normally seen, including tufted puffins and marbled murrelets. Black oystercatcher nesting sites have been identified here. It's a significant area for gulls, pigeon guillemots, diving ducks, grebes, common murres, western grebes, surf scoters and pelagic cormorants.

Klaskino Inlet

This inlet meanders for about 5 km (3 miles) into the forested mountains of Vancouver Island, ending in a muddy estuary. Recent logging is a factor. Numerous islands and rocks provide on-water attractions.

Almost half the length of the inlet consists of sand and gravel beaches or rock with sand and gravel, making it particularly good clam habitat. It's a significant commercial clam area. The inlet is a stopover for migratory birds and habitat year-round for gulls; shorebirds; alcids, including the marbled murrelet and common murre; diving ducks, including the surf scoter; and grebes, loons, mergansers and cormorants. Salmon streams contain chum, coho and pink, while several segments of the inlet are herring spawning grounds. Eelgrass is the most common marine vegetation.

Unfortunately, logging has stripped Red Stripe Mountain. The colourfully named Yaky Kop Cone shares a similar fate, as do portions of most other mountains here. A logging road skirts both sides of the inlet for the entire length. The area is slated for "visual rehabilitation."

Kwakiutl/Lawn Point Provincial Park: This park protects over 580 hectares (1,433 acres) of oceanfront, from the large, flat headland of Lawn Point to the twisted, rocky landscape of Kwakiutl Point. Between them is a significant area of old-growth forest. Crude trails lead between the points, but are difficult to find. Like many Vancouver Island parks, Kwakiutl/Lawn Point was established in 1996 out of the Vancouver Island Land Use Plan. Expect it to continue as undeveloped wilderness for many years. Notable wildlife includes sea otters and gray whales. Four eagle nesting sites have been identified in the park.

The east-facing beach at Lawn Point provides a sheltered beach and views across Brooks Bay.

Launches: A boat ramp is located near the eastern end of the inlet. A rough dirt road leads to a rough beach area. Rocks off the launch site make it difficult for anything but small boats or kayaks during lower tides. The only parking safely away from the logging road is limited to a tiny, unofficial notch near the ramp. It's not ideal, and some may be tempted to instead find the Side Bay launch.

Klaskino Anchorage

Tucked in behind Anchorage Island, Klaskino Anchorage is a popular stop for boats rounding Brooks Peninsula. Boats will have a much tougher time navigating the various reefs to reach the anchorage than kayaks. The islands here are quite pretty and have rough beaches. The anchorage is backed by the steep walls of Yaky Kop Cone. Four mooring buoys are provided.

Heater Point to Sapir Point

Numerous pretty beaches are located along this stretch, though many can be exposed to surf. One of the nicest is tucked in directly south of Heater Point. South of Heater Point, rock bluffs alternate with superb beaches. Another fine protected beach is located northeast of Gould Rock. Gould Rock is included in the Important Bird Area designation for this region. Just north of Sapir Point and east of Gould Rock is a beach with a wonderful waterfall that drops from a cliff directly onto the beach. If you need fresh water, here's a picturesque place to get it.

Camping: The most popular of the many beaches along this stretch is at Heater Point. Tucked in behind the point is a fairly secluded sand beach.

Klaskish Inlet

Steep shorelines enclose this inlet, but many attractive beaches line the north and east shores. Birds to be found here include marbled murrelets; gulls; shorebirds, such as the black oystercatcher; alcids, such as the pigeon guillemot; grebes; common murres; surf scoters; and pelagic cormorants. Herring spawn in the northern shoreline. Dungeness crab is harvested here commercially.

A deep, narrow channel as little as 20 m (65 feet) wide and bordered by imposing cliffs leads to Klaskish Basin, a long, narrow inlet with a steep shoreline. It ends in a drying flat at the Klaskish River estuary. The basin is a popular moorage; eight public mooring buoys are provided for mariners. Klaskish Narrows, Klaskish Basin and the East Creek estuary are expected to gain protection under the Land Act, though it can't come a moment too soon (see East Creek Valley below).

Place names: Klaskish Inlet was originally named Port Brooks in 1788 by Capt. Duncan of the *Princess Royal*. The name was adopted as Puerto de Bruks on Spanish charts in 1791. In 1862 it was changed by Capt. Richards who named it for the tribe that lived here. The name Brooks was given to the bay and the peninsula for reasons known only to Capt. Richards.

Klaskish Anchorage

Klaskish Anchorage is sheltered behind McDougal Island, a large, undeveloped island in the entrance to Klaskish Inlet. A rough beach on the Vancouver Island side of the anchorage houses an official Brooks Peninsula Provincial Park kiosk with a map of the park. The beach is very rough and the upland unsuitable for camping.

One of the few documented native archeology sites on the north side of Brooks Peninsula is located on Klaskish Indian Reserve 3, east of McDougal Island. Once used as a seasonal camp, it's marked by a 90-cm (3-foot) midden.

East Creek Valley

According to the Western Canada Wilderness Committee, this valley, which drains into Klaskish Inlet, is one of only six remaining large unlogged valleys out of an original 90 on Vancouver Island. Not for long. Two logging companies have been given the right to log it. LeMare Lake Logging Ltd. of Port McNeill is currently building a road into the watershed; the government has approved 32 km (20 miles) of road and 480 hectares (1,200 acres) of logging. Weyerhaeuser, meanwhile, holds the logging rights to the lower East Creek, which will be easier to log now a road is being built. Environmental groups are urging Weyerhaeuser to designate it an old-growth zone and refrain from logging it. An excerpt from the Sierra Club of British Columbia's Save East Creek website

Klaskish River Ecological Reserve: The reserve was established in 1990 and encompasses the lower 1.5 km (1 mile) of the Klaskish River, the north half of Klaskish Basin and the neighbouring valley slopes. The protected area is composed of 92 hectares (230 acres) of upland and 40 hectares (100 acres) of marine and foreshore waters. The estuary is in near-pristine condition and navigable by kayak. The reserve is most significant for housing wintering waterfowl, including trumpeter swans. Chinook, coho and chum spawn in the river, while the lower river and estuary are rearing habitat for juvenile salmon. Old-growth western hemlock can be found in the uplands.

campaign reads: "Hikers and kayakers describe East Creek as 'magical' because of the sense you get when experiencing such an ancient landscape. The coastline surrounding East Creek is the longest unbroken wilderness coastline anywhere on the North Island, but logging East Creek would cut that in half."

OUTER BROOKS PENINSULA

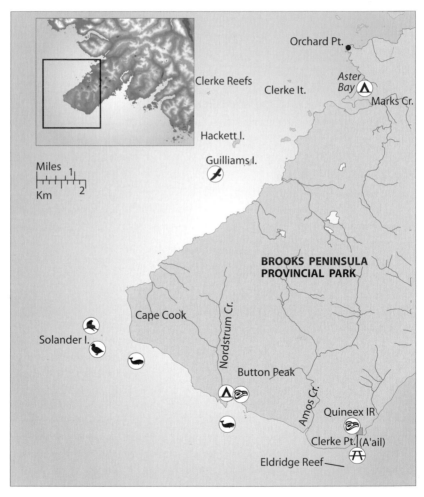

From Orchard Point to Clerke Point, the outer peninsula is exposed to the weather and prone to windy and stormy conditions. But timed properly it will yield treasures. In all likelihood you'll encounter a myriad of wildlife, from tufted puffins to gray whales in their extensive feeding grounds south of Cape Cook.

Aster Bay

The highlight of this bay is a long, white sand beach that protects the tide pools in the estuary for Marks Creek. Beaches, some of them rough and most quite exposed, continue southwest along the Brooks Peninsula shore until near Guilliams Island. The Brooks Peninsula shoreline from Guilliams Island to Cape Cook is steep and rocky. The few gravel and rock beaches are completely open to the weather, making Aster Bay the last reliable refuge before rounding Cape Cook.

Camping: While any beach along this stretch of Brooks Peninsula is a potential wilderness camping area, the finest is definitely at Aster Bay by the Marks Creek estuary. There are no amenities. As an alternative, the beaches within Klaskish Inlet offer more protection from the weather and surf.

Guilliams and Hackett islands

While some visitors might find a small beach on Guilliams suitable for a landing at high tide, these pristine islands are generally inaccessible. The surrounding waters are home mainly to seabirds and sea otters.

Cape Cook

Cape Cook is one of the prettiest points on the peninsula, with steep cliffs capped by trees. Many reefs are scattered along the waters south of the cape. From a distance they appear to be a solid toothed line, but they're actually quite dispersed.

Cape Cook is another notorious Graveyard of the Pacific. One of the victims was the barque *Thos. R. Foster*, which beached here in 1886. The crew survived 21 days eating mussels, crows, mice and seaweed until their rescue by natives. The whaling schooner *Jane Grey* would wreck here in 1893, killing 36 of the 61 on board.

Place names: On the morning of March 29, 1778, Capt. James Cook reached Vancouver Island to see a bay bordered by two significant points. The point to the south he named Breakers Point, now called Estevan Point; the one to the north he named Woody Point, now called Cape Cook.

Solander Island

This intriguing island lies 1.5 km (1 mile) off Cape Cook. It's a mostly barren rock rising 90 m (300 feet) from the sea. Solander is surrounded by numerous reefs and there are no beaches or access points. It's a major bird colony and ecological reserve. A permit is required to land. The island is home to a relatively new weather station, which provides updates on conditions for Brooks Peninsula. A light located atop the island flashes every 10 seconds.

Place names: Solander Island is named after Dr. Daniel Charles Solander, a Swedish botanist. Originally it was called Split Rock by Capt. George Dixon of the *Queen Charlotte*, who travelled the coast in 1787.

Solander Island Ecological Reserve: This reserve was created in 1971 to protect a large colony of breeding seabirds and their habitat. Two species live here in globally significant numbers. A survey in 1989 counted 70,000 pairs of Leach's storm-petrels, about 2.5 percent of the Eastern Pacific population. Cassin's auklets were also significant, with 34,000 pairs, about 1.9 percent of the global population. For Leach's storm-petrels, Solander Island ranks as the third-largest colony in B.C., and sixth for Cassin's auklets. It's home to the second-largest colony of tufted puffins in British Columbia (next to Triangle Island). About 3,000 pairs nest here. It's also home to colonies of fork-tailed storm-petrels, glaucous-winged gulls, pelagic cormorants, black oyster-catchers, common murres, horned puffins, pigeon guillemots, alba-trosses, shearwaters, cormorants and loons. Like many of the more remote islands, Solander Island is devoid of trees. The rocks to the north of the island are popular as a sea lion haulout.

Nordstrum Creek

Halfway between Cape Cook and Clarke Point is a bit of a cove into which Nordstrum Creek drains. Here, in amongst the reefs, lucky mariners can find a sheltered gravel beach perfect for a break or overnight shelter. The rocks in the water immediately outside the beach are numerous and can be tricky to navigate. Located just east of Nordstrum Creek and facing southwest along a short trail is a cave with a passageway that leads to a wider chamber. Fire-cracked rocks, clam shells and other cultural deposits indicate historic native habitation by the Chicklesaht. A midden can be found about 40 m (130 feet) west.

Camping: At Nordstrum Creek a wide stretch in the grass above the high tide line is suitable for tents. This is a wilderness site with no amenities. The creek provides fresh water. The surrounding reefs protect the beach from wave action.

Clerke Point

Clerke Point is distinctive for its 1 km (.6 mile) or more of rock platform and reefs that become visible at lower tides. The shore around the point is considerably flatter than other sections of Brooks Peninsula. If it's necessary to escape the water near Clerke Point, a sheltered gravel beach is located just east of the point. It's accessed through a channel in the rocky foreshore.

The north end of the beach is the Quineex Indian Reserve, and camping isn't an option. This reserve is the location of the only known former native village site on Brooks Peninsula. Trees indicate it hasn't been used for habitation since about 1750. It was almost certainly the village A'ail, used when fishing halibut.

The many shipwrecks on Brooks Peninsula prompted the construction of "shelter sheds," emergency shelters in small bights east of Clerke Point. The name "shelter sheds" is now often used by mariners to describe the bights between Clerke Point and Jackobson Point. They're occasionally used as anchorages.

Place names: Clerke Point is named after Commander Charles Clerke, the second in command on Capt. Cook's third and final voyage that proved fatal to them both. He died six months after Cook was murdered in the Hawaiian Islands. Clerke died of tuberculosis while exploring Alaskan waters.

Brooks Peninsula Provincial Park: Brooks Peninsula Provincial Park, created in 1986, is the largest coastal park on Vancouver Island, covering 74,000 hectares (183,000 acres) and including Nasparti Inlet, Battle Bay and the north shore of Ououkinsh Inlet. Mooring buoys have been provided. The only other amenities in the park are two kiosks with maps; one is at Columbia Cove and the other at Klaskish Anchorage. A rough trail leads from Columbia Cove to the nearby beaches. Otherwise the vast majority of the park can be enjoyed by water only. There are no designated campsites; wilderness and back-country camping are the only options.

CHECLESET BAY

Checleset Bay, the southern approach to Brooks Peninsula, encompasses a huge stretch of water from the Mission Group Islands to Clerke Point. Protected now as an ecological reserve, it also incorporates three large inlets and numerous small islands and islets. A key feature is the Bunsby Islands; Big Bunsby Island is a provincial marine park. Much of Checleset Bay is well protected from the worst of the open weather by the shelter of Brooks Peninsula, making this an ideal location to explore by paddle. Some excellent white sand beaches can be found along southern Brooks Peninsula. Numerous islets form a line in the exposed outer waters as far as 8 km (5 miles) from shore, earning them the name Barrier Islands.

Jackobson Point

Jackobson Point is the first prominent geographic location east of Clerke Point along the south coast of Brooks Peninsula. A beautiful stretch of white sand beach is located along the more exposed side of the point; the other side shelters Columbia Cove. The cove is popular

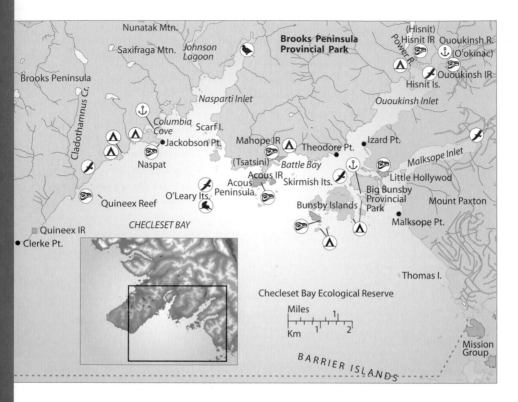

as an anchorage, and is equipped with three mooring buoys. It's backed by a tidal mudflat. A trail leads from the very southwest end of the mudflat to a nearby beach. Watch for numerous sea caves along the shoreline northeast of Columbia Cove toward Johnson Lagoon.

The caves located northwest of Quineex Reef were used as habitation. The first is located near the mouth of Cladothammus Creek, and measures 36 m (118 feet) in depth. A whale bone is among the cultural debris. It was also a burial cave. The second cave is 600 m (1,969 feet) southwest. It's more than 100 m (330 feet) deep. Shells have been carbon-dated at approximately AD 1640.

Hiking: A series of trails join the beaches west of Jackobson Point to Columbia Cove. The trailhead is at the map kiosk in Columbia Cove. The trail is well beaten to the first beach east of Jackobson Point. Another trail leads from the west end of that beach over a bluff to a protected gravel beach. From there the trail continues in rough form to another sand beach. The shoreline can be followed past this beach at lower tide to the mouth of a large cave.

Camping: Several superb beaches are located to the west of Jackobson Point. They can be exposed to moderate or high surf. The largest and most impressive beach is just west of Jackobson Point. About 1 km (.6 mile) southwest is another beach divided by a rock outcrop, which can provide some shelter from the surf. The beaches can be quite exposed, though wind breaks have been constructed by other campers from driftwood. If you're seeking complete shelter, there's a gravel beach in a small, deep bay between the two main beaches (it's the middle of the three tent icons near Jackobson Point on the map). While not as pretty, it offers shelter from everything but the worst southerlies.

Travel notes: While the beaches here are beautiful, a noticeably frustrating feature is the number of buoys, floats and plastic junk that has floated onto the beach. It arrives from all over the Pacific, as far as Japan. Glass balls, a type of float still used today in Japan, are treasured debris, but they're a rare find. The best time to seek them out is in the spring, before the beaches are picked over. The shores of Brooks Peninsula are a prime location for finding them.

Nasparti Inlet

A steep-sided fjord, Nasparti Inlet shelters the entrance to Johnson Lagoon, a tidal lagoon separated from Nasparti Inlet by a very narrow but pretty channel. With no road access and protected within Brooks Peninsula Provincial Park, Nasparti is one of the most secluded and pristine inlets on the coast.

Capt. Robert Gray arrived here in 1792 in the fur-trading vessel *Rediviva*. He had visited Columbia Cove in 1791, a visit that ended in an ill-fated encounter with natives. Gray claimed his party was attacked and was forced to kill many of the attackers. The squabble apparently erupted over the price of sea otter pelts. Gray eventually built Fort Defiance in Clayoquot Sound and constructed the ship *Adventure* (see page 271).

Caution: The current for Johnson Lagoon runs at several knots and is just about impossible to paddle against when in full flow.

Place names: Nasparti comes from the name for the tribe living near here in the time of the fur trade.

Sea otters: Sea otters are considered the smallest marine mammal but are the largest of the 13 otter species. They can weigh up to 45 kg (100 pounds) and reach up to 150 cm (5 feet) in length. They're often found in large social groups called rafts. Rafts are usually made up of females and pups, or males, but not both together. The males can travel over 140 km (86 miles) to create temporary breeding territories with females.

Rather than relying on blubber for insulation, sea otters survive through tiny bubbles trapped in the fur—fur that must be groomed frequently to maintain this characteristic. The fur is the thickest of any animal, with about 100,000 hairs per square cm (850,000 to 1 million per square inch), a feature that would be their downfall. Competition for the pelts would eventually cause their extinction off the Vancouver Island coast.

Starting in 1972, 89 sea otters captured in Alaska were reintroduced at the Bunsby Islands in three attempts. The population quickly established itself and is now estimated at up to 5,000. They can be found from God's Pocket to Clayoquot Sound.

Environmentally, their growth is good news for kelp, as sea otters eat sea urchins. Without sea otters as predators, sea urchins were able to graze on kelp beds without impediment, dramatically reducing the amount of kelp off the Vancouver Island coast. The kelp beds are the equivalent of sea forests, providing food and shelter for an entire ecosystem. Kelp beds are now returning, but not everyone is happy. Shellfish fisheries claim the sea otter is damaging about $200 million in business by reducing the numbers of sea urchins, Dungeness crab, geoduck, horse clams, sea cucumbers and intertidal clams. Controlling the population, especially around Quatsino Sound, is being considered. Shellfish harvesters argue that the environmental effect of sea otters could be achieved simply by increasing the volume of the sea urchin harvest.

Once again it seems sea otters are too successful for their own good.

Tamed only by a small weather station on its top, Solander Island is a wild island home to one of the most significant bird colonies on the British Columbia coast.

A crumbling housepost is a reminder of a culture lost on the Vancouver Island coast.

O'Leary Islets

This isolated and seemingly barren group of rocks is ecologically rich. Seals and sea lions haul out here, and many seabirds make their homes on the rocks. The islets are part of the Solander Island Important Bird Area.

Acous Peninsula

The waters here are dotted with beaches, coves, channels, islands, islets and reefs. Many are unnamed, including three prominent islands between Nasparti Inlet and Acous Peninsula. Much of the peninsula and an outlying island are Indian Reserves.

Checleset Bay Ecological Reserve: The reserve was created to protect habitat for sea otters. That need no longer exists, but the ecological reserve is under stress in other ways. While many islets previously supported nesting seabirds, recent surveys have found nesting on only four islets. They support about 7,300 pairs of Leach's storm-petrels, or about 1 percent of the eastern Pacific population of the birds. Twenty-three pairs of black oystercatchers represent 2 percent of the national population, and 341 pairs of glaucous-winged gulls constitute over 1 percent of the national population. Pelagic cormorants and pigeon guillemots are also found here. The marine waters are habitat for numerous seabirds and sea ducks, including marbled murrelets, harlequin ducks, sooty shearwaters and black-legged kitti-wakes, which roost on many of the rocky islets. About 98 percent of the reserve is open water, and includes about 40 islands and islets. Kelp and bull kelp beds, favourite sea otter feeding sites, are common.

A native village of the Checleset tribe was created here when the tribe moved from Checklaklis Island in the Bunsby Islands to Acous in the early 1800s. Though it was large and had a good water supply, the new village was abandoned when a powerful band member broke protocol by burying his wife and son there. The band moved again to Upsowis. Remnants of the village at Acous can still be seen, including carved houseposts. A nearby defensive site named Tsatsini was used by the tribe when an attack was expected. It was said to be difficult to navigate unless the channel was known. Tsatsini may have been used often, as the bay that sheltered it, Battle Bay, received its name for the many wars fought here.

Camping: A pleasant beach at Battle Bay stretches well past the borders of the reserve. The beach is ideal for wilderness camping.

Ououkinsh Inlet

Rarely travelled, this 8-km-long (5-mile), steep-sided inlet features the Hisnit Islands and two estuaries: Power River and Ououkinsh River. The inlet ends in a drying mudflat at Ououkinsh River. The head of the inlet is a safe anchorage. Dabbling ducks, loons, grebes, diving ducks, gulls, alcids, eagles and swans all frequent the entrance to the inlet. The Ououkinsh estuary is a rich marine environment, home to eelgrass beds, clam beaches and a significant herring spawning area. It's also sea otter and bald eagle habitat and a waterfowl wintering area.

The Chicklesaht had a village at the mouth of Ououkinsh River by the name O'okinac valued for the coho and dog salmon that ran here. Three house depressions and a midden are still visible, as well as the remains of a housepost. A fishing station was also located at the mouth of Power River.

Camping: Power River is a recognized wilderness camping area. The estuary provides a beach area suitable for camping.

Malksope Inlet

Another isolated, rarely visited inlet, Malksope Inlet ends in a drying mudflat. Logging and log booms are on the north and south shores. The northern shore of the inlet and the Malksope estuary are both used by migratory birds, as well as diving and dabbling ducks, eagles, grebes, mergansers and swans. It's a key clam and oyster collecting area. Kelp is plentiful at the mouth of the inlet, while herring spawn throughout the inlet. It's also sea otter habitat.

According to the Chicklesaht First Nation, the band moved to the Upsowis Indian Reserve on the north shore of the mouth of Malksope Inlet when they left Acous Peninsula. The reserve, now uninhabited, is known as Little Hollywood. Remnants of the village apparently still remain, including several collapsed houses and, as late as the 1980s, a carved human figure, but the site is overgrown.

BUNSBY ISLANDS

The Bunsby Islands are dominated by Big Bunsby Island. With rough shorelines that make access difficult, its main feature is a large and

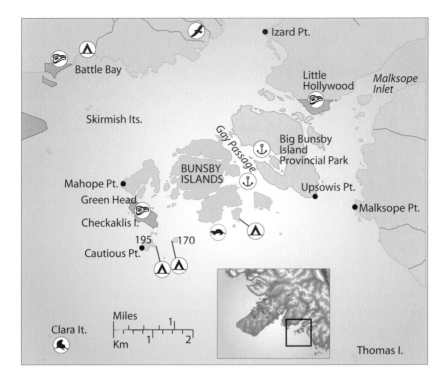

protected cove that's popular as an anchorage. There are no trails or amenities on the island.

Checkaklis Island, an Indian Reserve, is one of the prettiest islands in the group. Behind a sandy beach on the inside north shore are an occupied cabin and some outbuildings. Checkaklis was the first historic home of the Chicklesaht First Nation. At the north end of the island are 14 well-defined house depressions. The cove in the midst of the islands here is very pretty. Another significant native village was located on the southwestern shore of the middle Bunsby Island. Much of the evidence has been destroyed by logging.

Be sure to take a look at the unusual sea stack between the two islands known as Green Head.

There are four distinct smaller islands to the south of the main Bunsby Islands. They run generally in an east-west line, and contain most of the nicest beaches in the group. All the islands are unnamed. Elevation notations on the chart help differentiate them. The southwestern islands of "195" (Cautious Point) and "170" have particularly nice beaches facing one another. The island to the southwest of Big Bunsby contains a number of beaches, but the nicest is located facing east. An isthmus gives views to the outer waters.

Big Bunsby Provincial Marine Park: Big Bunsby Provincial Marine Park was established in 1996 to focus recreational use away from adjacent Checleset Bay Ecological Reserve. At Big Bunsby Park kayakers can discover all the attractions of more popular areas such as the Broken Islands Group without the crowds. Gray whales, bald eagles and, of course, sea otters are all regular visitors. The channels provide excellent opportunities for viewing intertidal marine life.

Place names: Bunsby Islands are named after Capt. John Bunsby, a humorous character in Charles Dickens' novel *Dombey and Son*, published in 1848. Bunsby's brig was *Cautious Clara*, which provided the names Cautious Point and Clara Islet. Gay Passage is named after Walter Gay, another character in the novel. These areas were named by Capt. Richards in 1862. It would only be a guess to suggest what he might have been reading at the time.

Camping: There's only one beach worth mentioning on Big Bunsby Island. It's on the southwest side in Gay Passage. Just north of a rock bluff you'll find a small but well-protected beach. The beach is nice enough, but quite isolated, with obstructed views. In a storm, however, it would be preferable to the more picturesque outer islets. The smaller outer islets have wilderness options on the beaches above the high tide line. There are no amenities. Island "195" features an east-facing beach, while "170" has a pocket beach facing west. The third island, below the central Bunsby Island, has a sand beach on the east side. Another nice cove with a rough beach is located slightly west. The beaches are generally protected from surf.

Thomas Island

Located southeast of the Bunsby Islands, midway toward the Mission Group Islands, Thomas Island is a remarkable open-ocean island. It supports an array of wildlife and is topped by Sitka spruce—rare tree cover for an exposed island. It's home to one of the largest sea arches on Vancouver Island shores. The cave runs right through the middle of the island.

The small outer Bunsby Islands are a pleasant place to pitch a tent, as someone did on the distant beach on the island marked "196" on the chart.

144   The Wild Coast

Kyuquot Sound

WHEN I ARRIVED AT THE MISSION GROUP ISLANDS IN 2003, I WAS RUNNING short of propane and hoped the folks at the tour camp at Spring Island might have a spare cannister; otherwise the nearest shopping would be in Tofino, several weeks away. They didn't have one, but offered to pick up a couple for me in Courtenay. One of the guides was making the trip and would be back in a few days. The delay allowed me the chance to leisurely explore the inlets of Kyuquot Sound before returning.

I had mixed feelings returning to inlets after so much time on the open coast. The buzz of motorboats, the tame shorelines, the comparative lack of wildlife—it didn't interest me as much as the outer waters. But I've fond memories of that visit: an aborted attempt to swim in Jansen Lake (I stopped at the wrong creek and hiked in looking for a lake that wasn't there); discovering a hidden waterfall at a makeshift campsite in Tahsish Inlet; watching dozens of eagles flying overhead in Centre Cove; stopping at the ruins of a whaling station and sharing the beach with a bear; and the highlight, discovering the incredible beauty of Rugged Point Provincial Park.

One day I'll return to paddle up Tahsish River; I know an adventure awaits deep inside Tahsish-Kwois Provincial Park. And one day when I need a break in the sand and the surf, I'll return to Rugged Point. The park is one of those truly special places that makes the west coast of Vancouver Island one of the finest destinations in the world.

GETTING HERE

Kyuquot Sound has only two launch sites. The quickest route by road is to the launch at Artlish River. Take the Atluck Main from the

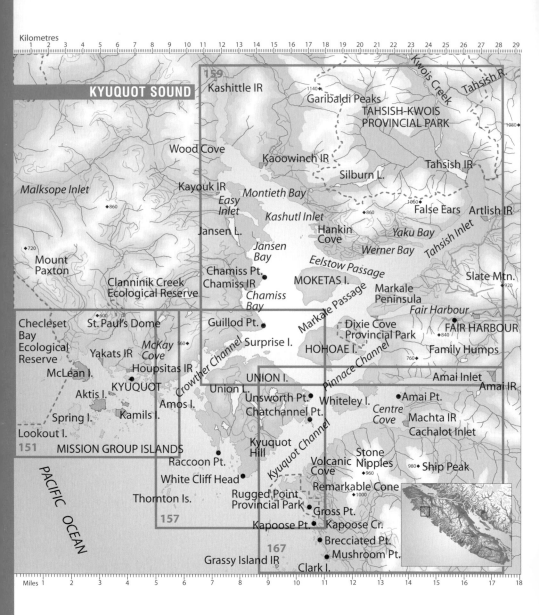

Kilometres
1 2 3 4 5 6 7 8 9 10 11 12 13 14 15 16 17 18 19 20 21 22 23 24 25 26 27 28 29

KYUQUOT SOUND

159

Kashittle IR

Garibaldi Peaks ◆1140

Kwois Creek

Tahsish R.

TAHSISH-KWOIS
PROVINCIAL PARK ◆1080

Wood Cove

Kaoowinch IR

Silburn L.

Tahsish IR

Malksope Inlet ◆860

Kayouk IR

Montieth Bay

Easy Inlet

Kashutl Inlet

False Ears ◆1060

Artlish IR

Jansen L.

Hankin Cove ◆860

Yaku Bay

Werner Bay

Tahsish Inlet

Jansen Bay

Mount Paxton ◆720

Chamiss Pt.
Chamiss IR

Clanninik Creek
Ecological Reserve

Chamiss Bay

MOKETAS I.

Eelstow Passage

Slate Mtn. ◆920

Markale
Peninsula

Markale Passage

Fair Harbour

Checleset
Bay
Ecological
Reserve

St. Paul's Dome ◆600

McKay Cove 560

Guillod Pt.

Surprise I.

Crowther Channel

Dixie Cove
Provincial Park ◆840

FAIR HARBOUR

HOHOAE I.

Pinnace Channel 760

Family Humps

McLean I.

Yakats IR

Houpsitas IR

UNION I.

Amai Inlet

Amai IR

Aktis I.

KYUQUOT

Union L.

Unsworth Pt.

Amos I.

Chatchannel Pt.

Whiteley I.

Amai Pt.

Centre Cove

Machta IR

Cachalot Inlet

Kamils I.

Spring I.

Lookout I.

151

MISSION GROUP ISLANDS

Kyuquot
Hill

Kyuquot Channel

Stone
Nipples ◆960

Ship Peak ◆980

Raccoon Pt.

Volcanic
Cove

Remarkable Cone ◆1000

White Cliff Head

Thornton Is.

Rugged Point
Provincial Park

157

Gross Pt.

Kapoose Pt.

Kapoose Cr.

Brecciated Pt.

167

Mushroom Pt.

Grassy Island IR

Clark I.

PACIFIC OCEAN

Miles 1 2 3 4 5 6 7 8 9 10 11 12 13 14 15 16 17 18

Island Highway. The turn is about 170 km (104 miles) north of Campbell River. Watch for the sign advertising the route to Zeballos. Once you're on Atluck Main, Artlish Main is a quick right. Artlish Main will lead directly to the Artlish River launch. The route to Fair Harbour is rather more circuitous. From Atluck Main, Pinder Main will lead to Zeballos (the route should be well marked). From there simply follow Fair Harbour Main back northward. It will eventually lead to the launch site.

EXPLORING BY KAYAK

Kyuquot Sound is a pretty area to explore, though most kayakers tend to head to Rugged Point and the Mission Group, leaving the other inlets unexplored.

Recommended trips

- *If you have a day:* Any day trips would be limited to near the two launch sites. From Artlish River, paddle up Tahsish Inlet to Tahsish River. From there explore the beautiful estuary and paddle up the river as far as energy or time permits.

- *If you have two days:* Reaching either Rugged Point or Spring Island is possible in an overnight trip, but it would be an unfortunate rush. It's about 25 km (16 miles) from Fair Harbour to Spring Island, and 20 km (13 miles) to Rugged Point. Instead, consider overnighting up the Tahsish River.

- *If you have three days:* Head to either Rugged Point or the Mission Group and set up a base camp, using the extra day for exploration. If you don't mind moving campsites, do a triangle—spend one night at Rugged Point and another at the Mission Group.

- *If you have five days:* Five days is enough to explore all Kyuquot Sound. A nice trip is to launch from Artlish River, visit Tahsish-Kwois Provincial Park, then head down the inlet for a night at the beach north of Hankin Cove on Kashutl Inlet. The next day you visit Easy Inlet and then travel to the Mission Group, spending two nights there. On the last night, stop at Rugged Point, then return to Artlish River. Of course, many people will want to head straight out to the Mission Group and spend the extra time exploring these islands, which is understandable. The most adventurous will want to head to the Bunsby Islands (see chapter 4).

- *If you have a week:* The best way to spend a week out of Kyuquot would be to launch from Fair Harbour or Artlish River then head to the Mission Group. Continue north (out of this chapter) to the Bunsby Islands and south Brooks Peninsula, then return. Also, plan a day or two at Rugged Point Provincial Park.

- *The ideal trip:* Since Kyuquot is the gateway to Checleset Bay and the southern shores of Brooks Peninsula, a launch from here should include the Mission Group, the Bunsby Islands and Jackobson Point on the south side of Brooks Peninsula. Add Rugged Point for good measure and you've got an unforgettable trip. A spectacular odyssey would be to launch from Quatsino, round Brooks Peninsula and return via Kyuquot. On the other hand, paddling up Tahsish River to Kwois Creek and deep into Tahsish-Kwois Provincial Park would be an adventure that has been shared by few.

THE BASICS

Geology and ecology

The main inlets and river valleys of Kyuquot Sound were carved by glaciers that also left beds of gravel along the valley floors. The retreat of the glaciers allowed the sea level to rise, creating the steep fjords and rocky islands. This has resulted in an ecologically rich environment with estuaries, salt marshes, sea grass beds, tidal flats, kelp beds, rocky reefs and upwellings—areas where colder, deeper water rises to the surface, bringing with it nutrients from the deeper water.

Eelgrass is the most common marine plant in Kyuquot Sound. Beds in lower intertidal areas and at the heads of inlets provide valuable habitat for a variety of species, from crabs and juvenile salmon to geese and swans. The reintroduction of the sea otter has increased the abundance of kelp and its associated ecosystem.

Dungeness crab is common in depths up to 100 m (330 feet) in areas with current and sandy bottoms. Sea cucumber species are also found in the sound, and the giant red California sea cucumber is harvested commercially. Chinook, coho and sockeye spawn here, while groundfish include halibut, ling cod, rockfish and sole. Herring also plays an important role in the Kyuquot fishery. Minke whales, Pacific white-sided dolphins, killer whales, Dall's porpoises and harbour porpoises are all regular visitors.

Kyuquot Sound plays a major role for seabirds and both resident and migratory birds. Migratory birds stop at the estuaries and marshes for rest or feeding in fall and spring.

Endangered species found here include the northern sea lion, northern right whale, common murre, marbled murrelet, eulachon, surf scoter, Cassin's auklet, tufted puffin, humpback whale and gray whale, as well as Northeast Pacific offshore killer whales and West Coast transient killer whales.

Weather

Kyuquot Sound shares the same weather pattern as neighbouring areas: moderate temperatures year-round and rare occasions of sub-zero temperatures. The village of Kyuquot is comparable to Tofino for precipitation, which receives about 3,300 mm (130 inches) per year. The amount increases inland. Fog is another consideration. Measures at Spring Island from 1953 to 1979 found fog 10 to 20 percent of the time year-round, with more in the winter. Winds are also strongest in the winter, when they tend to run southeast to northwest. It's generally calmer in the summer, but winds can whip up dangerously at any time of year.

Native overview

Kyuquot Sound is the land of the Nuu-chah-nulth. Fourteen local groups made up four tribes, and together they shared a summer village site at Aqtis (Village Island). The name for the entire group was Qa-yokwath (from which Kyuquot was derived). The inland sites, now long abandoned, provided winter shelter, while coastal sites were preferred in summer. Prior to European contact, these northern Nuu-chah-nulth had an economic advantage because of the dentalia shell beds located here. Dentalia shells were used as currency by many western North American native tribes.

After European contact Kyuquot Sound would briefly serve as a centre for fur and seal hunting, and for processing dogfish oil. The two remaining tribes amalgamated, but the decline of coastal resources hit Kyuquot particularly hard. Local processing facilities closed and the number of salmon boats declined. Now only two licensed and locally owned commercial trawlers remain in what was once a thriving fishing area. Most natives live at Houpsitas Indian Reserve #6 across from Walters Island, though less than half of the band members live on reserves in the Kyuquot Sound area. Reserves within the sound are former native village sites; for the sake of simplicity, not all are mentioned in the text.

Rock bluffs separate an assortment of beaches on the outer shores of Rugged Point Provincial Park.

THE SHORELINES

MISSION GROUP ISLANDS AND AREA

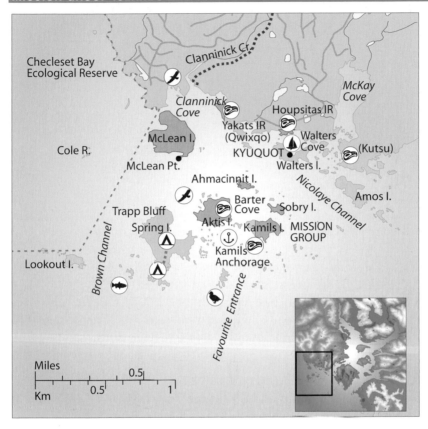

The Mission Group Islands are a mix of wave-pounded rocks, serene channels, sandy beaches and beautiful islands to explore, by foot and by water. Spring Island is the most used recreationally and is popular with kayakers, fishermen, scuba divers and beachcombers. Herring spawn throughout the area.

Spring Island

The largest and most visited of the Mission Group Islands, Spring Island offers camping, a cross-island trail, sea stacks, sea caves and beaches. The north-facing beach is a mixture of sand and gravel that becomes a muddy but ecologically rich intertidal flat at lower tides. It's the most popular area to visit, but nicer areas dot the island. An impressive sea arch is located on the island's north end and numerous

Spring Island is a recreational paradise, with beautiful beaches, reefs and islets to explore.

sea arches and scenic rocky bluffs line the north and western shores. The north-facing cove is used by West Coast Expeditions, which has an untenured camp set back from the beach. The camp is extensive, with numerous tent pads and a central area joined by a trail that fronts the beach. The staff is available for emergencies and general information.

Hiking: A nice 20-minute trail leads down the centre of the island and connects the campsites at the north and south ends of the island. Along the trail are foundations of old buildings, most likely from an old World War Two radar structure.

Camping: The north-facing bay is probably the most popular area. The commercial campsite is located here, as well as numerous well-outfitted fishing camps in summer. The muddy intertidal area can extend out quite a distance at low tide, forcing a slog with a kayak or dinghy. The commercial campsite shares its outhouse with other campers. A far more beautiful option is the sandy beach at the isthmus on the south end of the island (the isthmus appears as an island on most charts, but it's joined by a tombolo). The beach can be accessed from either the east or west sides, and both are usually quite sheltered thanks to the many neighbouring reefs. Camping can be on the beach above the high tide line or on one of several clearings on the grassy berm. The berm is quite well sheltered thanks to the surrounding shrubs and trees.

Lookout Island

The most remote of the Mission Group Islands, Lookout Island has a wonderful but exposed sand beach facing northeast. A navigation beacon is on the east side of the island.

Aktis Island

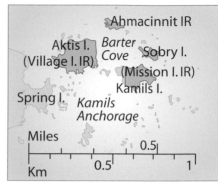

Often referred to as Village Island, Aktis has a long and colourful history as a native village site. It's an Indian Reserve and home to a handful of people who live along the east side of the island. Many of the homes are derelict. Sandy beaches are located along most of the shorefront, with a particularly nice beach facing Spring Island, but these beaches are off-limits. The tidal mudflats, which are extensive along the east shore of Aktis Island, are home to significant eelgrass beds and clam beaches. Dentalia is found on the north of Aktis Island.

Aktis Island was the summer village of the Kyuquot people. Twenty-seven houses were located here, and were identical to the houses at the winter village, right down to the beam and post carvings. They were apparently arranged in a single row along the waterfront, with just two houses in a second row. Aktis was used from the early 1800s, probably due to the growing importance of dogfish oil, shark oil and the fur trade.

The Mission Group is a collection of some of the most pleasant islets, reefs and sand beaches on Vancouver Island.

Kamils Island

Kamils Island is mostly reserve land, though the west portion is public land and includes a significant sandy area and drying mudflat suitable for exploration. Spring, Aktis and Kamils islands create an ideal shelter known as Kamils Anchorage. The best access for boats, not too surprisingly, is via Favourite Entrance, which passes between two unnamed islets to the east of Spring Island. Otherwise the anchorage is surrounded by potentially dangerous reefs. Kamils Island, also known as Mission Island, was called Tcaxhwotaql, meaning 'going after drinking water by canoe.'

Camping: A few of the islets to the east of Spring Island have wonderful sand beaches, and can make for isolated wilderness camping.

Sobry Island

Located to the north of Kamils Island, this is also reserve land and has generally rock shoreline. It can become joined to Kamils Island at lower tides.

Barter Cove was the site of one of the last but most destructive native battles on the coast. In 1855, after numerous raids between the Kyuquots and their Clayoquot neighbours, the Clayoquots planned a surprise attack. They were joined by the Hesquiats, Moachat, Ehatisaht and Checleset. The armada paddled to an island, almost certainly Sobry, and timed the raid for midnight at low tide so they could cross the sandbar to the village sites. The Kyuquot lost some 60 to 70 warriors, and their village and canoes were destroyed. It's still referred to as the last war.

Favourite Entrance

Named for the favoured passage into Kamils Anchorage, several rugged and exposed islets flank the route. It's marine bird habitat, known for Leach's storm-petrels, pelagic cormorants, pigeon guillemots and black oystercatchers. The unnamed islet at the western mouth of the entrance is home to a small tufted puffin colony.

Clanninick Cove

This sheltered, uninhabited cove is protected by McLean Island, an Indian Reserve. A drying mudflat at the head of the cove is a rich intertidal environment. The Clanninick Creek estuary has a large eelgrass bed, habitat for alcids, gulls, dabbling ducks, diving ducks and grebes. It's a waterfowl wintering area and frequently used by bald eagles and sea otters. A trail leads alongside Clanninick Creek to the ecological reserve. Yakats reserve was a winter village for tribes that summered in Amai and Cachalot inlets.

Camping: If you want to avoid the crowds of Spring Island, you could pitch a tent on the beach near the head of the cove. McLean Island is off-limits, since it's reserve land.

Walters Cove

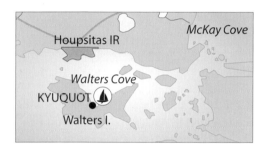

Clanninick Creek Ecological Reserve: This ecological reserve was created in 1976 to protect a small but exceptional stand of old-growth Sitka spruce. It's set about 2.5 km (1.5 miles) inland from Clanninick Cove along a glaciated valley. The reserve is 1 km (.6 mile) in length and has one low waterfall. The Sitka spruce here reach as much as 3 m (10 feet) in diameter and 75 m (246 feet) in height. The creek is used for spawning by a small number of chinook and pink salmon and a much larger coho and chum population. The land around it has been logged, resulting in severe blowdown. The reason for creating the reserve may soon be gone.

This is the population centre of Kyuquot Sound and home to most of the sound's 220 permanent residents. Walters Cove is flanked by Kyuquot Village to the south and Houpsitas Indian Reserve #6 to the north, once a winter tribal village. Federally operated wharves are located at both Walters Island and Houpsitas. The cove is also filled with private docks, commercial and industrial docks and a telecommunications line. The MV *Uchuk III* has a passenger and freight ferry terminal on Walters Island. Floatplanes regularly use the cove. Private land is concentrated along the shoreline facing Walters Cove. There are also several privately owned islands at the entrance to the cove. A well-stocked store and post office are located at the end of the government dock. A pay telephone and garbage disposal site are located on the outer end of the dock. Slightly west of the dock is Miss Charlie's, a restaurant named for the tame resident seal.

Caution: Entry into the cove can be difficult due to the submerged rocks. The only entry for most boats is from the east. Kayaks and dinghies can enter at both the east and west entrances.

McKay Cove

This deep cove's mouth is pocked with islets and reefs, making entry difficult for mariners. It's also subject to strong tidal currents that extend around the nearby islands. The north shore of McKay Cove is used by migratory birds, and is part of a Canadian Wildlife Service area of interest for conservation. The east entrance was a village site, Kutsu.

Amos Island

This island guards the west entrance to Crowther Channel. Clam beaches can be found on the north side of the island. A bird colony is located on an islet southwest of Amos. While most of Amos Island is composed of volcanic granite rock, there's a section on the east-facing cove that's composed of fossil-bearing sedimentary rock. Look for the black rock. For more on this anomaly, see Grassy Island (page 170).

UNION ISLAND

The largest island in Kyuquot Sound, Union Island is a considerable breakwater for the more peaceful channels of the inner sound. The outer shores are spectacularly rugged.

Crowther Channel

The northern entrance to Kyuquot Sound has numerous small coves and islets to explore. The largest island, Surprise Island, has been extensively logged, but there are still oyster beaches and herring spawn on both the south and north shores. Look for the eagle nest. There's a shellfish scallop aquaculture operation on the north end of the island. Steep shores on the Vancouver Island side have kept the channel mainly undeveloped, though log handling and storage is allowed. A First Nations shellfish reserve is on the islet on the west side of Union Island. A floating fishing lodge, Slam Bang Lodge, operates in the channel alongside Union Island June through August.

Logs were once hauled from the bush by rail to Crowther Channel, and evidence of an old track can still be found at British Creek.

Camping: A number of beach areas can serve as campsites along this stretch of Vancouver Island shore, particularly behind Meyer Island. Most sites have pleasant beaches and are well protected from breaking surf, but they aren't as scenic as the outer campsites in the Mission Group.

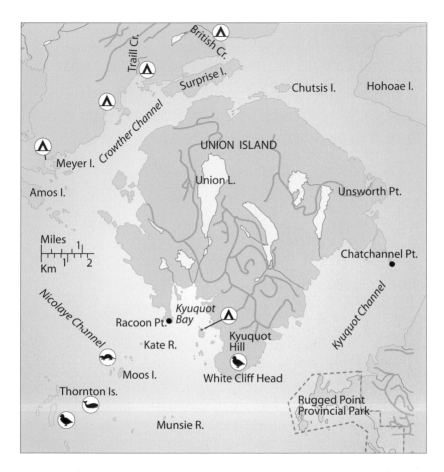

Thornton Islands

These are the largest of a series of islets and rocks in the exposed waters off Union Island. Sea otters and harbour seals use the islets, but they're most significant for the breeding populations of four bird species—black oystercatchers (about 125 pairs, or 2 percent of the world's population), glaucous-winged gulls, pigeon guillemots and pelagic cormorants. Fork-tailed storm-petrels, Leach's storm-petrels and tufted puffins also nest here. The rocks, pocket beaches and intertidal areas provide habitat for migrating shorebirds, particularly black turnstones. Ten other shorebird species have been recorded here. A 1988 survey found 200 roosting Brandt's cormorants, 500 common murres and 480 California gulls. Marbled murrelets and Harlequin ducks can also be seen in the surrounding waters. Near Moos Islet sea otters raft, and the entire stretch is an important gray whale feeding and migration area.

White Cliff Head

Abutting Kyuquot Channel, the area around White Cliff Head features steep, rocky shoreline with numerous pocket coves to explore. Bird colonies are located atop the head.

The aptly-named White Cliff Head hugs the outer shore of Union Island, offering beautiful scenery.

Kyuquot Bay

The exposed side of Union Island is probably the prettiest. Kyuquot Bay is dotted with numerous islands and inlets to explore.

Camping: Wilderness camping is possible on the northeast side of the largest island in the bay. A very pleasant beach is set on the sheltered side of the island, while a quick scramble onto the rocks to the north will provide you with pleasant views out to the open ocean—perfect for sunsets.

THE INNER SOUND

Kyuquot Sound is the least inhabited of the five major sounds on Vancouver Island, and this translates into mostly pristine shorelines. There are, however, isolated pockets of industrialization and much evidence of logging along the mountains. The central sound is dom-

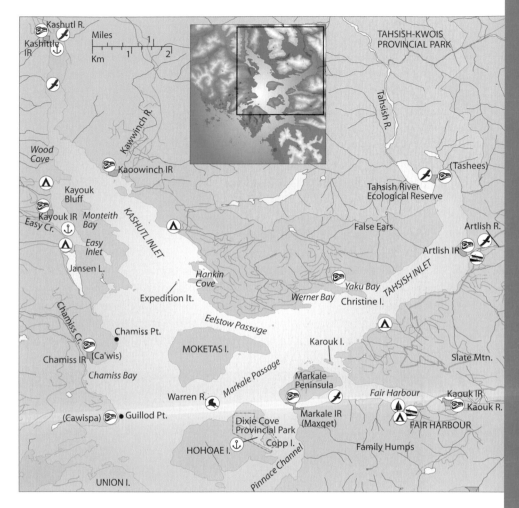

inated by two large uninhabited islands, Moketas and Hohoae. A provincial marine park on Hohoae protects Dixie Cove, a quiet anchorage; the north end of Tahsish Inlet is protected by Tahsish-Kwois Provincial Park.

Caution: The five inlets are protected from the open ocean swell, but winds can funnel down them, making for difficult conditions.

Chamiss Bay

Chamiss Bay is one of the few developed areas in the inner sound. International Forest Products Ltd. (Interfor) has an active camp, with up to 50 seasonal employees and 30 seasonal tree-planting staff. The region's log handling is focused in this bay. Logs are towed here and then barged out. Chamiss Bay has two documented eagle nesting sites and a clam beach. Seals use Chamiss Point as a haulout.

A winter village was located near Guillod Point; local groups from Kashutl Inlet assembled here. One of them, the Ca'wisath, resided at the Chamiss Creek mouth.

Moketas Island

The most impressive feature of this mountainous, steep island is the huge rock bluff to the east. A beach can be found on the north shore of the island.

Moketas is being eyed for its high aquaculture potential, so fish or prawn farms are likely to be part of the future landscape here. Shrimp are harvested commercially in Kyuquot Sound by traps and trawl gear. Shrimp are generally found on sloped, rocky ocean bottoms between 75 and 150 m (250 and 500 feet) down, making the waters around Moketas and Hohoae islands excellent for prawn harvesting. Other areas in Kyuquot where prawns are harvested are Tahsish Inlet and Chamiss Bay. Seals and sea lions use Warren Rocks as a haulout.

The back door into Dixie Cove Provincial Park is through a route best navigated by paddle. This view is out the passage toward Family Humps.

Hohoae Island

Like Moketas Island to the north, Hohoae Island is characterized by steep, rocky shoreline with numerous rough pocket beaches. The north shore of the island is well used as a route linking Kyuquot and Chamiss with Fair Harbour. Marine Harvest Canada operates a salmon farm on the south point of Hohoae Island and across Pinnace Channel. The waters between Hohoae and Union islands and off Guillod Point are used by migratory birds. Particularly notable is a pelagic cormorant colony at the south end of Hohoae Island.

Dixie Cove Provincial Park: Dixie Cove on Hohoae Island is an all-weather anchorage popular for its sheltered waters and views of the surrounding mountains. There are actually two coves here. The first is reached through a narrow channel south of Copp Island (the channel north of Copp Island can only be navigated by kayaks or small boats). The park protects 89 hectares (220 acres) of upland with pockets of old-growth forest, but the uplands are without trails for exploring.

Kashutl Inlet

Extending northwest into Vancouver Island, Kashutl Inlet is divided, in a sense, into an upper and lower section. The upper leg continues past a narrow section of the inlet for about 4 km (2.5 miles) to the drying mudflat of the Kashutl River estuary. Both stretches are prone to strong outflow winds. It's also one of the few areas on the coast where the surface water can freeze due to the amount of fresh water entering the inlet. Evidence of industrialization includes a gypsum mining operation and logging operations. Over half the nearby forest remains mature.

Hankin Cove

This cove is easily overlooked as the access is quite small. It's occasionally used as an anchorage. A creek feeds into it, providing a suitable environment for ducks, gulls, grebes and swans.

Camping: A beautiful sandy beach—probably the finest in the interior of Kyuquot Sound—is found on the shore to the north of Hankin Cove. The beach stretches for a considerable distance, with views down the sound. Camping is wilderness above the high tide line. Surf from ocean swell shouldn't be an issue, but wind waves might be a factor if conditions are poor.

Monteith Bay

A small gypsum mining operation includes a barge-loading dock and facility. Expect the possibility of noise from trucks working at the mine.

Easy Inlet

This deep, narrow inlet has two estuaries and many nice beaches to explore. Winds can channel down the inlet. Look for two eagle nests. A clam beach is at the mouth of Easy Creek. Jansen Creek (which leads to Jansen Lake) supports the only sockeye salmon run in Kyuquot Sound. Migratory birds use the entire inlet, with eelgrass beds on the west side of the inlet. Jansen Lake is a large, warm freshwater lake accessible via a short walk.

Camping: The most accessible of numerous beaches suitable for camping is near the northernmost curving beach at the entrance to the inlet. Other spots can be found alongside the estuaries, particularly at Jansen Creek.

Kauwinch River Estuary

This is a valuable location ecologically, but the shoreline surrounding the estuary is being heavily modified by logging, which has left unstable terrain and drainage issues. Chum and coho are the primary fish species found in Kauwinch River, along with a smaller chinook run. Clam beaches can be found at the western edge of the Kauwinch estuary.

Easy Inlet's various estuaries provide grassy areas to stretch the legs on a windy day with white-caps whipping up Kashutl Inlet.

Kashutl River Estuary

This area is rarely visited, and the narrow inlet and steep shoreline create a great sense of seclusion. Log handling can take place here. There are three known eagle nesting sites, and the entire upper arm of Kashutl Inlet is important migratory bird habitat attracting ducks, gulls and swans.

Tahsish Inlet

Tahsish Inlet is set amid a highly mountainous section of Vancouver Island. Peaks such as False Ears (over 1000 m / 3300 feet tall) and Slate Mountain provide dramatic backdrops. Two boat launches ensure a steady flow of recreational boat traffic. Tahsish-Kwois Provincial Park protects the Tahsish River estuary and the Vancouver Island interior behind it.

Tahsish Inlet has been heavily logged. There are nine tenures for log handling and storage here, and helicopters are used for log drops along the north shore of the inlet. A log booming ground is located at Artlish River. Fortunately, Tahsish-Kwois protects the pristine views up the estuary into the surrounding mountains.

In 1862 Lt. Philip Hankin and surgeon Charles Wood of HMS *Hecate* crossed from Tahsish Inlet to Fort Rupert, becoming the first Europeans to cross Vancouver Island by land. It was an attempt to survey the interior of the island, but results were understandably crude.

Yaku Bay

Yaku Bay is a pristine bay with a beach alongside the estuary. It's a significant clam area. The bay can be used as an anchorage. The lower bay, Werner Bay, is backed by a nice sand beach, but evidence of logging includes a log dump ramp and floating drums. A native village was located at Yaku Bay; it's not a reserve today.

Camping: Both Yaku Bay and Werner Bay have beaches at the head that could serve as a campsite in a pinch, but they aren't highly recommended. Another option is across the inlet in a small cove. A rough beach fronts a grassy area suitable for tents. The area behind has been clear-cut and is only just beginning to recover, but there's an interesting waterfall just to the north of the beach. It would make a beautiful place to visit, but unfortunately no trail yet exists to provide access to the waterfall. Hopefully this area will evolve.

Artlish River

The nearby mountains drain into this river, creating a large river system and estuary. The estuary is slightly developed, with a road and boat launch. This and Fair Harbour are the only two real points of access to the waters of Kyuquot Sound, so the launch tends to be quite busy. There's a log booming ground at the river, plus a commercial dock and barge grid.

The estuary is home to a significant eelgrass bed, and the river attracts mergansers, swans, gulls, shorebirds, dabbling and diving ducks, geese and eagles. A clam beach is located at the mouth of the river. Significant old growth can still be found in the upland areas.

Chum and coho are the primary fish species here. The Artlish River has historically been a fine chinook-bearing river, with counts in the mid-1960s as high as 3,500. Over the last 15 years that has fallen to about 130 fish, with counts of less than 50 in seven of the last 15 years. It's a problem facing the entire west coast of Vancouver Island. Very low ocean survival rates—less than 1 percent from smolt to adult—bring the risk of extinction. Coho, on the other hand, has been recovering since 1998, with marine survival at about 10 percent. Chum survival has also been stable.

Tahsish-Kwois Provincial Park: At 10,829 hectares (26,760 acres), this park is one of the largest on Vancouver Island, and features two lakes, a scenic river canyon and a mountain-enclosed valley. It was established to protect a key watershed flowing into Kyuquot Sound. The south end of the park surrounds the Tahsish River Ecological Reserve, which is the main access into the park. There are no roads or maintained trails. Wilderness recreational opportunities abound, including viewing wildlife, old-growth forest, backcountry hiking, camping and freshwater fishing. The park protects one of the most important Roosevelt elk winter ranges on Vancouver Island.

Tahsish River estuary

Protected by a new provincial park and an ecological reserve, the Tahsish River estuary is one of the major ecological features of Kyuquot Sound, with the intertidal sloughs providing refuge for birds and fish alike. The eelgrass bed in the estuary supports chum, coho, some chinook and a range of birds including mergansers, swans, gulls, shorebirds, ducks, geese and eagles. The estuary is navigable and provides a gateway into one of the most scenic regions of Vancouver Island—an area without road or foot access. Snow-capped mountain peaks continue into the distance of the valley. Both the Tahsish and Kwois rivers (the Kwois River continues north of Tahsish River) are recognized canoe and kayak routes.

Tashees, Chief Maquinna's fishing village, was located at the head of Tahsish Inlet. A trail

Tahsish River Ecological Reserve, set at the mouth of Tahsish River, is the entrance to Tahsish-Kwois Provincial Park. The estuary serves as interesting intertidal habitat.

from the head of the inlet once led to the Nimpkish River, providing First Nations one of the few routes across Vancouver Island to the eastern shores.

Place names: *Tahsish* means trail or passage, a reference to the trail leading to Nimpkish River. Capt. Vancouver named the village Tahsheis on his charts in 1798. Capt. Richards used the name Tahsish when surveying here in the early 1860s.

Camping: The shoreline to the north of the estuary and along the north end of Tahsish Inlet is a long stretch of sand and gravel beach. The difficulty is in finding a level area above the high tide line, as the growth is thick behind the beach. This is a wilderness area with no amenities.

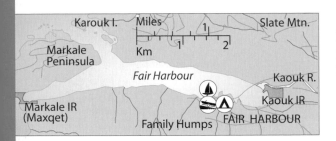

Fair Harbour

Fair Harbour is one of two main entry points into Kyuquot Sound. It's not a community. Formerly a recreation site with a campground and boat launch, it has since been privatized and developed with a dock, fuel facilities and a small store that sells basic foods and fishing tackle. A fee is charged for most uses, including parking. Marine access to the harbour is through a narrow and islet-strewn channel northeast of Markale Peninsula.

The nearby Kaouk River estuary has been modified with road construction and a causeway, but it still remains important bird habitat for swans, dabbling ducks, diving ducks and geese. Kaouk River is a salmon migration route. The area surrounding the harbour has been heavily logged, particularly to the waterline of Family Humps. Markale Peninsula has also been well trimmed. The higher portions of Family Humps remain intact and provide a dramatic backdrop for most of Kyuquot Sound.

Fair Harbour was the site of a major village, Maxqet, on the isthmus of Markale Peninsula. Numerous groups that were spread across Kyuquot during summer assembled here for the winter.

Launches: The boat launch is dirt and gravel with a small beach area to the side suitable for loading and unloading kayaks. A fee for parking applies.

Camping: Sites at the privatized forest recreation campground are generally for RVs and campers, used as a base for fishing excursions. A few secluded sites suitable for tents are located along the waterfront just east of the dock.

KYUQUOT CHANNEL

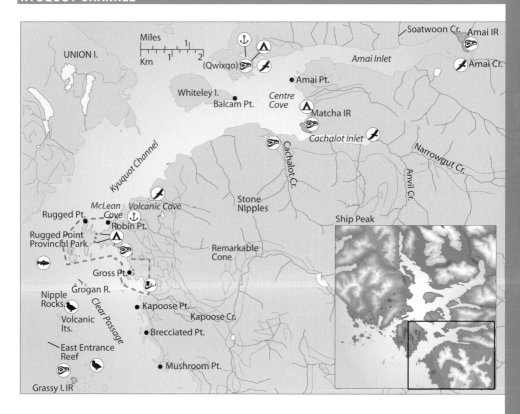

The southern entrance to Kyuquot Sound is exceedingly pretty, with a multitude of coves and beaches to explore. Rugged Point Provincial Park at the south entrance to Kyuquot Channel protects an incredibly beautiful white sand beach on Vancouver Island. At the north end of the channel are other inlets and islands to explore, including Cachalot and Amai inlets.

Centre Cove

Not often named on charts or maps, Centre Cove is the central body of water outside both Amai Inlet and Cachalot Inlet. A particularly nice feature is the tiny unnamed cove to the northwest, which attracts a large number of eagles. The cove was Qwixqo, the winter home of the three local groups from Amai and Cachalot inlets. A fish farm is located off Whiteley Island.

Camping: Several nice beaches along the east shoreline of Centre Cove could be used for camping. The Ministry of Forests has set aside the upland area as a recreation site, but it hasn't been developed. The shore here can be exposed to westerlies. A very sheltered option is the tiny cove to the northwest of Centre Cove. A small island becomes landlocked at lower tides by a gravel and shell bar. A beach provides access to a flat, grassy area suitable for a tent.

Amai Inlet

Amai Inlet is one of two fairly small, narrow inlets that extend off Centre Cove. The inlet features nice beaches and the Amai Creek estuary at its head. There's some industrial activity here, including a Marine Harvest Canada salmon farm operation and several log handling and storage areas. Remnants of a log dump are at the mouth of the inlet.

The eelgrass bed at the head of the inlet attracts cormorants, gulls and grebes. Clams and oysters can be found on beaches at the mouth of Amai Creek and another stream on the south shore. Amai Creek and Soatwoon Creek on the north shore are both anadromous (fresh-water breeding) fish-bearing streams. Prawns are harvested in the inlet, and seals and sea lions use Amai Point as a haulout.

Place names: Amai Inlet may still be referred to as Deep Inlet. It was named Deep Inlet on the British Admiralty Chart in 1863 and on B.C. maps in 1919, but was changed by Hydrographic Services in 1947 to avoid a duplication.

Cachalot Inlet

Exploring this inlet is limited due to the lengthy stretch of drying mudflat and a fish farm that dominates the inlet outside the intertidal area. The large eelgrass bed at the inlet's head (73 hectares/180 acres) supports a population of migratory birds including dabbling ducks, gulls and swans. Both Cachalot and Narrowgut creeks are anadromous fish streams. Eight eagle nesting sites have been found here.

Two local groups of the Kyuquot had sites here—the north shore at the Machta reserve and the southern shoreline at the mouth of Cachalot Creek. A whaling station and pilchard processing plant were located here, and ruins are visible from the shoreline.

McLean and Volcanic coves

McLean is the largest of several small coves along the Vancouver Island side of Kyuquot Channel. A considerable portion of the cove dries in lower tides. The upland is quite flat, and has been recently logged to near the shoreline, leaving a narrow scenic buffer. The area is being eyed for tourism development. Floating lodges and base camps are possibilities being considered. Both McLean and Volcanic coves are provincial boat havens.

This whole stretch of shore attracts pelagic cormorants, alcids, mergansers and grebes. This is herring spawning ground and geoduck is harvested here.

Place names: Volcanic Cove earned its name from the many volcanic cones in the area, leftovers of the volcanic activity that formed this region.

Caution: The entrance to Kyuquot Channel is exposed to swell. Conditions can become rough if the current meets opposing winds.

Rugged Point

Rugged Point is a forbidding rock shoreline, but there are beautiful beaches on both sides of the adjoining peninsula. The most popular beach occupies the northern side between Rugged Point and Robin Point. Two other larger beaches to the south are exposed to the open ocean. A well-groomed trail from the north to the south beach is a five-minute hike. Small trails also join various segments of the south beach and cross Gross Point by way of a short but challenging climb to the southernmost portion of the park.

The Ehetisat and Nuchatlet traditional territory begins south of Rugged Point. Traditional cahqos, dentalia fishing grounds, are located on a beach just southeast of Rugged Point, by Kapoose Creek and on Grassy Island.

Caution: In the summer this area is prone to strong winds. This means that in the morning the northern beach is likely to be affected by outflow wind, while the southern beaches will be protected. In the afternoon the reverse will be true. These outflow and inflow (diurnal) wind patterns can affect all the channels and inlets of Kyuquot Sound.

Camping: Camping is on the beaches above the high tide line. Amenities include a pit toilet, an information kiosk and a picnic shelter on the north beach. The beach on the north side is generally more protected from surf; on the breathtakingly beautiful southern beaches the surf can be moderate to high. Water is available at Kapoose Creek south of Gross Point.

Clear Passage

A long stretch of submerged rocks, reefs and islets lies in a line 2 km (1.2 miles) or less from shore. The area inside the reefs is easily navigated, with the apt name Clear Passage. The reefs can be forbidding, but make for interesting exploration. The most impressive sight is Grogan Rock, a stone pillar that towers 8 m (26 feet) from the ocean. The area is a bird haven. Nipple Rocks, Volcanic Islets, Diver Islet, Calm Rocks, Grassy Island, Clark Island and the east side of Clear Passage shelter colonies of glaucous-winged gulls, Leach's storm-petrels, pelagic cormorants, tufted puffins, pigeon guillemots, black oystercatchers and dabbling ducks. Herring spawn in kelp beds around Rugged Point. Kapoose Creek and Porritt Creek are both anadromous fish streams. Gray whales use this as a feeding area and a migration route.

Grassy Island

Set in among a maze of reefs, Grassy Island offers a beautiful crushed-shell beach facing southeast toward Vancouver Island. It's one of those special places on the coast, but caution should be observed to avoid disturbing nesting birds. It's an Indian Reserve but is often used recreationally. Visitors should keep in mind they're trespassing.

While volcanic rock is dominant in this area, a few pockets of sedimentary rock are exposed. The sedimentary rock is notable because the fossils weren't crushed in the process of heat and pressure that created the rock; creatures that are millions of years old are easily visible. An example can be found by the crushed-shell beach on Grassy Island. Other examples extend as far north as Amos Island.

Nootka Island

JUST THE NAME NOOTKA EVOKES IMAGES—OF ANCIENT WHALERS AND warriors who plied the waters around Nootka Island in canoes; of sheltered coves where early explorers anchored trading ships; of deep inlets carved into mountainous land. Today Nootka Island still maintains that frontier image. It's a place where history and wilderness collide, creating a rich atmosphere where the echoes of life before European influence can still be felt. Two towns and several small settlements dot the waters around Nootka Island, but much of the coast is as it has always been. Impenetrable rocky shorelines characterize much of the outer coast, but areas like Catala Island and Nuchatlitz provincial parks offer exceptional wilderness camping experiences on undeveloped beaches.

On my trip down the coast in 2003 I had a graphic illustration of the two very different worlds of Nootka Island. I turned the corner at Tatchu Point and paddled to Catala Island, where I found more kayakers than I had seen in the previous eight weeks along the north coast. Recreational boat traffic was like a plague of gnats in Gillam Channel and down Esperanza Inlet. I could count five fish farms in sight from one point in Hecate Channel.

And then I turned another corner and entered Nuchatlitz Inlet. Civilization melted away and I felt the closest I had yet been to an inlet untouched by civilization. This sense of undisturbed isolation can be found in numerous points around Nootka Island: where Espinosa and Little Espinosa inlets meet; at the former native village site of Ehatisaht; in Tahsis Narows; and naturally, down the outer coast of Nootka Island.

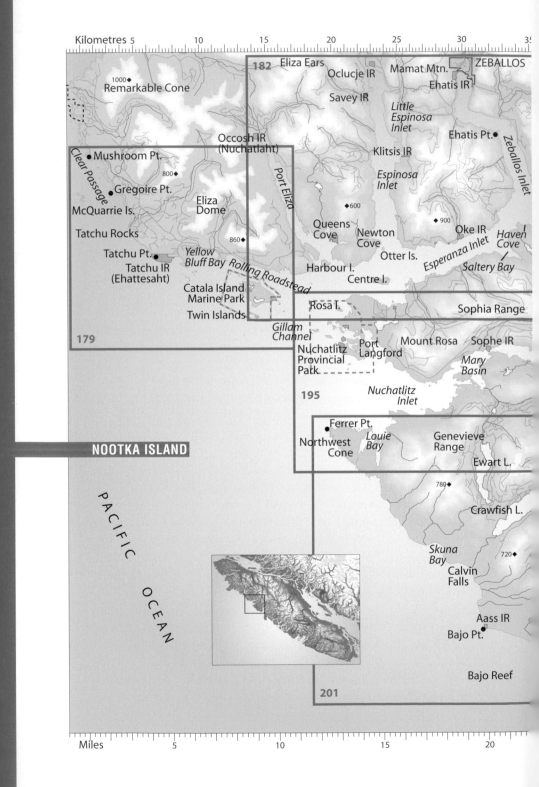

Kilometres

182
179
195
201

Eliza Ears
Oclucje IR
Savey IR
Mamat Mtn.
ZEBALLOS
Ehatis IR

1000◆
Remarkable Cone

Little
Espinosa
Inlet

Ehatis Pt.

Occosh IR
(Nuchatlaht)

Klitsis IR

Zeballos Inlet

Mushroom Pt.

800◆

Gregoire Pt.

Espinosa
Inlet

Clear Passage

Eliza
Dome

Port Eliza

McQuarrie Is.

Tatchu Rocks

600◆

900◆

Oke IR

Haven
Cove

Queens
Cove
Newton
Cove

860◆

Tatchu Pt.

Tatchu IR
(Ehattesaht)

Yellow
Bluff Bay

Otter Is.

Esperanza Inlet

Saltery Bay

Rolling Roadstead

Harbour I.

Centre I.

Catala Island
Marine Park

Rosa I.

Sophia Range

Twin Islands

Gillam
Channel

Nuchatlitz
Provincial
Park

Port
Langford

Mount Rosa
Sophe IR

Mary
Basin

195

Nuchatlitz
Inlet

Ferrer Pt.

Northwest
Cone

Louie
Bay

Genevieve
Range

Ewart L.

NOOTKA ISLAND

780◆

Crawfish L.

P A C I F I C

O C E A N

Skuna
Bay

720◆

Calvin
Falls

Aass IR

Bajo Pt.

Bajo Reef

Miles

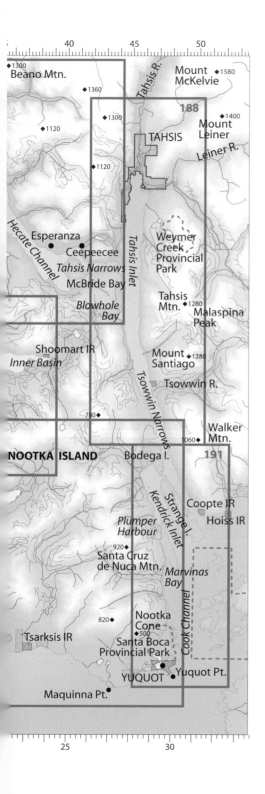

40   45   50

◆1300
Beano Mtn.

◆1360

188

Tahsis R.

Mount ◆1580
McKelvie

◆1400

◆1300

◆1120

Mount
Leiner

TAHSIS

Leiner R.

◆1120

Esperanza

Hecate Channel

Ceepeecee

Tahsis Narrows

McBride Bay

Tahsis Inlet

Weymer
Creek
Provincial
Park

Blowhole
Bay

Tahsis ◆1280
Mtn. Malaspina
Peak

Shoomart IR

Inner Basin

Mount ◆1280
Santiago

Tsowwin R.

Tsowwin Narrows

780◆

NOOTKA ISLAND

Bodega I.

1060◆ Walker
Mtn.

191

Strange I.

Kendrick Inlet

Coopte IR

Hoiss IR

Plumper
Harbour

920◆
Santa Cruz
de Nuca Mtn.

Marvinas
Bay

Cook Channel

820◆
Nootka
Cone
◆500
Santa Boca
Provincial Park

Tsarksis IR

YUQUOT   Yuquot Pt.

Maquinna Pt.

25   30

GETTING HERE

Two full-service communities are located on the inlets to the north of Nootka Island. Zeballos is the most difficult to access, as it means a lengthy drive on the highway north of Campbell River (170 km/ 105 miles) then a 42-km (26-mile) drive south along a logging road (the Atluck/Pinder mains; be sure to turn right after the Nimpkish River bridge). Marginally more accessible is Tahsis, reached via Gold River. From Gold River a wide, well-groomed, but active forest service road leads to the town. The route is well marked. Head through Gold River by staying on the main highway, cross a bridge and turn left at the T-junction. Another quick right will take you up a steep hill that becomes the gravel forest service road. The drive to Tahsis is 63.5 km (40 miles), or a bit more than an hour under normal conditions. Other options are the launches in Nootka Sound, particularly Cougar Creek on Tlupana Inlet. See chapter 7, Nootka Sound, for more details on those options.

EXPLORING BY KAYAK

The inlets north of Nootka Sound and Nootka Island are among the best paddling opportunities on the entire British Columbia coast. Catala Island, Nuchatlitz Provincial Park and Nuchatlitz Inlet are all easily accessible. For those who prefer protected waters, the channels offer miles of exploration with majestic mountain views.

Recommended trips

- *If you have a day:* You'll just be teasing yourself, but launching from Tahsis and exploring Tahsis Narrows is a nice way to spend the day. If you prefer to depart from Zeballos, you can explore the narrows from the other direction (a much longer venture, about 17 km/10.5 miles to the entrance of the narrows). If you launch into Little Espinosa Inlet you can spend a relaxing and rewarding day in the sheltered waters there. A day trip to any of the outer destinations would be difficult. For non-paddlers, the MV *Uchuk III* leaves Gold River and has a three-hour stopover at Yuquot on Wednesdays and Saturdays.

- *If you have a weekend:* An overnight stay allows you to depart from Little Espinosa Inlet and stay at Catala Island or Nuchatlitz Provincial Park (too short a time to truly enjoy it, however). It's just over 16 km (10 miles) to Catala. To stay in protected water, consider leaving Tahsis and overnighting at the Santiago Creek Recreation Site.

Nuchatlitz Provincial Park is a picturesque collection of reefs and islands perfect for paddling.

- *If you have three days:* The best trip would be to travel to Catala or Nuchatlitz Provincial Park from Little Espinosa, using the extra day to explore the islands.

- *If you have five days:* For casual visits, I recommend visiting Catala Island and Nuchatlitz provincial parks, with a side trip (or a stay) in Nuchatlitz Inlet. A more sheltered route is a trip down Tahsis Inlet to the Spanish Pilot Group (covered in the next chapter), with a side trip to Yuquot and possibly Maquinna Point.

- *If you have a week:* A trip around Nootka Island is a wonderful way to spend a week, but it's a trip for veteran paddlers only. Consider departing at Tahsis and overnighting at Garden Point, Catala Island, Nuchatlitz Park, Calvin Falls, Yuquot and Santiago Creek. Plan for foul weather days as well. Less adventurous paddlers could have a satisfying week exploring Catala Island, Nuchatlitz Provincial Park and Nuchatlitz Inlet.

- *The ideal trip:* The ideal would be an extended visit of Catala and Nuchatlitz, with lots of time to explore the areas casually and spend time relaxing on the beaches. If you could combine this with a circumnavigation of Nootka Island, you'd have an unforgettable kayaking experience. This trip should include Bligh Island and the Spanish Pilot Group, of course. This would be a wonderful two-week getaway.

THE BASICS

Geology and ecology

Nootka Island contains most of the coastal environments typical for the west coast of Vancouver Island. These include rocky shorelines, exposed and protected island groups, steep fjords and ecologically rich estuaries. The result is a variety of ecosystems including some of the largest kelp beds off the west coast of Vancouver Island, at Tatchu Rocks, Escalante Point and Bajo Reef. Bajo Reef and Esperanza Inlet are important salmon feeding grounds. Remarkably, Nootka Island and Nootka Sound lack major seabird breeding colonies. There are just four small breeding locations: Cameron Rocks, Ensanada Islet, Justice Rock and White Rock. Even so, the shore areas are used by dozens of species, with the island playing a role by way of migratory corridors, staging areas and both summer and winter habitat. The waters around Nootka Island are used by marine mammals, including killer whales, humpback whales, porpoises, gray whales, sea lions and sea porpoises.

Weather

Like most of the coast, the weather in Nootka is dominated by the two major weather systems, the Aleutian Low in winter and the North Pacific High in summer. The result is a mild maritime climate and coastal region prone to high winds. While the prevailing summer westerlies are common along most of the coast, the lighthouse at Yuquot sees a different picture: southwesterlies during summer and northerlies during winter. This shows the influence of local winds on the lighthouse, where the outflow winds originate from the north in the winter and onshore winds are generated by the differential heating of the land and sea during the summer. Winds greater than 30 km per hour (18 miles per hour) are common year-round. Precipitation can total 3,000 to 4,000 mm (120 to 157 inches). Temperatures rarely drop below freezing at lower elevations but seldom average above 15°C (60°F) in the summer.

Native overview

Today they're the Mowachaht/Muchalaht, Nuchatlaht and Ehattesaht First Nations, the descendants of the Nuu-chah-nulth warriors and whalers who lived in Nootka Sound. The name of Chief Maquinna dominated the earliest written history of this region, a time when the sound was a thriving and well-populated area.

The political and social divisions of the Nuu-chah-nulth constantly shifted, but a structure, based on a series of migrations over the

Replicas of houseposts can be found inside the tiny heritage church at Yuquot.

course of the year to follow resources, was fairly constant. Local groups would form confederations, usually to ensure access to resources. In February groups would move near the outer coast for shellfish, bottomfish, chinook, herring and migratory birds. In April they moved to camps on the outer coast. In late August or early September they would return to local villages for the salmon runs. Until the end of December attention would turn to rituals and ceremonies. By late February, with provisions running low, there would be a move to coastal areas to start the process again.

Three confederacies have survived within the Nootka Sound area. The Mowachaht/Muchalaht territory includes Muchalat Inlet, Tlupana Inlet, Nootka Sound and Tahsis Inlet. The Nuchatlaht lived on the northwestern portion of Nootka Island, in Nuchatlitz Inlet and along a portion of Esperanza Inlet. The Ehattesaht inhabited the northwest side of Esperanza Inlet, Zeballos Inlet, Espinosa Inlet and Port Eliza. Many of their descendants continue to live in the area— the Mowachaht/Muchalaht at Tsaxana near Gold River, the Nuchatlaht at Ocluje on Espinosa Inlet and the Ehattesaht at Ehatis, a reserve neighbouring Zeballos. Former native village sites dot the inlets; if not mentioned in the text, many of the village names are on the maps.

THE SHORELINES

THE NORTHERN APPROACH

South of Mushroom Point, starting at McQuarrie Islets, a line of reefs turns toward Vancouver Island, eventually forming Tatchu Rocks. The shoreline here is wild and exposed. Swell and reefs combine to restrict the area to veteran paddlers and mariners only. Their reward is beaches, headlands and reefs that are rarely explored.

McQuarrie Islets

Kayakers may find a beach here for a break, but be cautious not to disturb the seabird colonies. Cormorants, tufted puffins and pigeon guillemots nest here.

Jurassic Point

Beautiful but exposed beaches along this stretch are slightly protected by reefs. A sheltered spot can be found south of Gregoire Point. The mouth of Tatchu Creek is protected by Tatchu Rocks, which create a bar that can be impassable at lower tides. There's wonderful

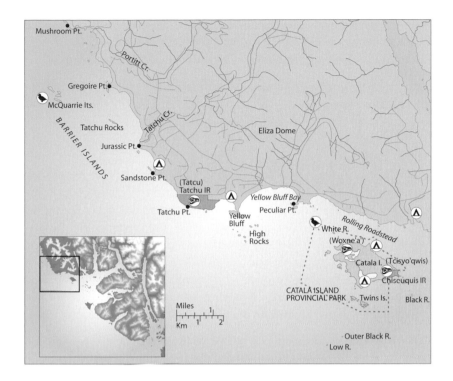

wilderness camping here for veteran kayakers willing to brave the outer waters. Large kelp beds are located off Tatchu Rocks.

Tatchu Point

Marking the northern entrance to Esperanza Inlet, Tatchu Point is characterized by numerous troublesome reefs and shallow waters. The Crown land from Tatchu Point to Sandstone Point is earmarked for lodges and commercial recreation.

Tatchu Point was Tatcu, the home of a group of skilled whalers. Through a merger with the Ehattesaht, Tatcu became the Ehattesaht's summer village. The whalers were allowed a home to winter at Hohk (on the north shore of Esperanza Inlet), and the Ehattesaht extended their range to include the halibut fishing and whaling possible from Tatchu Point.

Caution: Tatchu Point is one of the many problem points of the west coast of Vancouver Island. A shallow ocean floor combines with weather and currents from both Esperanza Inlet and the Pacific Ocean, often resulting in steep swell and confused waters. A bar of semi-exposed rocks extends from the point. The point is best rounded in the morning before the wind and swell rise. A crossing at or near slack tide is also recommended. Even then it can be tumultuous.

Place names: Tatchu Point was derived from the word *tatchtatcha*, 'to chew.' This was a great fishing place and a great deal of food was consumed here at feasts and gatherings.

Yellow Bluff

This is a pretty area with a rugged bluff set between two large beaches. High Rocks, a number of submerged rocks and reefs, stretch in a line from Tatchu Point into the entrance of Esperanza Inlet, making for difficult navigation. The reefs act as a breakwater for Rolling Roadstead to the east. Rolling Roadstead's name is derived from the break the swell gets from the surrounding reefs and islands. It's a major recreation route for boats and kayaking traffic. A logging road runs behind Yellow Bluff Bay. A logging operation and camp are located near Peculiar Point. There's an abandoned airstrip on the upland area.

Camping: The beaches on either side of Yellow Bluff are suitable for pitching a tent. The most protected is the beach northeast of the bluff. Pocket coves lie northeast from Catala Island and are a little-used alternative to the more crowded beaches at the provincial park. Wilderness camping is possible on the beach above the high tide line.

Catala Island

Catala Island has two faces: a jagged and exposed shoreline surrounded by reefs on the outer side, and sheltered waters with accessible beaches on the inside. Because of the shelter, paddlers can explore right up to some very interesting geological features. Numerous sea stacks, caves and other features lie to the east of a spit facing Rolling Roadstead. Major geoduck beds are found near Catala Island, and dungeness crab thrive in Rolling Roadstead. Sea otters extend throughout this region.

Catala Island Marine Provincial Park: Created in 1995, it protects 850 hectares (2,100 acres) on Catala Island plus nearby features including Halftide Reef, Twin Islands and White Rock. White Rock is one of the few seabird breeding colonies in Nootka Sound. The eastern corner of the island is a First Nation reserve. A lake and a bog can be found in the centre of the island.

Two native sites were located on Catala Island; an Ehattesaht village to the northwest and a Nuchatlet site to the southeast. That site, Tcisyo'qwis, is now a reserve.

The cobble spit on Catala Island offers impressive views up Rolling Roadstead to Esperanza Inlet.

Camping: The most popular location is on the east side of the spit facing Rolling Roadstead. Camping is on the flat cobble and sand area above the high tide line. It can comfortably accommodate a multitude, and quite often a multitude will be camped here. Amenities are a pit toilet in the trees behind the beach. Another popular camping location is the beach just north of Twin Islands. A long, sandy beach stretches east from the point, but the favoured location is right at the point, where there are several areas to pitch a tent on the uplands. The beach can be exposed to moderate surf. There's no accessible fresh water on Catala. A number of streams are across Rolling Roadstead on Vancouver Island. Yellow Bluff Bay has a nice river for water not far from Peculiar Point.

Hiking: Rough trails include a route to a lake from the northern spit. The access point is to the left of the pit toilet along the cliff edge.

Place names: The island is named for Rev. Magin Catala, a Franciscan monk. He spent 45 years as a missionary on the coast. One year was spent at Nootka as chaplain during the brief Spanish occupation. Eliza and Malaspina added the name Isla de Catala to their 1791 charts. Catala is often mispronounced. The correct way to say it is KAT-a-la, with emphasis on the "kat," not ka-TAL-a.

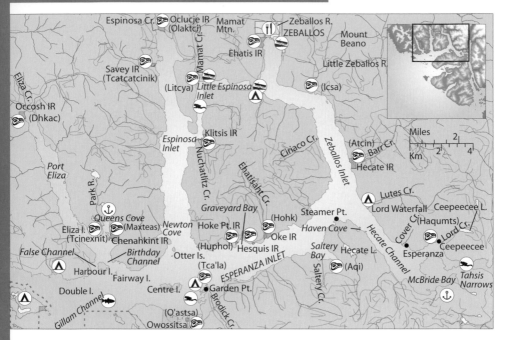

Esperanza Inlet is caught between two worlds. As a major transportation corridor into Nootka Sound, it's prone to heavy traffic. It's also wilderness, with long, undisturbed sections of shoreline. The entire length of the inlet is currently free from development, though there's evidence of logging. Commercial fisheries, both prawn and shrimp, are important in the inlet. Prawns are found at the 50- to 150-m (165- to 492-feet) depth of the upper portion of Esperanza Inlet (toward Hecate Channel). Shrimps are found in the outer area. A commercial fishing ground for hook-and-line (longline) groundfish gear is located at the entrance to Esperanza Inlet. A popular recreational fishing area is in Gillam Channel.

Place names: When Capt. Cook explored this region in 1778 he found a harbour and gave it the name Hope Bay. The Spaniards translated the name to Esperanza, and the inlet was so-named by Malaspina. He explored here in 1791, along with officers Espinosa and Cavallos.

Port Eliza

Called a port rather than an inlet, Port Eliza is the smallest of the waterways surrounding Nootka Island. While interesting because it's narrow and bordered by steep mountainsides, logging has left its mark and Western Forest Products has a waterside dryland sort here.

Like many long inlets, Port Eliza offers diminishing rewards for travelling the full length as the scenery doesn't change and it ends in a drying mudflat. Queens Cove, tucked into the southeastern side of Port Eliza, is most popular as a sheltered anchorage. The area is inhabited, and houses hug the shoreline. Park River can be explored by kayak or small boat. Eliza Creek was once the site of a Nuchatlet winter village, Dhkac.

Place names: Port Eliza is named after Spanish Lt. Francisco Eliza, who was in command of three vessels: *Concepcion*, *San Carlos* and *Princessa Real* (the captured *Princess Royal*). He was sent from Mexico to reoccupy Nootka in 1790. The ships arrived April 5, and the old fortifications and barracks were restored. Eliza would later explore Alaska and Juan de Fuca Strait. Scurvy and a lack of supplies cut that expedition short. A survey sketch of Port Eliza was made by Malaspina's officers in 1791 when the port was named by Malaspina during his stay here.

Garden Point
The southwestern stretch of Esperanza has a pretty selection of sandy bays, coves and rocky shoreline. Garden Point is among the prettiest, with a sandy beach and a bar connecting the point to an outlying islet. The point is a forest recreation site, with very basic amenities. Garden Point is one of the top diving areas in Nootka Sound. It's also a key area for sea otters and a herring spawning area, as is nearby Owossitsa Creek.

Camping: Camping is possible on the beach above the high tide line or in a cleared area in the forest behind the point. A variety of sheltered spots can be found along a short trail. Amenities include a pit toilet.

Saltery Bay
The south coast of Esperanza Inlet from Garden Point to Steamer Point is characterized by numerous pocket beaches, but few are suitable for camping.

Saltery Bay, earmarked for both finfish and shellfish aquaculture, supports a herring spawn. A Nuchatlitz village was located here.

Ehatisaht

The shoreline between Espinosa and Zeballos inlets is steep, with breaks only at Graveyard Bay and Ehatisaht Creek. Both are former native village sites. At Ehatisaht Creek the stream has created a gravel bar and beach. A meadow lies to the east, where there's evidence of a failed farming operation.

Ehatisaht Creek is the site of Hohk, the main winter village of the Ehattesaht. About 14 houses were crowded into the tight space between the stream and a high bluff.

Espinosa Inlet

Espinosa Inlet is pretty enough, but development reduces its wilderness appeal. Western Forest Products has a dryland sort at the head of the inlet and a shellfish aquaculture tenure exists for Little Espinosa Inlet. The highlight is Little Espinosa Inlet, where steep, mountainous shorelines press down upon the narrow waterway. Pink salmon is abundant here, and clams can be found in both Espinosa and Little Espinosa inlets. They're also the best places to find shrimp in Nootka Sound, along with the waters around Bligh Island (see chapter 7). Sea otters are active from Little Espinosa to Catala Island.

Espinosa and Little Espinosa are a popular diving area known as "The Garden." A small forest service site, located at the very head of the lagoon, is run co-operatively with the village of Zeballos. The picnic area includes a rough boat launch to the lagoon. Former native village sites dot the inlet.

Caution: The upper portion of Little Espinosa Inlet is prone to tidal rapids. It's referred to locally as a reversing waterfall as the water floods and ebbs over the shallow bar to and from the lagoon.

Launches: The launch at Little Espinosa Inlet near Marmat Creek is a popular way for small boats and kayaks to reach locations such as Catala and Nuchatlitz provincial parks. To get to the launch, follow the Zeballos Main south from Zeballos. It will turn west as it becomes the Fair Harbour Main Line and hug the south shore of Little Espinosa Inlet. The launch is located where the logging main bridges the inlet at the narrows.

Zeballos Inlet

Zeballos Inlet runs basically north-south more than 12 km (7.5 miles) from the community of Zeballos to Esperanza Inlet. This is a busy

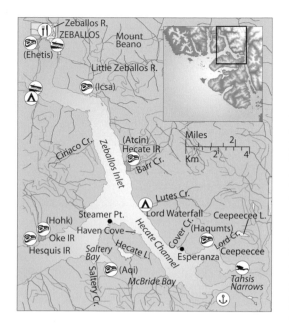

waterway, with a great deal of recreational and commercial traffic, plus development such as fish farms, especially where Zeballos, Hecate and Esperanza inlets meet. Western Forest Products has dryland sorts on the inlet.

Zeballos River supports a sockeye salmon run as well as chinook, coho and sea-run cutthroat. Little Zeballos River has a winter steelhead run, while Zeballos River has a summer run. Prawn fishing takes place in this inlet, and there's an experimental sea cucumber harvest (here and in Tahsis Inlet). Zeballos River estuary is elk habitat and winter habitat for diving and dabbling ducks. Zeballos is a mineral-rich area; there's a historic mineral mining camp in the upland area of the inlet.

Three former native village sites are located on the inlet.

Zeballos

An iron mine gave birth to the modern-day Zeballos in 1964. Hotels, associated restaurants, public floats, a post office, a liquor store, water taxis and a general store can be found here.

Zeballos was settled in the 1930s when gold was found in the nearby hills. The resulting rush created a town that swelled to a population of about 5,000 in its heyday, though it was short-lived. The gold rush was cut short by the war in 1939. By the early 1940s the mines had all shut down, mostly because the price of gold plummeted. In all, about $11 million in gold was taken from the hills.

Camping: Zeballos village operates a full-service RV park. Call **250-761-4299** for information. Cevallos Campsite, also run by the village, is located near the centre of town on the Zeballos River. It has 10 campsites, an outhouse, fire pits, firewood and picnic tables. A fee applies. Resolution Park Recreation Site is a managed site with no

Little Espinosa Inlet is a pretty introduction to the waterways north of Nootka Island.

fees, located about 3 km (2 miles) south of Zeballos on the west side of the inlet. There are seven sites, fire pits, picnic tables, outhouses and a boat launch.

Launches: Kayakers can launch at Resolution Park Recreation Site or in Zeballos on the east side of the head of the inlet at a municipal launch.

Hecate Channel

Hecate Channel and Tahsis Narrows connect Esperanza Inlet and Tahsis Inlet. It's well used by recreational and commercial boats alike. Aquaculture is predominant here. Five fish farms and their associated buildings are all visible simultaneously in the channel. Prawns are fished here. Hecate Channel is one of about a half-dozen key diving destinations in Nootka Sound.

Lord Waterfall

Lord Waterfall is a beautiful waterfall on the north end of Hecate Channel. It's set back about 100 m (330 feet) in the bush. A trail leads from a rough beach through the understorey to a steep climb by rope down to Lutes Creek. At the gravel bar at the bottom is a deep pool directly below the waterfall. If you plan a swim, be warned that the water is chillingly cold!

Camping: A very small, grassy, flat bank is located south of the beach that provides access to Lord Waterfall. The flat area is suitable for a single tent. The nearby fish farm tends to attract traffic and runs its noisy generator till late in the day. It's not an ideal location, but there are very few alternatives in this area.

Esperanza

This tiny community is tucked into the north shore of Hecate Channel. It's a non-denominational mission and school that offers a place of refuge for individuals and families in crisis. A summer and family camp is also offered each year. The mission can be contacted at **250-934-7792**.

A small hospital was built here in 1937 by the Shantymen's Christian Association and called the Nootka Mission Hospital. A hotel was built beside it in 1938; it burned down in 1960. The Shantymen purchased the property and built a community centre. The hospital closed in 1974 but the centre is still run by the Shantymen.

McBride Bay

The bay provides a protected anchorage and is considered a sensitive marine area. While it has been used for log booming, current planning is to designate it for public recreational use. Remnants of an old sawmill are on the south shore of the bay.

Ceepeecee

This tiny and picturesque community of little more than a dozen homes and cottages is sandwiched between tall peaks on the north shore of Tahsis Narrows. It's accessible only by boat.

The Canadian Packing Corporation, a subsidiary of the California Packing Corporation, opened a pilchard-reduction plant here in 1927. The plant burned down in 1958. The post office, which opened in May 1926, was eventually moved to Esperanza and renamed Esperanza Post Office.

Hiking: A 1.5-km (1-mile) trail runs from the community of Ceepeecee to Ceepeecee Lake, then along the lake's shore.

Place names: The Canadian Packing Company operated here in the 1920s, and the community (a post office, steamer landing and settlement) picked up the phonetic rendering of the C.P.C. name. The local nickname was accepted by the post office, and adopted by the *B.C. Gazetteer* in 1930.

Tahsis Narrows

The narrows is just under 2 km (about a mile long). It's as little as a few hundred yards wide in some stretches and is bounded by tall peaks on either side, making for an impressive journey. Incredibly,

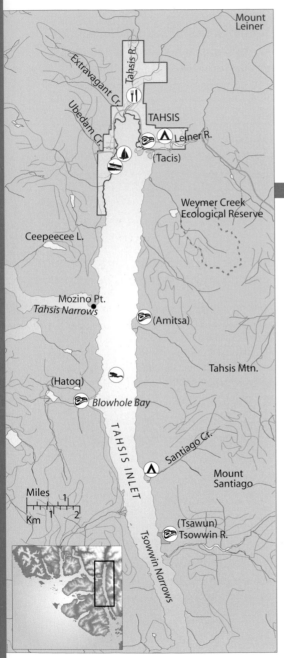

Tahsis Narrows is exempt from strong currents, despite it being a narrow waterway between two huge bodies of water strongly affected by tide. The water from Tahsis Inlet travels south, creating strong currents at Tsowwin Narrows instead. Tahsis Narrows is a popular dive location.

TAHSIS INLET

Tahsis Inlet is an impressive 20-km (12-mile) stretch of water bounded by mountainous peaks on both sides. The full-service community of Tahsis is located at the head of the inlet, but the vast majority of its length is undeveloped. Recreational traffic can be high, especially toward Tahsis. Tahsis River has one of the largest coho spawning runs in Nootka Sound and one of the largest chum runs, including a late winter run. Prawns are fished in Tahsis Inlet, and a long-term experimental harvest of sea cucumbers is taking place here.

Leiner River

The river ends in a drying mud-flat that's a rich marine environment. Leiner River is home to a sockeye run, a summer and winter steelhead run, a coho run and cutthroat. The northern section of Tahsis Inlet is habitat for the endangered Keen's long-eared myotis. Paddling opportunities are limited, but there's a recreation site slightly up the river that's accessible by road.

North of the river was Tacis, once home to the legendary Chief Maquinna. It was here that Maquinna hosted captains Vancouver and Quadra in 1792.

Camping: The Leiner River Recreation Site is a user-maintained site with a string of eight pretty campsites near the river. It's accessible by road but not water. Amenities are pit toilets, picnic tables and fire pits. It makes a staging area for launches from Tahsis.

Tahsis

The community of Tahsis sits along the Tahsis River mouth below the impressive peaks of Mount Leiner and Mount McKelvie. Economically, Tahsis has become a victim of the downturn in the forest industry's fortunes, and the mill on the waterfront has closed and is being dismantled.

The first sawmill at Tahsis was built in 1945 and was initially a floating logging camp. It was sold several years later to the Tahsis Company, a subsidiary of the East Asiatic Company, a corporation headed by a Danish prince. The company also owned the pulp mill at Gold River. In 1967 Princess Margrethe and Prince Henrik of Denmark visited the mill at Tahsis, along with an entourage of industrialists, Danish officials and an ambassador. The visit is most memorable for the princess touring the mill wearing a hard hat.

Tahsis is a full-service community with a general store, hotel, pub, marina, bank, government dock and post office. Laundry and showers are located at the marina.

Launches: The best access to the water is on the west side of Zeballos Inlet south of the government dock. The launch is a large, vacant tarmac area with adequate parking located across the road.

Hiking: A number of well-marked local trails run off the main road through Tahsis. The Coral Cave Recreation Trail is a short hike from a rough road north of Tahsis. Bring your flashlight. The West Bay Recreation Trail runs for 2 km (1.2 miles) from the south end of town through the forest along Tahsis Inlet and provides access to the beach there.

Tsowwin Narrows

The Tsowwin River has pushed a large delta of sediment into Tahsis Inlet, which serves as both a landmark and a navigational roadblock.

The narrows is one of the largest clam areas in Nootka Sound. Tsowwin River is important elk habitat and there are numerous bears along this stretch of the inlet. Native village sites dot the inlet.

A significant log tie-up is located at Tsowwin Narrows and a logging camp is located at Blowhole Bay. This stretch of Tahsis Inlet is quite stunning, but the amount of logging visible on Nootka Island is one of the worst examples on the Vancouver Island coastline. The Vancouver Island side of Tahsis Inlet is also logged, but the height and drama of the peaks (such as Mt. Santiago and Tahsis Mountain) keep the view interesting.

Caution: Tidal streams can run as high as 3 knots through the narrows, making passage difficult if you're opposing the current. Other than the current, you'll encounter nothing worse than a few rips.

Camping: Most of Tahsis Inlet is steep-shored and rocky. Tsowwin Narrows is mostly intertidal and the foreshore is best left pristine. The best camping is at Santiago Creek, where there's a recreation site on a flat, grassy headland. It has several tent sites, picnic tables and a pit toilet. It's not maintained. Blackberry is encroaching on the grassy clearing and at last look, in 2003, one of the two picnic tables was almost completely overrun. Without maintenance the area will soon be entirely overgrown. Access is from a rough beach on either side of the headland.

COOK CHANNEL

Cook Channel separates the Spanish Pilot Group from Nootka Island. The waterway isn't wide and is relatively sheltered from the open ocean swell. There are two small developments here: the community of Nootka and Yuquot at Friendly Cove.

Kendrick Inlet

Two large islands lie alongside Nootka Island here. One is Bodega Island, which is separated from Nootka by a narrow and shallow channel that turns muddy at lower tides. Bodega Island in turn is separated from Strange Island by Princesa Channel, a picturesque but rock-strewn waterway. Boats will have a far tougher time here than kayakers.

Kendrick Inlet is a key herring spawning location and one of the largest clam areas in Nootka Sound. Dungeness crab is found here in high numbers. There's a large dryland sort near Plumper Harbour.

North Kendrick Inlet is a provincial boat haven. Jewitt Cove, on Strange Island, is another anchorage. The area around the cove is designated for recreational use.

Camping: A very nice gravel beach is located along the south shore of Strange Island west of a bluff dominated by Salter Point. There are no amenities.

Marvinas Bay

With three creeks leading to the bay, Marvinas is rich in marine life, particularly marine birds. It's a herring spawning area. The Moachat village site of Mawun was located at the head of the bay. Commander W. R. Broughton refitted his sloop of war *Providence* here in 1796. The American ship *Boston* was captured in the bay in 1803 by Maquinna, who killed all but two of the crew. One of the survivors, John R. Jewitt, was forced to sail *Boston* to Friendly Cove. The ship was burned there and Jewitt spent two years as a slave. Eventually he was freed and later wrote a popular account of his ordeal.

Camping: Tucked into the bay is a choice of beaches. The nicest is on the north end. It's very well protected. It's not a designated camping area. An alternative is Strange Island.

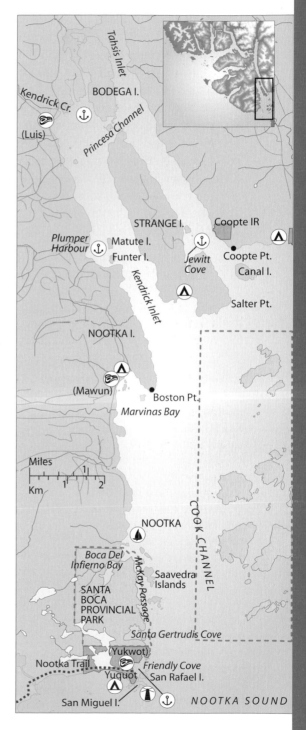

Nootka

This tiny community is tucked into a cove just outside the entrance to Boca del Infierno Bay. A few homes line the waterfront. A small marina that sells fuel is on the south side of the peninsula. The largest of the Saavedra Islands is privately owned and is a resort.

Boca del Infierno Bay is reached via a narrow channel subject to an extremely powerful tidal stream that can make it impassable. Once inside there's little to see. The tree line and understorey extends to the high tide line, allowing little exploration of the shore. The head of the bay is a drying mudflat. Given the difficult access and lack of attractions once inside, exploration isn't recommended unless you want to navigate the pretty channel into the bay at slack tide. If the tide turns against you, you may be stuck there for six hours, so beware.

Place names: The tide rushing through the narrow entrance at the mouth of the bay earned it the name that translates to 'Bay of Fury' or 'Bay of Hell' (though some translate it as 'mouth of the inferno'). The Spanish name was adopted because it was more palatable. A 1933 memo from H. D. Parizeau of the Canadian Hydrographic Service states, "While the name translated means Bay of Fury or Bay of Hell, and therefore is objectionable, being in a foreign language its objection isn't so transparent."

Santa Gertrudis-Boca del Infierno Provincial Park: Commonly referred to as Santa Boca Provincial Park, it's a little-known and even less visited park that encompasses both Boca del Infierno Bay and Santa Gertrudis Cove. Created in 1996 and encompassing 440 hectares (1,087 acres), it lies north of the reserve at Yuquot and protects an old-growth forest, coastal marine habitat and some native heritage sites. There's only one small trail within the park— from Santa Gertrudis Cove to Jewitt Lake. The visual highlight is the tidal rapid through the mouth of Boca del Infierno Bay. Sheltered anchorages can be found in both Boca del Infierno and Santa Gertrudis.

Santa Gertrudis Cove

This pretty cove has a number of small islands in its centre that can become joined to Nootka Island at low tide. It's a protected anchorage and a nice place to explore by kayak. A trail leads from the cove to Jewitt Lake.

Friendly Cove

This protected cove is part of a Mowachaht reserve that puts out the welcome mat for visitors. The community consists of a pair of houses, the manned lighthouse and a pretty church. There's a dock for mooring boats and an extensive gravel beach for landing kayaks. Friendly Cove is the southern end of the Nootka Trail, and is often busy with boats picking up and dropping off hikers. The MV *Uchuk III* stops here. The Mowachaht First Nation charges a landing fee.

Six cute little cabins along the trail west of Yuquot, abutting either Jewitt Lake or the oceanfront, contain both fireplaces and propane heaters. They can be rented from the Mowachaht First Nation by calling **250-283-2015**.

The original Roman Catholic Church was built here by Father Brabant in 1889, but it burned down in 1954. A new church was built in 1956, and today doubles as a museum. It has a number of interesting features, including native totems (replicas from the village of Yuquot). Two ornate stained glass windows were donated by the Spanish government. One depicts a Franciscan monk preaching to natives, while another shows the cove being transferred from Spain to England by Capt. Quadra and Capt. Vancouver. A cornerstone commemorates the spot where John Meares of the Royal Navy built and launched the first European ship to be built on the northwest coast of North America in 1788, the schooner *Northwest America*. It was later seized by the Spanish and renamed *Gertrudis*.

The trail from Yuquot leads past burial grounds that are remarkable. Many of the families of the deceased left items of importance in the life of the departed on or near the tombstones. These include a sewing machine, a gramophone and a canoe. Personal items have also been draped over the tombstones. (Please treat the cemeteries with respect and don't trespass or disturb artifacts.)

The Nootka Lighthouse on the rocks of Yuquot Point was built in 1911. It's a manned lighthouse and supplies the marine weather reports for the region under the name Nootka. A plaque, the Captain

The entrance to Boca del Infierno Bay is a pleasant area—at slack tide.

Cook monument, can be found near the lighthouse. It's believed to be built on the same location as one of the cannons used to protect San Miguel Fort located here in the 1700s.

Friendly Cove, called Yuquot, was the summer village site of the Moachat confederacy. In the time of Capt. Cook 13 big houses lined the waterfront here and the village was home to about 1,500 people. The cove became known as Friendly Cove due to their welcoming nature. The ships *Resolution* and *Discovery* arrived under the command of Capt. James Cook in 1778, establishing relations with the famous Chief Maquinna. Goods were traded for sea otter pelts. The sailors used the furs for bedding, then sold them in China for prices as high as $120 a skin. The result was an immediate sensation. A year after the publication of Cook's account in 1784, numerous ships were setting sail for Nootka Sound in search of this new-found treasure.

A trading post, Santa Cruz de Nutka, was located just north of Fort San Miguel. Built in 1789 by the Spanish and abandoned in 1795, it was the only Spanish fort ever built in Canada, with barracks and 16 guns. To exert Spanish authority, Capt. Esteban José Martinez, in charge of the fort, captured four British vessels (the *Iphigenia*, *Northwest America*, *Argonaut* and *Princess Royal*) for infringing on the rights of the crown of Spain in its exclusive right to trade on the coast. The seizure prompted the start of the Nootka Controversy that almost caused a war between England and Spain. Friendly Cove was the centre for the sea otter trade until 1795, when both Spain and England essentially abandoned the coast. The last sea otter trading vessel departed here in 1825.

Albert Leon, a Russian counterfeiter of some notoriety, purchased an abandoned farm near Friendly Cove in 1908. With the help of two accomplices acting as distributors, his fake $20 bills flooded the U.S. Officials eventually caught up with him, resulting in a lengthy stay at Leavenworth Prison.

Place names: Yuquot is an ancient word, derived from *yukwitte*, meaning 'to blow with wind,' and *aht*, or 'people.' It has been spelled over the years in a variety of ways: Yucuat, and in 1792 Yucuatl by Galiano.

Camping: An open meadow is located north of the historic church and is available for tenting. It's primarily used by hikers leaving or entering the Nootka Trail. As an alternative, many hikers stay on the beach to the west of the reserve, near the lagoon, to avoid a fee.

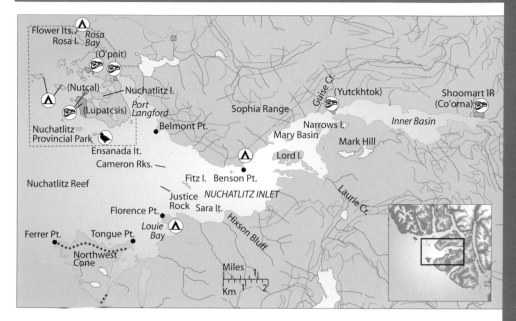

This portion of the outer coast of Nootka Island is among the kinder, gentler of the open ocean segments of Vancouver Island. The Nuchatlitz Islands, plus numerous reefs and islets are protected in Nuchatlitz Provincial Park. It's not all parkland, however; there's an Indian Reserve within the park boundaries plus the community of Nuchatlitz, which is subdivided into cottages and homes. O'pnit was a campsite that was the southern extremity of the Ehattesaht territory. Nuchatlet sites included Lupatcsis, a village location where the Nuchatlet groups from Port Eliza and Espinosa Inlet gathered for sea hunting and fishing in the summer. At the turn of the last century the site shifted north to Nutcal, or Nuchatlitz, for which the area was later named.

While most inlets on the west coast of Vancouver Island tend to be busier and more developed than the areas open to the ocean, Nuchatlitz Inlet is a glimpse into what all these inlets might have been several centuries ago. There's almost no development here and just as little evidence of logging on the surrounding hills. The shoreline shares many of the more dramatic features of the exposed sections of the coast, including sea caves and beautiful sand beaches. The inlet can be explored all the way to Inner Basin, a sheltered lagoon bordered by steep mountain slopes.

A major geoduck bed is located at the mouth of Nuchatlitz Inlet. Herring spawn in Nuchatlitz, Port Langford and Mary Basin. Outer Nuchatlitz Inlet is an important crab area and sea otters congregate here.

Nuchatlitz Islands

Most of the islands are unnamed, and for the purpose of identification are referred to by the elevation number of the island on the Esperanza Inlet chart. There are several islands with the same elevation notations; in those instances, they're referred to by "north" and "south" to distinguish them.

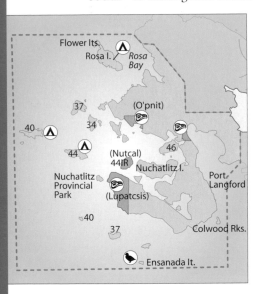

- *Rosa Island:* Rosa Island is the largest of the islands within the park and the closest to Esperanza Inlet. A nice pocket sand beach faces northeast. The southwest side is rocky and strewn with islets and rocks. The water north of Rosa Island is extremely popular for recreational fishing, and dozens of boats are likely to be trolling here during the summer.

- *37:* This island sits off the westernmost tip of Nootka Island's Nuchatlitz peninsula. It's rarely used recreationally, and it and the surrounding islands require careful navigation. Watch for reefs that extend northwest.

- *40 North:* This pretty island lies well out toward open water and has several nice beaches facing east.

- *44:* Arguably the nicest of the islands, this island is directly west of the reserve (44IR) and becomes connected to it by a drying sand bar at low tides. Beaches surround the island but the most popular beaches are to the north and west. Trails cross the headlands between the beaches, so it's possible to walk around the entire island.

- *44IR:* This reserve is located east of island 44. The ruins marked on the chart are the remnants of a small community that was built in recent history. The homes are now crumbling. The beach is popular for strolls, especially since it connects to 44 during low tide.

- *Nuchatlitz Island:* This island, set deep in the bay tucked in behind the reserve, is a bit of an anomaly for this area. The island has been

A group of kayakers debates heading out from Island 44 as the winds pick up in the afternoon. Quite wisely they stuck to protected waters.

subdivided and is strewn with homes and cabins of varying quality. The nearby bay is very pretty and pristine except for some aquaculture. Island 46 to the north of Nuchatlitz looks like it might be circumnavigable, but the passage to the east is just a dribble. The cove to the south of Nuchatlitz Island has a narrow entrance and an island in its centre to paddle around.

- *Ensanada Islet:* There are numerous reefs that extend south of 44— so many, in fact, that it can be difficult to navigate even by kayak. The best bet, if you're heading south into Nuchatlitz Inlet, is to go southeast toward 37 and duck out between 40 South and 37. Ensanada Islet is fairly well set out from the others, and is one of the few bird colonies in Nootka Sound, with black oystercatchers, pigeon guillemots and glaucous-winged gulls.

Camping: While most beaches on these islands are suitable for camping, several stand out. The closest to Esperanza Inlet is Rosa Island's northeast beach, which is quite small but very sheltered and has room for perhaps a dozen tents in fairly close quarters. A popular camping island is 44, which has a beach along the entire north end of the island. Another nice camping island is 40 North, the westernmost island in the group. A nice beach faces east. All camping is wilderness on the beach above the high tide line.

Travel notes: Two B.C. kayakers, Andrew Camp and Blake Rawlyk, died in this area in May 2003. Though it will probably never be known exactly what occurred, the two camped in Nuchatlitz Provincial Park before they went missing on a planned trip around the outside of Nootka Sound. Their bodies were found near Ensanada Islet. They were apparently travelling on a day when high winds were expected. The reefs around Nuchatlitz are a maze, and it would be very easy to leave a protected area unprepared for the high swell and hidden rocks just around the corner. It's a lesson to never take unnecessary risks, listen to weather forecasts, be sure of the waters before you head into them and always give reefs the respect they deserve.

Nuchatlitz Provincial Park: This park protects the northwest corner of Nootka Island and the associated islands and reefs that surround it. It's a picturesque area, attracting boaters, campers, sports fishermen, kayakers and wildlife viewers to its shores. There are no amenities, but the park has many beaches suitable for wilderness camping. It was made a park in 1996, and in total protects 2,105 hectares (5,200 acres).

Cameron Rocks

These two bare rocks, each 8 m (26 feet) and 3 m (10 feet) high, were originally called Bare Rocks but were renamed after David Cameron, the chief justice of Vancouver Island from 1853 to 1856. The rocks are one of a handful of seabird breeding colonies in Nootka Sound and are home to black oystercatchers and pigeon guillemots. Justice Rock, south of Cameron Rocks, is home to black oystercatchers.

Port Langford to Benson Point

Port Langford is a deep bay that cuts well into the northwestern peninsula of Nootka Island. The shore along the southeastern stretch between Belmont Point and Benson Point has numerous sea caves, pocket beaches, sea stacks and cliff bluffs to explore. Watch for a particularly pretty cave with a waterfall pouring over the cave entrance. If you play it right you could paddle underneath and fill up your water bottle without leaving your kayak.

Camping: While there are numerous beaches ideal for wilderness camping, the best and most popular beach is near Benson Point. The beach is particularly sandy and protected, and a flat area in the grass behind the beach is ideal for setting up camp away from the more exposed shore. Numerous rock bluffs to the west of the beach make a great area to scramble, explore and watch sunsets.

Mary Basin

This portion of Nuchatlitz Inlet is very protected, thanks in part to Lord Island. Two large estuaries drain into Mary Basin, as well as the waters of Inner Basin. As a result the tidal currents can be felt around

Lord Island and toward Narrows Island south of Guise Creek. The area around Guise Creek becomes a gravel bar at low tide and the shallow water increases the current. It's a pleasant place and not often visited. A large clam area is located in Mary Basin. The small peninsula near Guise Creek was a Nuchatlet village site.

Hiking: A trail is said to lead up Laurie Creek to a pleasant swimming hole, but I haven't had an opportunity to hike it myself. Like all non-maintained wilderness trails, expect it to be rugged, overgrown and wet.

Inner Basin

This long, narrow waterway is quite pleasant, but a little more featureless than the outer shoreline of the inlet. The current at the entrance can run as high as 3 knots. If you're travelling against the current, keep to the sides and a short fight should get you into the basin. A beach is located just north of the entrance. Another is located at the drying head on the east side of the basin. The basin is a winter area for sea otters.

Louie Bay

Louie Bay is filled by an extensive drying mudflat south and west of Tongue Point. A sheltered lagoon off the main bay is used frequently by floatplanes, particularly for charters dropping off hikers to the north entrance of the Nootka Island Trail. South of Florence Point are several nice beaches. An interesting sea cave is located at Tongue Point. Pieces of the hull of a large ruined ship lie scattered across the shallow beach south of Tongue Point. The bay is a rich clam area.

Numerous sea caves line the north shore of Nuchatlitz Inlet.

The neck of land that supports Northwest Cone is shown on some charts (particularly the Esperanza Inlet chart, 3674) as being separated from the rest of Nootka Island. Louie Bay's mudflat becomes narrower and narrower, finally becoming almost a tidal stream. While the water of Louie Bay never actually connects with the open coast, the nature of the channel indicates that water from the open ocean does indeed get washed into the channel, probably during particularly violent storms. So it's not so much a separate island as it's broken by a storm channel.

The trailhead of the Nootka Trail is located at the far end of the lagoon, indicated by a cluster of markers. A sign states that the trail isn't maintained. The trail leads to Third Beach, where a grassy area is ideal for camping.

Camping: The beaches south of Florence Point make for a beautiful camping area, particularly if you like watching sunsets. The beach is open to the western winds, and the surf can be moderate. To avoid the worst, tuck behind the rocks on the north side of the beach. Another option is south of Tongue Point. This unusual area is a private campground, the Esperanza Mission Camp. A shelter and minimal amenities are offered for a fee. To register, follow the instructions on the sign and use a marine radio to book your spot.

Hiking: From the Esperanza Mission Camp at Tongue Point, a trail leads to an abandoned World War Two radar station, then to Ferrer Point. It's likely overgrown. Otherwise, if you want to see the outer coast from the shelter of Louie Bay, just follow the storm channel to the far side. A trail runs along the shoreline and through a pretty rocky area with several sea stacks and views to the open Pacific.

OUTER NOOTKA ISLAND

South of Ferrer Point is 35 km (20 miles) of open coast until the all-weather shelter of Friendly Cove and Yuquot. Of particular concern to kayakers is the lack of shelter should winds pick up. While potentially dangerous, the outer coast can be a supremely rewarding journey. Very few boats travel the outer route, so the few people you encounter are likely to be hikers on the Nootka Trail.

Caution: The marine charts for Nootka Island (Esperanza Inlet) and Nootka Sound miss a portion of the outer shore of Nootka Island. The portion left off the map is south of the channel at Louie Bay to near

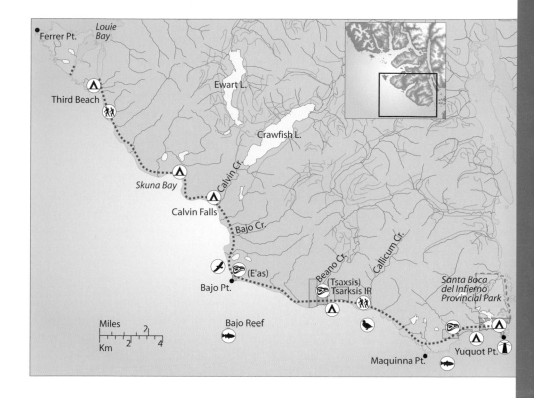

Calvin Falls. You can always buy the third chart (3603), which has just that small section of land but is otherwise mostly open and useless water. Or you can travel by sight. If you stay near shore you should have no difficulty as the shoreline isn't convoluted and most major geographic locations, such as Calvin Falls, can be easily identified. Another option, of course, is preprogramming waypoints into a GPS.

Ferrer Point

The point is bordered by extremely rocky coast. It's a major recreational fishing area.

Caution: This stretch of water is one of the problem areas of the coast. The waters from Nuchatlitz Inlet, Gillam Channel and the open Pacific combine with the shallow ocean floor to create steep and irregular swells. Conditions can be dangerous and are best attempted in the morning before the seas and winds build.

Calvin Falls

This is the first easily accessible resting spot on the coast south of Nuchatlitz Inlet. While there are beaches along the entire length, all are exposed to the open ocean and are subject to high surf. The waterfall itself is a beautiful site. The falls is the most popular area for hikers to congregate and camp. A roped trail leads up the south side of the falls to a swimming hole.

Camping: The sweeping beach surrounding Calvin Falls is one of the largest on the coast. Just pick your spot. Most of the sprawling beach is also open to the Pacific, but there's an area on the very northwest corner that abuts a rock shelf, which acts as a breakwater. Here the surf will be low to moderate, especially when the tide is lower and more of the rock shelf is exposed.

Bajo Point

This area would appear to be a problem point, but it's not. Maquinna Point is where the waters of Nootka Sound and the open Pacific become a problem. Along Bajo Point the shore is a combination of rough beach (generally sand, gravel and cobble with drift logs at the high tide line) and rock bluffs. Landing is difficult anywhere along this stretch. Just offshore is Bajo Reef, one of the largest areas of canopy kelp on the west coast of Vancouver Island. Herring spawn here, one of the few exposed coastal areas where herring spawning has been recorded. A heron rookery is located at Bajo Point.

Bajo Point is the site of E'as, a once significant native village. The people here and at Tsaxsis (Tsarksis reserve to the east) are credited with inventing the art of whaling and discovering the Shaman's Dance. Or rather, they're said to have received it from the Wolves. They lived year-round here, having no territories in the more sheltered areas.

While not considered a "Graveyard of the Pacific," Bajo Point has attracted its share of tragedies. The British ship *King David* hit Bajo Reef in 1905. The crew went ashore and lit fires, but dwindling supplies prompted seven of the crew to leave in a lifeboat. They were never heard from again. The other 18 were finally rescued by the *Queen City*, which investigated the fires. One more died on the return journey.

Beano Creek

This area is a potential break for paddlers. The beach is protected from the worst of the prevailing westerly weather. A ridge off Beano

Creek shelters much of the beach. A private cabin is located in the trees here (a section of the beach is private property).

Tsarksis reserve is the site of a major traditional native village, Tsaxsis. The residents were associated with the E'as'ath to the west.

Maquinna Point

This is arguably the prettiest stretch of Nootka Island, with numerous sea caves and sea stacks in among pocket beaches enclosed by jagged bluffs. For those just nosing out around the south waters of Nootka Island, this stretch is bound to be the highlight of a day trip. For those rounding Nootka Island, it's a scenic ending to the open ocean portion of a counterclockwise trip.

Caution: The waters off Maquinna Point tend to be jumbled, even at the best of times. Waters from Nootka Sound clash with the open Pacific, often creating sharp, rip-like waves. There are also numerous reefs surrounding the shoreline here.

Yuquot Point

The shoreline between Maquinna Point and Yuquot Point is almost entirely beach. Many reefs are located in the waters of the bay between the points. The beach can be exposed to moderate surf, though pockets of low surf are likely easily found in the shelter of reefs.

HIKING THE NOOTKA ISLAND TRAIL

The Nootka Island Trail is a wilderness trail, maintained by its users. It crosses through Crown land, not parkland, with some areas on Indian Reserves. A rise in popularity has transformed the trail from a bushwacking adventure to a beaten path, but there are still no aids like the many bridges and stairs that adorn the West Coast Trail. That means three to five days of rough sections over headlands, wet marches from the trailhead and slogging along cobble and sand beaches that slide away with every footstep. Because it's wilderness it's also not patrolled, so there are no checkpoints or park staff for safety. Cell phones won't work here. When you travel here you're on your own.

Trailhead at Louie Bay: If you arrive by floatplane (Nootka Air from Gold River) you'll be required to do some wading to the trail head. From there it's about an hour to Third Beach. This is a popular place to stay on the first night.

Hara Creek: South of Third Beach the trail becomes headlands with some beach areas passable only at low tide. The overland portions of the trail can be rough.

Skuna Bay: As you approach Skuna Bay the trail becomes easier, with portions traversing rocky shelving or beach. The beach at Skuna Bay is often used as a campsite, though most hikers prefer to continue on to Calvin Falls.

Calvin Falls: The falls itself is a visual highlight of the trip. The river running along the beach is tidal, and crossing is best done at low tide. A trail leads up the rocks on the south side of the falls to a popular swimming hole.

NOOTKA ISLAND TRAIL

Bajo Point: Rocky shelving and rough beach characterize this stretch. The point was once a native village site, E'as, and you may be able to pick out where the houses once stood.

GETTING HERE

There are two popular methods to access the trailheads. One is water taxi. For a fee you can arrange to be picked up from Gold River, Tahsis or Zeballos and dropped off at the trailhead. Several days later you can be picked up at the other side. This tends to be quite a costly option, especially for small groups. Another popular option is taking a charter flight with Nootka Air from Gold River and landing at the lagoon at Louie Bay. Once at Yuquot you have a choice of a water taxi home or taking the MV *Uchuk III*. It arrives only on Mondays and Wednesdays, so timing is crucial. Conversely, some water taxi operators will equip you with a marine radio so you can call to arrange for a pickup at any time, and possibly from any location if you're injured or can't complete the trail.

Beano Creek: This cobble beach makes for a difficult walk. Beano Creek is most easily crossed at low tide. West of the creek is reserve, and signs discourage crossing. Stick to the beach and you shouldn't have any problems.

Yuquot: The final leg is simple hiking. Camping is possible on a large field outside the heritage church overlooking Friendly Cove. A fee applies. Camping on the beach near the lagoon is free.

Callicum Creek: This stretch of trail is the start of several difficult sections over the headlands toward Maquinna Point. Callicum Creek is best crossed at low tide.

Tidal lagoon: This lagoon has the appear-ance of a river at its mouth, and is quite deep. The best time to cross is at low tide.

Maquinna Point: Here the trail leads over high, rocky headlands. Signs point to sea caves, a side trip worth taking.

Sea stacks and sea caves line the northeast shore of Catala Island, making it a sheltered place to explore some dramatic coastal features.

Nootka Sound

MY FIRST VISIT TO NOOTKA SOUND WAS A WARM AND SUNNY PADDLE IN THE middle of January. I left Cougar Creek in morning fog, but that burned away into an interesting mist that hung over the nearby hills. I reached Hanna Channel to see an eagle take flight from Camel Rock, the bird framed amid fluffy clouds, mountainous peaks and a meandering ocean channel. It was a picture-perfect moment, one that for me will always define Nootka Sound.

It's not an area without faults for those seeking a wilderness experience. Development dots various protected coves, with houseboats, fishing camps, log sorting facilities and fish farms tucked around every corner. A real sense of isolation can only be found on the outer waters and within Bligh Island Provincial Park and the Spanish Pilot Group.

Any visitor to Nootka should be prepared to face mountainsides scarred by logging. The central charm remains, however. As a result Nootka Sound is growing in popularity as one of the premier kayaking and travel destinations on the West Coast. The history of Nootka Sound also beckons. This region is the birthplace of modern British Columbia, where Spanish and British explorers vied for trade, where conflicts erupted and where, ultimately, Britain took control from Spain.

GETTING HERE

Nootka Sound is marginally more accessible than Kyuquot and Quatsino sounds, but most visitors, especially those taking a ferry from the mainland, will require the best part of a day just to arrive at the launch site. From Nanaimo take the Island Highway to Campbell River. From there take Highway 28 west to Gold River. One launch option is Muchalat Inlet west of Gold River. Simply drive through

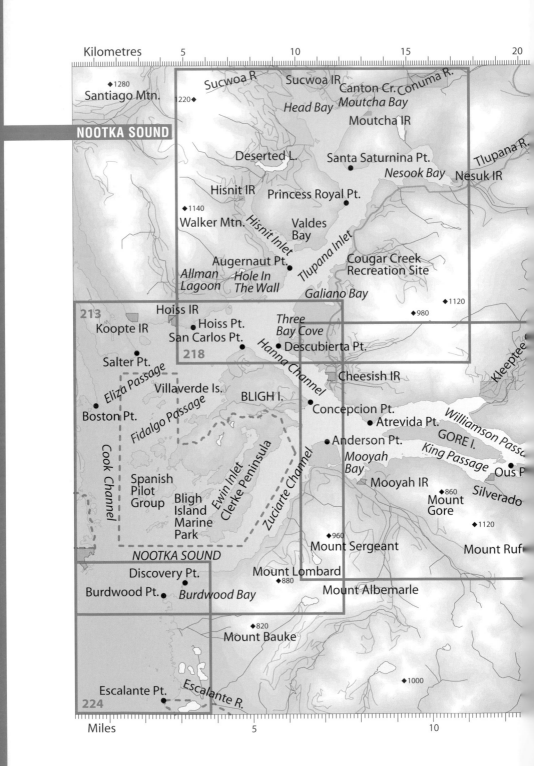

Kilometres 5 10 15 20

◆1280
Santiago Mtn.

1220◆

Sucwoa R.

Sucwoa IR
Canton Cr. Conuma R.
Head Bay Moutcha Bay
Moutcha IR

Deserted L.

Santa Saturnina Pt.
Nesook Bay
Nesuk IR

Tlupana R.

Hisnit IR

Princess Royal Pt.

◆1140
Walker Mtn.

Valdes
Bay

Hisnit Inlet

Augernaut Pt.

Tlupana Inlet

Cougar Creek
Recreation Site

Allman
Lagoon

Hole In
The Wall

Galiano Bay

◆1120

◆980

213

Hoiss IR

Koopte IR

Hoiss Pt.

San Carlos Pt.

Three
Bay Cove

218

Descubierta Pt.

Kleeptee

Salter Pt.

Hanna Channel

Cheesish IR

Eliza Passage

Villaverde Is.

BLIGH I.

Concepcion Pt.

Williamson Pass

Boston Pt.

Fidalgo Passage

Atrevida Pt.

GORE I.

Anderson Pt.

King Passage

Ous P.

Cook Channel

Spanish
Pilot
Group

Ewin Inlet

Clerke Peninsula

Zuciarte Channel

Mooyah
Bay

Mooyah IR

Silverado

◆860
Mount
Gore

Bligh
Island
Marine
Park

◆1120

NOOTKA SOUND

◆960

Mount Sergeant

Mount Ruf

Discovery Pt.

Mount Lombard

Burdwood Pt.

Burdwood Bay

◆880

Mount Albemarle

◆820
Mount Bauke

◆1000

Escalante Pt.

Escalante R.

224

Miles 5 10

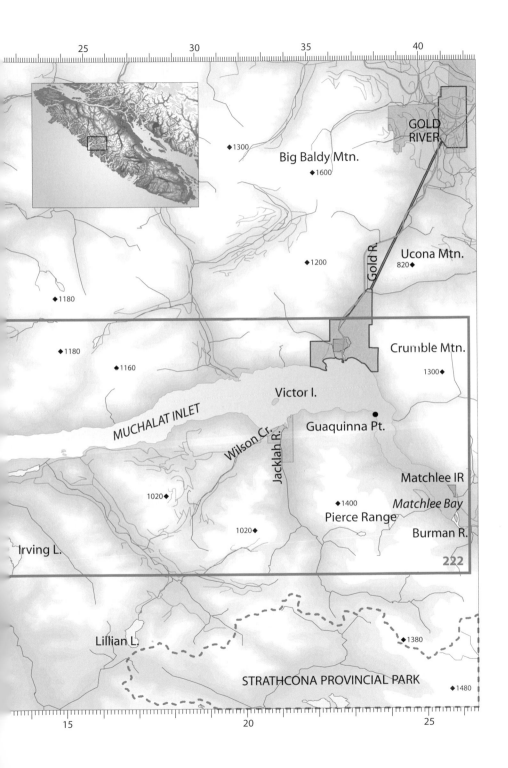

25 30 35 40

◆1300

Big Baldy Mtn.

◆1600

GOLD RIVER

Gold R.

◆1200

Ucona Mtn.
820◆

◆1180

◆1180

◆1160

Crumble Mtn.

1300◆

Victor I.

MUCHALAT INLET

Guaquinna Pt.

Wilson Cr.

Jacklah R.

Matchlee IR

1020◆

Matchlee Bay

◆1400

Pierce Range

Burman R.

1020◆

Irving L.

222

◆1380

Lillian L.

STRATHCONA PROVINCIAL PARK

◆1480

15 20 25

Gold River to find that launch site. For the Cougar Creek Recreation Site launch into Tlupana Inlet, continue on the highway without entering Gold River. At the T-intersection at the bridge just past Gold River, turn left, then take a quick right up a hill onto the gravel forest service road. Follow it for about 25 km (16 miles) to Tlupana Main. Take it past the log sort at Nesook Bay for another 7 km (4.5 miles) until you arrive at the Cougar Creek Recreation Site. An alternative closer to Bligh Island is Tatu Marina. Simply continue on the same logging road past Cougar Creek. This is a private marina, so restrictions and fees apply. Other launch options are in Zeballos and Tahsis in the northern inlets. See chapter 6, Nootka Island, for more information on those sites.

EXPLORING BY KAYAK

Bligh Island and the Spanish Pilot Group are the strongest magnets for explorers in Nootka Sound. The inner inlets, such as Tlupana Inlet, are pleasant enough, but human use and development affect the charm. Many waterfronts are still pristine, but most nooks and crannies of Nootka Sound are filled with development. Bligh Island Provincial Park is the wonderful exception.

Recommended short trips

- *If you have a day:* Choose from two relaxing trips: visit Hisnit Inlet from Cougar Creek or Matchlee Bay from Gold River. If you're adventurous, you could circumnavigate Bligh Island, but it's a daunting 38-km (24-mile) trip.

- *If you have a weekend:* For a pleasant overnight trip, paddle down Tlupana Inlet from Cougar Creek, camp at Hoiss River and return by the same route the next day. You could conceivably overnight at the Spanish Pilot Group. It would be a rushed visit.

- *If you have three days:* A trip to the Spanish Pilot Group is a must. Launch from Cougar Creek. Spend the middle day exploring the islands or Ewin Inlet.

- *If you have five days:* This time can be comfortably spent at the Spanish Pilot Group. Count on two days of travel (arriving and departing) and three days of exploring. One day should include Yuquot on Nootka Island, and perhaps even the outer coast as far as Maquinna Point on Nootka Island. For a change of pace, spend a night at the beautiful sand beach at Burdwood Bay. This would make for a relaxing holiday.

- *If you have a week:* You can explore almost all of the Nootka region in a week, including the northern waterways such as Esperanza and Tahsis inlets. For a gentle holiday, consider a launch at Tahsis, an exploration down to Strange Island, a stay at the Spanish Pilot Group, a circumnavigation of Bligh Island, a visit to Yuquot and as much of the outer coast of Nootka Island as you feel comfortable with, then a return up Tahsis Inlet. Launching from Cougar Creek instead would cut down on the amount of travel.

- *The ideal trip:* A trip recommended for veterans only is a circumnavigation of Nootka Island. Itineraries are suggested in chapter 6, Nootka Island. A modification would be a launch from Cougar Creek. A counter-clockwise circumnavigation of the island is recommended to take advantage of the prevailing winds.

THE BASICS

Geology and ecology

A combination of glaciation and tectonics are responsible for creating the landforms around Nootka Sound. Movement of the tectonic plates that form the earth's crust created the high coastal relief. Glaciers carved the steep fjords that run perpendicular to the coast. The result is a variety of landforms from exposed rocky platforms and island groups to steep fjords, sheltered estuaries and the occasional sandy beach.

Nootka Sound is significant for its salmon, with major sockeye, chinook and chum runs in most of the major rivers. Strangely, there are no seabird breeding colonies in Nootka Sound itself; for those one has to look to a few rocks and islets on the north side of Nootka Island. Nootka Sound, however, is a relatively new home for a thriving population of sea otters. These mammals were reintroduced at Checleset Bay to the north, and they have expanded their territory into Nootka Sound. This is now one of the best areas to see sea otters, especially around Bligh Island and the Spanish Pilot Group.

Weather

See the weather section for Nootka Island (page 177).

Native overview

Nootka Sound is the land of the Mowachaht/Muchalaht First Nation, the result of a long series of amalgamations. The many local groups in Nootka Sound, Tahsis Inlet and Tlupana Inlet united to become the Mowachaht. Groups in Muchalat Inlet and Gold River united to form the Muchalaht confederacy. In the 1890s the two confederacies joined at Yuquot on Nootka Island. Between the 1960s and 1990s they lived at Ahaminaquus on Gold River, and today have moved to Tsaxana. The current band numbers above 500, with about 170 on the Tsaxana reserve at Gold River.

The Mowachaht and Muchalaht were historically bitter foes, feuding over adjoining lands and fishing rights, particularly at Gold River, where food was plentiful. Battles between the two tribes took their toll on the Muchalaht; so did raids by the Ahousat and the Hopatcisath of Sproat Lake (inland Vancouver Island), who attacked the Muchalaht in retaliation for the massacre of some of their tribesmen. The tribe was reduced to 30 to 40 able-bodied men, who assembled at a fortified home at Gold River to await the final battle. The Mowachaht chief died, however, before the Muchalaht were exterminated, and as a result they were left alone.

With peace established, the Muchalaht began to rebuild, moving to a winter village at Tcecis on Hanna Channel (see page 217). Marriages between the Muchalaht and Mowachaht increased the relationship between the tribes until they united in the late 1800s.

THE SHORELINES

NOOTKA SOUND

Three arms extend from the sound: Tlupana, Muchalat and Tahsis inlets. The sound is dominated by Bligh Island and dotted with other islands, most notably the Spanish Pilot Group, protected as a provincial marine park. Bligh Island has a number of historic areas and inlets to explore, the most interesting of which are on the provincial park side of the island. The rest of Bligh Island has been or is being logged, and much of the shore is used for log sorting and storage. The surrounding mountains have been logged, making for a less-than-pristine backdrop. Even so, Nootka Sound is growing in popularity as a kayaking destination.

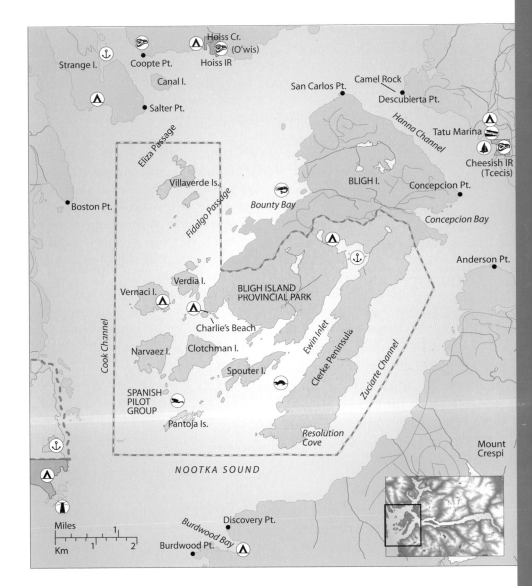

Strange I. · Coopte Pt. · Hoiss Cr. · (O'wis) · Hoiss IR · Canal I. · Salter Pt. · San Carlos Pt. · Camel Rock · Descubierta Pt. · Hanna Channel · Tatu Marina · Cheesish IR (Tcecis) · BLIGH I. · Concepcion Pt. · Boston Pt. · Eliza Passage · Villaverde Is. · Fidalgo Passage · Bounty Bay · Concepcion Bay · Anderson Pt. · Verdia I. · Vernaci I. · BLIGH ISLAND PROVINCIAL PARK · Charlie's Beach · Cook Channel · Narvaez I. · Clotchman I. · Ewin Inlet · Clerke Peninsula · Zuciarte Channel · Spouter I. · SPANISH PILOT GROUP · Pantoja Is. · Resolution Cove · Mount Crespi · NOOTKA SOUND · Miles · Km · Burdwood Bay · Discovery Pt. · Burdwood Pt.

Spanish Pilot Group

These islands offer a maze of channels and reefs ideal for exploration by kayak. Vernaci and Verdia are the most protected islands, while the outer Pantoja Islands are subject to swell from the open Pacific, giving a hint of what the outer waters are like. Aside from a few pocket beaches there are few places to pull out of the water. Most of the islands are ringed by steep, rocky shorelines; many, like Clotchman Island, are virtually inaccessible.

Camping: There are only a few beaches suitable for camping in the Spanish Pilot Group. On a small, rough beach on the east side of Vernaci Island are numerous clearings for tents within the cover of the trees upland of the beach. There are no facilities.

Bligh Island

Bligh Island, 10 km (6 miles) end to end, has numerous features to enjoy and a few best ignored. The provincial marine park is to the south and a working forest lies to the north. Bligh Island is unlikely to receive more protection in the near future. Much of the shoreline is being eyed for rural development, particularly the area along Fidalgo Channel south of Bounty Bay.

Bligh Island is one of three major shrimp-fishing areas in the Nootka region. The others are Esperanza and Espinosa inlets. Both Bligh Island and the Spanish Pilot Group are favoured areas for sea otters, and they can often be seen cavorting in the waters here. These islands are also popular diving locations.

Place names: Bligh Island is named after the famed Vice Admiral William Bligh, who was master of HMS *Resolution* on Cook's third voyage. Bligh would become notorious for the mutiny he suffered on the *Bounty*. He was set adrift with 18 companions; without a chart they sailed 5,823 km (3,618 miles) before being rescued.

Concepcion Bay

The area of Bligh Island south of Concepcion Point is used by Western Forest Products as a log tie-up area and an associated dry-land sort. The north shore facing Hanna Channel is also used for log handling and storage.

Bounty Bay

The shorefront here to the north, known as Bounty Bay, is primarily a log storage and handling area. The area south of Bounty Bay is ear-marked for upland resort and cottage development. One resort is already located here. Utopia Bay Lodge offers accommodation, kayak rentals and guided trips. Call **1-800-661-9393** or visit **www.utopiabay.ca**.

The Spanish Pilot Group is growing in popularity as a relaxed wilderness paddling destination.

Ewin Inlet

This inlet stretches more than 5 km (3 miles) along Clerke Peninsula into Bligh Island. In places it becomes quite narrow. At the head is a bit of a cove with islets and a rich intertidal area to explore. The inlet is a key herring spawn area. The intertidal zone along this inlet is particularly rich, so be sure to take a close look at lower tides. Expect to see anemones, chitons, starfish, jellyfish and numerous other marine creatures. Ewin Inlet is considered the best anchorage in the area, rivalling Friendly Cove on nearby Nootka Island.

Camping: On the west side of the cove at the head of Ewin Inlet is a nice beach with a multitude of tent sites scattered in the trees. A stream is available for water through most of the year. The view across the cove is quite pretty, but the area can be prone to mosquitoes. Considering it's several miles just to get in and out of Ewin Inlet, it's rather inconveniently located if you wish to use this a base camp for exploration. An alternative and more popular camping area is on the very southwest point of Bligh Island. Tucked in behind the south side of the point opposite Clotchman Island is a beach (known locally as Charlie's Beach). Numerous pretty tent sites are scattered in the woods behind the beach. Amenities include an outhouse.

Resolution Cove

The southern end of Clerke Peninsula is particularly scenic, with steep rock bluffs pounded by swell. On the east end of Clerke Peninsula is Resolution Cove, an unassuming cove famous for its history. There's a pleasant beach at the head of the cove.

It was here, in 1778, that HMS *Resolution* was refitted from March 31 to April 26 during Capt. Cook's third voyage. Cook was searching for the Northwest Passage. The repairs were needed after a severe storm. The foremast of the ship was replaced by trees felled from Bligh Island. Bligh was the master of the *Resolution* at the time. Cook's visit to what he called Ships Cove made him the first European to set foot on B.C. soil. His survey of Nootka Sound conducted during this visit—an extremely detailed work—wouldn't be superceded until the British Navy survey in 1862. A bronze plaque set on a large rock overlooks the cove marking Cook's stopover here in 1778. The rock is visible on the chart of Nootka Sound. The peculiar thing is the plaque is extremely difficult to visit. It's located on a steep-sided rock with no easily found trail.

When Cook sailed into the sheltered cove, natives investigated and saw a man with a hook nose and a humpback, characteristics of the dog salmon and humpback salmon, and they named the newcomers fish-come-alive-as-people. Resolution Cove was known to the natives as Kathniaktl, meaning 'a place of driftwood.'

Burdwood Bay is almost certainly Nootka Sound's finest beach, though take care landing in the surf.

Eliza Passage

This stretch of water separates Vancouver Island and Bligh Island, and at points is as narrow as 1.6 km (1 mile) across. It's often used by commercial vessels, including log barges. The Vancouver Island shore is dominated by Coopte Point and Hoiss Creek's estuary. Hoiss Indian Reserve, now uninhabited, was the Moachat winter village called O'wis.

Camping: Just west of Hoiss Creek is a gravel and sand beach. On the upland is a flat, wooded area with a half-dozen makeshift camping locations set among the trees. A few tables have been made from debris.

Hanna Channel

This pretty stretch separates the north side of Bligh Island from Vancouver Island. There are some interesting reefs around Camel Rock and wonderful views down the channel. Across the channel is Cheesish Indian Reserve, the site of the traditional Muchalat village called Tcecis.

Launches: Tatu Marina on Hanna Channel offers a launch site. It's privately operated. Fees and restrictions apply.

Camping: Tatu Marina offers vehicle-accessible campsites in the forest on the hill above the marina. The spots can be quite pretty. A fee applies.

Zuciarte Channel

This stretch of water is bordered by rock ledges that drop straight into the water. The recreational highlight is Burdwood Bay, which has a white sand beach—probably the finest in Nootka Sound. The stretch of coast around Burdwood Bay is littered with sea caves, including several within the bay. The channel, along with southeast Nootka Island, is known for its sea urchins.

The freighter *Schiedyk* was wrecked on the west side of Zuciarte Channel after hitting a rock ledge in 1968. The remains can still be seen.

Place names: Zuciarte is adopted from the native name Ze-sa-at, a clan of the Muchalats who were historic rivals of Maquinna and his people.

Camping: You can camp at the beautiful beach at Burdwood Bay, but surf can be moderate to high and the beach is open to the prevailing northwesterly winds. If you wish to avoid the surf, there's a very narrow beach set between some rocks on the southwest shore of the bay.

There's no access to the main beach and the strip of sand is quite narrow. The main beach is expansive, with camping anywhere above the high tide line. There's also a cleared area within the forest on the beach's northeast side. Burdwood Bay offers pleasant views toward Yuquot. There are no amenities.

TLUPANA INLET

This inlet is lined with interesting coves and side passages to explore. You'll find houseboats, floating resorts, fish farms and other evidence of human occupation in just about every sheltered niche. Still, some passages remain largely ignored, such as Hisnit Inlet. A launch site and associated campground at Cougar Creek makes Tlupana Inlet a

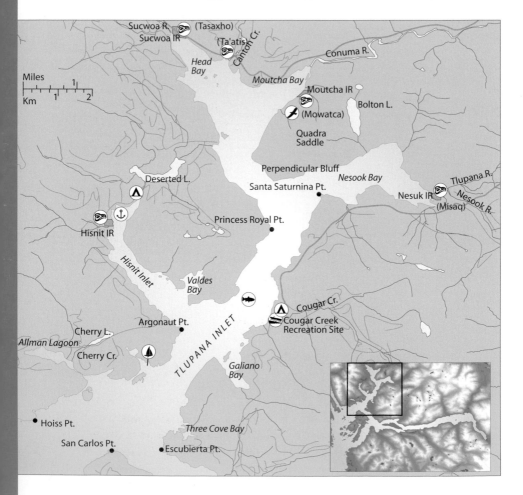

popular entry point into Nootka Sound. The inlet is a major salmon holding area. Every year about 75 tonnes of clams are harvested from Nootka Sound, with Tlupana Inlet contributing a considerable portion of that.

Capt. Vancouver visited the area on September 27, 1794. He was accompanied by Brigadier General Don Jose Manuel Alava, the new governor of Nootka and Quadra's successor. Alava didn't like what he saw. Rowing up the inhospitable inlets with huge precipices and gloomy ravines, Alava repeatedly expressed his surprise that such forbidding country could ever have placed Great Britain and Spain on the verge of war.

Place Names: Either Capt. Eliza or Malaspina in 1791 first named Tlupana Inlet "Fondo de Clupananul." Galiano's chart in 1792 called it "Brazo de Tluplananulg." By 1841 it was known as Hapana Reach, eventually evolving to its name today.

Allman Lagoon
A long river-like passage accessible by small boat at higher tides leads to the lagoon. Aquaculture, houseboats and even a marina are situated near the lagoon's entrance. The marina is located in a cove known locally as Hole in the Wall or Critter Cove after the Critter Cove Marina, which has a lodge, cottages, cabins and suites. Call **250-283-7364** or visit **www.crittercove.com**.

Hisnit Inlet
This deep and curving inlet is probably the least visited area of inner Nootka Sound. Except for remnants of logging operations, the inlet is undeveloped. This is a key crab area, many species of ducks winter here and the inlet supports a valuable clam-harvesting industry. Valdes Bay is a designated provincial boat haven.

Hisnit Inlet's north shore is the site of Hisnit, a former Moachat village and now a reserve.

Camping: A wilderness camping area is located at the head of the inlet, where rough campsites are carved out of the forested upland. Logging roads have allowed considerable recreational use. Junk, such as abandoned chairs, has been left by unthinking campers. Camping is possible along the expansive beach, a better alternative. Public road access is slated to be deactivated.

Head and Moutcha bays

This pretty area is marked by a large logging camp, a dryland log-sort facility and log storage in the northwestern section of Head Bay. Quadra Saddle and Perpendicular Bluff, a huge cliff jutting straight into Tlupana Inlet, are visual highlights. Bald eagles are common here, as is other marine and bird life. Conuma River supports one of the largest coho spawning runs in Nootka Sound and is a popular recreational fishery. There are also chinook, chum and steelhead runs, with a late winter run of steelhead. The Sucwoa River has a significant summer run of steelhead. Both the Conuma and Sucwoa estuaries are key elk habitat.

This area has several historic village sites of the Mowachat. One at Conuma River called Mowatca became the namesake of the Mowachat. Mowatca is derived from the word *moo-ach*, meaning 'deer.' Deer were plentiful here, and as a result the Mowatca were 'people of the deer.'

Camping: Moutcha Bay Marina, RV Park and Campground is located on the waterfront in Moutcha Bay and offers both RV camping and tent sites, many on the water. Log cabins are another option. Phone **250-923-2908** or visit **www.moutchabay.com**.

A rainbow of mist falls onto a houseboat at Hisnit Inlet.

Nesook Bay

Like Head Bay, logging has left its mark here. A dryland log-sorting facility is located on the southeast shore of the bay. Tlupana River is a popular fishing river with a significant summer steelhead run. The Tlupana estuary is an important crab area and elk are common here. Many species of dabbling and diving ducks winter in the estuary.

Cougar Creek Recreation Site

This is a well-developed and well-used site, with campsites, a beach, a dock and a boat ramp. There are 47 campsites with pit toilets. The rocky beach is popular for clam digging. It's a managed recreation site and fees apply from late June to the end of September.

Launches: The launch ramp is gravel with a good-sized beach for loading kayaks. The site is well sheltered and parking is available for a fee. The overnight parking fee is equivalent to the camping fee, based on the assumption that if you're not in the campground you're still sleeping somewhere and should pay for it. For the most current information, contact **Forests.ForestPracticesBranchOffice@gems3.gov.bc.ca**.

Galiano Bay

This bay is pretty, but don't look for pristine wilderness: most protected pockets of Galiano Bay are developed. At Three Cove Bay, south of Galiano Bay, there's a shellfish aquaculture tenure, and the area is being considered for foreshore and upland cottage development. The bay is the only location in the upper inlets of Nootka Sound where herring spawn.

MUCHALAT INLET

Running 30 km (18 miles) east to west, Muchalat is a formidable stretch of water. There are no formal camping sites and just as few makeshift possibilities. Its steep shorelines are backed by impressive peaks. The inlet has become famous in recent years for being home to Luna, a killer whale that separated from L Pod in July, 2001. Growing increasingly friendly with boats and floatplanes, government officials became concerned over the damage he was causing and his own safety. Plans to move Luna to reunite him with his pod in Juan de Fuca Strait made international news in 2003, but protests, particularly by members of the Muchalat band, delayed the process. In spring 2005 plans for Luna remained stalled.

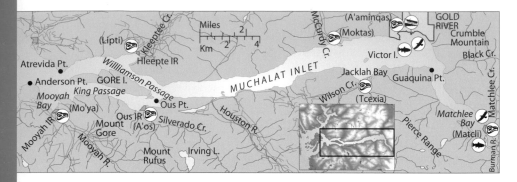

Historic native village sites are marked on the map (the names are in brackets).

Caution: Wind is the largest factor to consider when navigating Muchalat Inlet. The mountains can channel the wind, creating adverse wind waves and current.

Matchlee Bay

Matchlee Bay is nestled between two tall, steep mountain ranges at the very eastern end of Muchalat Inlet. Though close to the civilization and industrialization of Gold River (log handling takes place here), it's still a beautiful stretch to explore.

Burman River, along with nearby Gold River, are significant fish-bearing rivers, with one of the largest coho and chinook runs in Nootka Sound and winter and summer steelhead runs. Burman River is home to the largest spawning population of pink salmon in the sound. The estuary supports winter populations of both dabbling and diving ducks. Numerous elk inhabit the estuary.

Gold River

Gold River is a pretty, mountain-enclosed town about 14 km (9 miles) from Muchalat Inlet and 91 km (56 miles) from Campbell River by road (355 km/220 miles from Victoria). It's a full-service community, but it has been struggling since the closure of the pulp mill in 1998. A hotel, restaurant, grocery store, gas station and other amenities can be found here. Western Forest Products has dryland sort facilities at the Gold River pulp mill site and at McCurdy Creek, Kleeptee Creek and Houston River on the inlet.

The Gold River estuary was the site of A'aminqas. It was here during the low fortunes of the Muchalat in the 1870s that they assembled and built a fort, with a double palisade of cedar timbers around one house. They issued notice to the Moachat, their enemies at the time, to fight them to the finish "for we are ready to die." But the Moachat leader had died, and the challenge was never answered.

If you're travelling by car, the Upana Caves are located 17 km (10.5 miles) from Gold River on the road to Tahsis. Watch for the turnoff and small sign (easily missed). The caves are a maze of about 15 entrances joined by trails.

Launches: You can launch from Gold River at the public wharf near the pulp mill. It's about 14 km (8.7 miles) from the town.

Houston River
The stretch of Muchalat Inlet along here is very steep-sided, dropping directly into deep water. Most estuaries with gravel bars are log-sorting areas. A major log tie-up is located at Rufus, about halfway between Houston and Jacklah rivers. A dryland log sort is located at Houston River.

Gore Island
Gore Island is the biggest island in Muchalat Inlet. It's steep-sided, and the major estuaries to either side, Kleeptee and Silverado creeks, are subject to industrial activity. Kleeptee is a dryland log sorting facility, while Silverado has an existing mineral tenure with mining in its past.

Place names: In 1862 Capt. Richards used a common thread for three names. Gore Island was named for Capt. John Gore, first lieutenant of HMS *Resolution*, Cook's vessel that was refitted in Nootka Sound in 1778. The neighbouring passages, King and Williamson, were named after the second and third lieutenants of the *Resolution*.

Mooyah Bay
This is a popular recreation area that's also used for log handling, plus there's an existing mineral tenure. It's also considered a sensitive marine coastal wetland habitat, making for a mixture of demands and uses. A recent land use plan for Nootka Sound allows log handling and industrial use of the bay, and encourages new uses, such as shellfish aquaculture in the bay and adjacent to Gore Island. The plan also states that an objective is to maintain the wetland environment. It's questionable how both can be achieved.

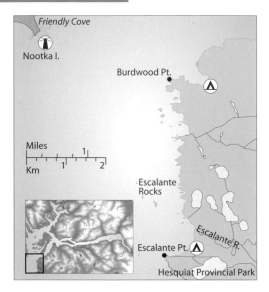

The outer shore south of Nootka Sound is an impressive mix of beaches, rock bluffs and reefs. It's the northern stretch of a long expanse of coast along Hesquiat Peninsula. (The rest of the peninsula is covered in more detail in chapter 8, North Clayoquot Sound.)

Escalante Point

The nicest beach, without question, is north of Escalante Point. Unfortunately, it's quite open to the weather, but adventurous travellers might find it a wonderful camping location. There are large kelp beds around Escalante Point. Escalante River has a late winter run of steelhead. Herring spawn along this stretch.

Caution: This entire stretch is open to swell and has numerous reefs. Beaches are exposed and prone to high surf.

A view up Fidalgo Passage toward Tlupana Inlet.

North Clayoquot Sound

CLAYOQUOT SOUND WAS THE FIRST WEST COAST SOUND THAT I HAD THE chance to explore by kayak. Rain and clouds followed my partner and I for most of the trip, but it was still an unforgettable experience. There was something about the light that made it a magical place, and photo enlargements from that trip still have a place of honour on the wall. After travelling the coast more extensively and returning to Clayoquot for yet another visit in 2003, I was expecting the crowds to be a distraction. While tour boats buzzed by with startling frequency, the number of kayakers and recreational boaters wasn't overwhelming. The scenery was. Simply put, after visiting all the other sounds, I was left in awe upon returning to Clayoquot.

Even without debating which sound is prettiest, Clayoquot certainly has more routes, more attractions, more areas to explore and more diverse surroundings than any other sound on Vancouver Island. It has more protected areas and more secluded waterways. Even in peak season you're likely to find yourself alone along the more remote northern stretches, such as Sydney and Shelter inlets. And the light here had the same effect the second time: the green hues during the day and the purples and oranges during sunset seem unique to this region.

Those are my reasons for visiting Clayoquot. If you visit here, chances are you'll find your own.

GETTING HERE

There are no vehicle access points to the portion of Clayoquot Sound covered in this chapter. A launch from Tofino is really the only option. To get to Tofino, see chapter 9 (page 278).

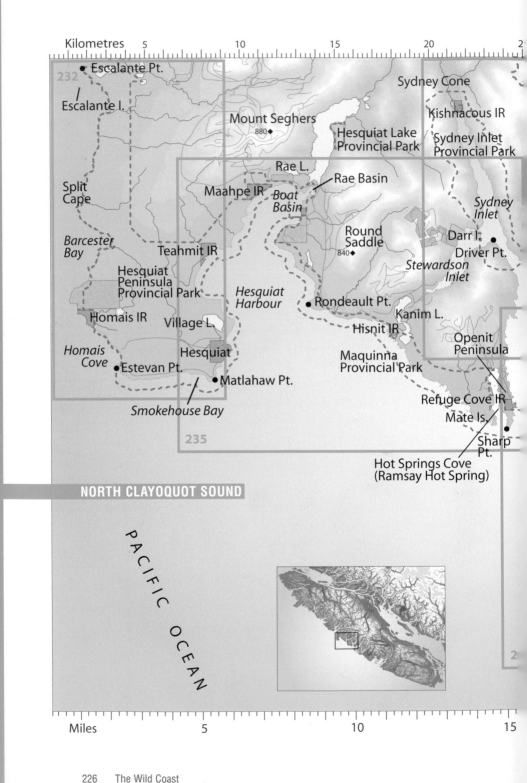

Kilometres 5 10 15 20 2

232

Escalante Pt.

Escalante I.

Sydney Cone

Kishnacous IR

Split
Cape

Mount Seghers
880◆

Hesquiat Lake
Provincial Park

Sydney Inlet
Provincial Park

Rae L.

Maahpe IR

Rae Basin

Boat
Basin

Sydney
Inlet

Barcester
Bay

Teahmit IR

Round
Saddle
840◆

Darr I.

Driver Pt.

Stewardson
Inlet

Hesquiat
Peninsula
Provincial Park

Hesquiat
Harbour

Rondeault Pt.

Kanim L.

Homais IR

Village L.

Hisnit IR

Openit
Peninsula

Homais
Cove

Hesquiat

Maquinna
Provincial Park

Estevan Pt.

Matlahaw Pt.

Refuge Cove IR

Mate Is.

Smokehouse Bay

235

Sharp
Pt.

Hot Springs Cove
(Ramsay Hot Spring)

NORTH CLAYOQUOT SOUND

P A C I F I C   O C E A N

2

Miles 5 10 15

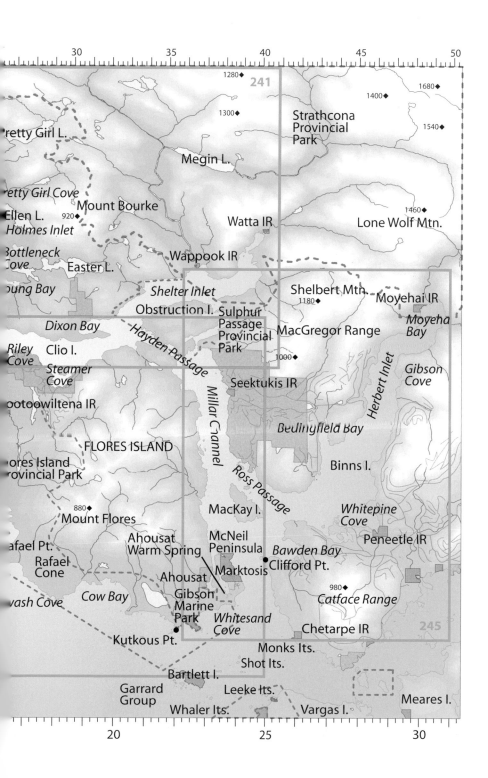

30 35 40 45 50

1280◆ **241**

1680◆

1400◆

1300◆

Strathcona Provincial Park

1540◆

retty Girl L.

Megin L.

retty Girl Cove

1460◆

Mount Bourke

Ellen L. 920◆

Watta IR

Lone Wolf Mtn.

Holmes Inlet

Bottleneck
Cove

Wappook IR

Easter L.

Shelter Inlet

Shelbert Mtn.
1180◆

Moyehai IR

Dixon Bay

Obstruction I.

Sulphur
Passage
Provincial
Park

*Moyeha
Bay*

MacGregor Range

ung Bay

Hayden Passage

*Riley
Cove*

Clio I.

Herbert Inlet

*Gibson
Cove*

1000◆

*Steamer
Cove*

Seektukis IR

ootoowiltena IR

Millar Channel

Bedingfield Bay

FLORES ISLAND

Binns I.

ores Island
rovincial Park

Ross Passage

880◆

MacKay I.

*Whitepine
Cove*

Mount Flores

Peneetle IR

afael Pt.

Ahousat
Warm Spring

McNeil
Peninsula

Bawden Bay

*Rafael
Cone*

Marktosis

Clifford Pt.

Ahousat

980◆

vash Cove

Cow Bay

Gibson
Marine
Park

*Whitesand
Cove*

Catface Range

245

Kutkous Pt.

Chetarpe IR

Bartlett I.

Monks Its.

Shot Its.

Garrard
Group

Leeke Its.

Meares I.

Whaler Its.

Vargas I.

20 25 30

EXPLORING BY KAYAK

Without launch access, you must either take a water taxi (an increasingly popular way to get to remote areas) or travel through south Clayoquot Sound to get here. The most popular point of entry is Tofino.

Recommended short trips

- *If you have a day:* Day trips are next to impossible in this stretch of Clayoquot Sound, as the nearest launch is at Tofino. One option is to take the water taxi *Ahousaht Pride* from Tofino to Ahousat and stroll to the warm spring and Whitesand Cove (recommended). Other options are tours to Hot Springs Cove or whale watching off Flores Island.

- *If you have a weekend:* Overnight trips are difficult in this region. Conceivably you could launch from Tofino, overnight at Whitesand Cove and return the next day. My advice instead would be to travel to Vargas Island (see chapter 9, South Clayoquot Sound) and take the time to enjoy the trip. A water taxi to Flores Island and overnighting at at the hostel at Ahousat or on the beach at Whitesand Cove is another option.

- *If you have three days:* No matter the route, it's going to take almost a full day of paddling to get from Tofino to Flores Island. You can camp two nights at Whitesand Cove and take the extra day to explore the nearby waters. Consider heading to Rafael Point to see the gray whales on the middle day.

- *If you have five days:* If you rush, you could get to Hot Springs Cove. Set up a base camp on Flores and visit the hot spring on the middle day. Hot Springs Cove, while a major draw, is congested, and you might want to avoid it. Instead, consider touring Sulphur Passage, Sydney Inlet or Megin River. All three are highly recommended.

- *If you have a week:* A circumnavigation of Flores Island is a must. If you launch at Tofino, overnight at Whitesand Cove and then head up Millar Channel to Shelter Inlet. Consider a side trip to Megin River or Sydney Inlet and its various channels. Head to Hot Springs Cove if you must, but if you've gone that far be sure to visit the shoreline of Maquinna Provincial Park. You could conceivably make it as far as Hesquiat Harbour. Return via the outer shore of Flores Island, maybe overnighting at Cow Bay, and then via Vargas Island to Tofino. This would make for a fabulous holiday that involves a great many miles. Be sure to build in a few foul weather days.

A bull kelp forest surrounds the lava rocks at Kutcous Point.

- *The ideal trip:* By combining the best elements of north and south Clayoquot Sound you'll have a world-class wilderness holiday. The places to take in include Vargas Island, Cleland Island, Whitesand Cove, Obstruction Island, Megin River, Sydney Inlet, Hot Springs Cove, Maquinna Provincial Park, Hesquiat Harbour and Cow Bay. This is one of the most spectacular trips on the coast, and an incredible way to spend 10 days to two weeks or more.

THE BASICS

Geology and ecology

Clayoquot Sound has one of the most celebrated and controversial environments in North America. It's famous for being one of the last great temperate rainforests in the world. The towering western red-cedar, Sitka spruce and western hemlock can be over 1,000 years old. Protests in 1993 to stop the logging evolved into the largest case of civil disobedience in Canadian history.

Clayoquot Sound is composed of two physical regions: the coastal plain and the Vancouver Island Mountains. The coastal plain is almost flat and divided into islands and peninsulas by inlets and channels. The plain is often broken by steep, rocky hills, though Hesquiat Peninsula is low elevation throughout its length. The Vancouver Island Mountains are deep, eroded troughs, with ridges rising to as high as 1,700 m (5,577 feet) within Clayoquot's boundary. Rock ranges from coarse metamorphic and intrusive rock to older volcanic and sedimentary rock (look for volcanic samples, for instance, at Kutcous Point on Flores Island). Glacial till commonly covers the bedrock.

Western hemlock is the dominant species along with western red-cedar, amabilis fir, yellow cedar, Sitka spruce, Douglas-fir and red alder. The almost continuous old-growth forests are rich in biomass—that is, dead and decaying trees that support numerous species. The uneven canopies created by falling trees lead to a variety of ecological processes, particularly understorey development and the rebirth of new trees, a process that can take 300 to 1,000 years. Forty-seven species—37 birds and 10 mammals—in Clayoquot Sound use the cavities of large trees, both living and dead, to raise offspring or hibernate.

Weather

Clayoquot Sound is typical for the west coast of Vancouver Island, with a year-round mild climate and a great deal of rain. In any given year it's likely to rain for more than 200 days and be above freezing for 310 of them. Over the year 3,200 mm (125 inches) of rain is likely to fall, with the least in July at 76 mm (3 inches) and the most in December at 451 mm (18 inches). Those values are for Tofino. Typical for Clayoquot will be sunshine on the outer coast and cloud cover over the mountains, so expect your chance of rainfall to increase significantly if you venture into the deeper channels in the interior of the sound. The average temperature peaks in July at 14.4°C (58°F), while the coldest month is January with an average temperature of 4.5°C (40°F).

Native overview

This is the land of the Hesquiaht and Ahousaht. The Hesquiaht were originally several independent groups located near Hesquiat Harbour, and were considered about the poorest of the Nuu-chah-nulth, as all but one group lacked dogfish rivers. They didn't turn to the land for hunting, instead focusing all efforts on hair seal and porpoise hunting. They were also renowned whalers. The Ahousaht, on the other hand, grew through a series of wars to become one of the strongest Nuu-chah-nulth nations, rivaling the Clayoquot (today's Tla-o-qui-aht), with the centre of the Ahousaht civilization on Flores Island. A third group, the Otsosat, became extinct largely through war with the Ahousaht. Their main home was at Siwash Cove, near Cow Bay.

Today most of the Ahousaht band members live at Marktosis, a thriving community on Flores Island that has a community hall, church, band office, cultural centre, two gyms and a soccer field. The Ahousaht originally lived on the outside of Flores Island. One popular account of their name means 'people living with their backs to the land and mountains.' A 1934 B.C. Hydrographic Service note states natives repudiated the claim, and it was simply a "whiteman's invention."

The Hesquiaht abandoned the village of Hesquiat in Hesquiat Harbour after World War Two in favour of Refuge Cove in Hot Springs Cove.

THE SHORELINES

HESQUIAT PENINSULA

This incredible stretch of oceanfront is rugged and exposed. There are unique reef structures, unspoiled beaches and wind- and surf-pounded rock ledge shoreline, with expansive sandy beaches that cry out for

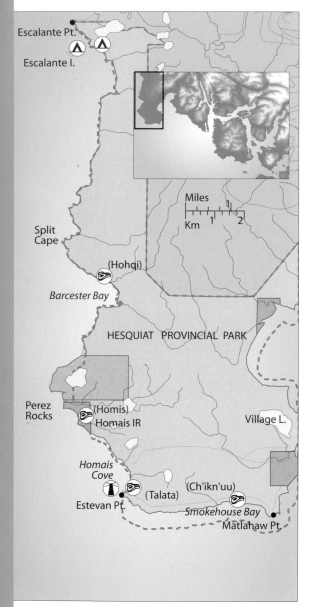

at least one tent per summer (not all get them).

Caution: Most of the outer coast of Hesquiat Peninsula is open to the full brunt of the weather and the prevailing westerlies. The shal-low ocean ledge of the peninsula can mean steep swell. It's a stretch recommended for experienced kayakers only. Bays are protect-ed under some conditions, but expect high surf. Avoid travel in the afternoon, when the winds rise.

Escalante Island

This pretty island is highly remote, located south of Escalante Point amid a scatter-ing of reefs. The island and reefs are partial protection for the bay south of Escalante Point.

Camping: A nice little beach on the inside of Escalante Island, facing Vancouver Island, makes a protected wilderness camp setting. An alternative is the beach on the bay east of Escalante Island. It's relatively sheltered, though more exposed than the island.

Barcester Bay

This deep bay is only partially sheltered. The curving beach could be used as a camping area, but the shore is exposed to westerly weather. North of the bay Split Cape gets its name honestly. The rock at the cape has clearly separated from the shore.

Perez Rocks

These are some of the most interesting reefs on the Vancouver Island coast. On one reef the rocks appear to be stacked like sandbags or the ruined foundation of some old building. There are grassy stretches accessible by a crushed-shell beach. On the shore here was the winter village of a group of renowned sea otter hunters, the Homisath.

Estevan Point

Estevan Point is a desolate stretch of low-lying shore. Very few areas are accessible from the water. It was here on August 8, 1774, that natives on Vancouver Island first saw a European ship. It was the *Santiago*, carrying Captain Juan Perez on his search through northern waters. The natives paddled out in three canoes. The Franciscan Tomas de la Penne recorded, "they remained at some distance from the ship, crying out and making gestures that we should go away." And the next day they did—a storm arose, forcing Perez to leave.

The lighthouse at Estevan Point was built in 1909. It has a unique flying buttress design, with iron braces covered by concrete. The lighthouse has the distinction of being the only location in North America to be bombed during World War Two. In 1942 a Japanese submarine tried to shell the light station and an attached World War Two radio station. About 25 80 pound, 5.9-calibre shells were fired from about two miles offshore, but the aiming was poor and the lighthouse escaped the attack, thanks in part to the quick-thinking lightkeeper, R. M. Lally, who turned off the light. Several of the shells landed beyond the station near Hesquiat Village, though no one was injured. Except for a few shell fragments hitting buildings no damage was done. A shell fragment recovered in 1973 is now on display at the Maritime Museum of British Columbia. (This shelling is a magnet for conspiracy theorists, many of whom have surmised that the bombing was in fact "friendly fire" undertaken to help wartime recruitment efforts.)

Place names: The point is named after Capt. Perez's second lieutenant, Estevan Jose Martinez, the nephew of Don Manuel Antonio Flores, the viceroy of Mexico. Martinez was later dispatched to Nootka to secure the sound from British traders, resulting in the Nootka Controversy that almost led to war between England and Spain.

Hesquiat Harbour contains miles of beaches that are rarely visited.

Matlahaw Point

Guarding the western entrance to Hesquiat Harbour, a long rib of reefs extends outward from the point. It's best given a wide berth. Multiple tiers of breaking waves can be encountered along the shore. West of Matlahaw Point on a rock at Smokehouse Bay is a petroglyph. The bay was Ch'ikn'uu, a winter village site.

HESQUIAT HARBOUR

This sheltered waterway is almost entirely surrounded by beaches, offering a multitude of recreational opportunities. Sections of the harbour are shallow and prone to breaking waves, but otherwise many of the shorelines are calm and enticing. Portions are Indian Reserve and historic sites dot the harbour. Hooksum Outdoor School operates out of Hesquiat Harbour in the traditional territory of the Kiniqwastakumulth clan of the Hesquiaht First Nation. The school teaches indigenous knowledge, remote surfing, technical tree climbing, coastal hiking, natural history, guiding, leadership, wilderness first aid, sea kayaking and life saving. Contact Hooksum Outdoor School, Box 352, Tofino, BC, Canada V0R 2Z0, or phone **250-670-1120**.

The First Nations who historically lived at Hesquiat Harbour were a merging of several independent groups. The main group was located at Kiqina, west of Antons Spit. In the summer the group moved to Hilwina, north of Hesquiat Point, for the spring salmon, halibut and codfish. Heckwi was a winter village site.

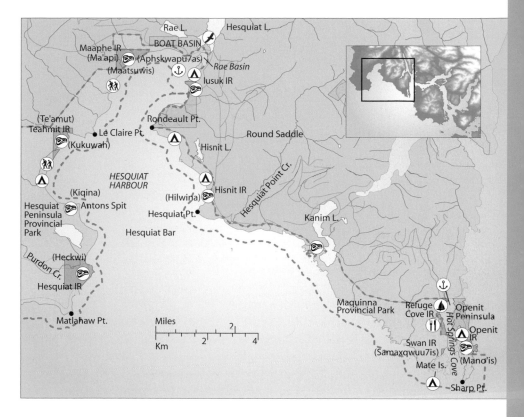

The first mission on the west coast of Vancouver Island was at the village of Hesquiat. The church and residence were built in 1875, and A. J. Brabant (see page 304) would serve the various native communities on the coast for more than 30 years.

The barque *John Bright*, carrying lumber from Port Gamble to Valparaiso in February 1869, was wrecked during a heavy southwest gale outside Hesquiat Harbour. All on board were killed. Officials in Victoria believed that natives had murdered the survivors as they reached the shore, as the bodies of ten men and one woman were found near the wreck on the beach, some of them headless. HMS *Sparrowhawk* went to examine the bodies and brought back seven native prisoners to Victoria. Two were sentenced to death and were hanged on July 29. The gallows were built near the head of Hesquiat Harbour, and the entire native community was brought out to witness the execution as a warning. The natives, however, said the bodies had been mangled in the storm and they had simply dragged the victims to shore.

The tall ship *Lady Washington* sits at anchor in Hesquiat Harbour exactly 200 years after the original *Lady Washington* anchored here.

Place names: Hesquiat is derived from the word *hishkwii*, which means 'to tear with the teeth.' Hesquiat Village was blessed with a saltwater grass called segmo that drifted into shore. During the herring spawn, the local people would strip the segmo with their teeth to separate the attached herring spawn from the grass. This was considered a great delicacy. The name describes the crunching sound made when chewing off the herring.

Hesquiat Peninsula Provincial Park: This park, established in 1995, encompasses 7,899 hectares (19,518 acres) from Escalante Point to Hesquiat Harbour. Here can be found old-growth stands of Sitka spruce, lodgepole pine, white pine and yellow cedar plus a freshwater lake. Shoreline features include extensive offshore reefs, sea caves, sheltered bays, kelp beds, sand beaches and drying mudflats. Included in the park boundary are Hesquiat Harbour, Rae Basin and Boat Basin. There are no facilities, but a very rough trail follows the beach from Boat Basin to Escalante Point (see page 224).

Antons Spit

North of Matlahaw Point the rolling swell of the open ocean is likely to find its way in as far as Antons Spit, where it will get steeper and form breaking waves as it hits the spit and the shallows, Hesquiat Bar. The spit itself runs dry in lower tides. North of the spit the beach is cobble until it turns toward Le Claire Point, where it gradually transforms into beautiful white sand.

Caution: Surfers claim every seventh wave is a big one, and that every seventh large wave is extra large. Whether mathematically correct or not, many waves are larger than others, and this is definitely a factor at shallow bars that extend for a great distance, such as Antons

An interesting array of sea caves, rock features and pocket beaches line the shore of Maquinna Provincial Park.

Spit. Kayakers or other boaters may think they're travelling well outside the breakers, but when that big one comes—and it will –you'll be facing an unusually large breaking wave when you thought you were safely outside the breakers. Oops.

Camping: The entire beach between Antons Spit and the Maahpe reserve is suitable for wilderness camping. Two rivers at Maahpe reserve offer fresh water.

Maquinna Provincial Park: Maquinna Provincial Park is most famous for Ramsay Hot Spring at Hot Springs Cove. But in 1992 as a result of Clayoquot Land Use Decision the park would be expanded from the 29 hectares (72 acres) at Openit Peninsula to more than 2,667 hectares (6,667 acres) stretching toward Hesquiat Harbour. This addition contains some of the most impressive waterfront on the west coast of Vancouver Island. Pocket beaches are hemmed in by magnificent rock bluffs, which have been eroded into a variety of sea caves, sea stacks and interesting formations. If you visit Hot Springs Cove, an hour or two spent north of the cove will be time well spent.

The sea caves here were formerly burial sites, though the remains have since been reinterred. Archeologists studying the burial caves along the shoreline have determined that a native in this area had a life expectancy of little more than 21 years. The Hesquiat Band has removed all cultural and skeletal items from the caves due to vandalism, so the caves can be visited without violating their sanctity.

Boat Basin

This inner portion of Hesquiat Harbour is among the most protected. A few homes are located at Boat Basin. There are no amenities.

This is the traditional territory of the Ma'apiath, who summered at Hilwina near Hesquiat Point. The group thrived until an Ahousaht raid wiped out much of the population. The remnants moved to Heckwi near Matlahaw Point, joining with another local group, the Kiqinath.

In 1915, the pioneer settler known as Cougar Annie arrived at Hesquiat Harbour and homesteaded on a wilderness property at Boat Basin. She bore eight of her 11 children here, had four husbands and outlasted them all, and created a garden out of five acres of rainforest. The garden is now a heritage site and tours can be arranged through the Boat Basin Foundation. An interpretive day-trip is offered through Ocean Outfitters in Tofino. Call **1-877-906-2326**. The garden is the subject of a book, *Cougar Annie's Garden*, by Margaret Horsfield. The Temperate Rainforest Field Study Centre is located at Rae Lake near the garden. For more information contact **1-888-638-2804** or visit **www.cougarannie.com**.

Camping: Several pleasant, sheltered beaches are located on the eastern shore of Boat Basin. There are a few areas with level clearings behind the beach for camping in shelter. Several uninhabited Indian Reserves may seem ideal for camping, but care should be taken not to trespass.

Hiking: The Hesquiat Peninsula Trail extends 32 km (20 miles) from Boat Basin to Escalante Point. In practice, however, it's rarely used and likely to be overgrown in the areas where the trail (loosely defined) passes rock bluffs. Otherwise, the beaches serve as the trail. Expect to have to bushwhack sections if you attempt to hike here. Another little-used trail leads from Boat Basin to Refuge Cove along an old telegraph line, but it has all but disappeared. A few old telegraph buildings along the route have also collapsed. None of the reserves on the Hesquiat Peninsula Trail are currently inhabited except as fishing camps by band members who are usually happy to see visitors, but as it's reserve land it's recommended to get advance permission to cross reserve property. Call the Hesquiaht First Nation band office at **250-670-1100**.

Rae Basin

This pretty cove is likely to be the far end of a journey to Hesquiat Harbour. At higher tides the stream to Hesquiat Lake can be attempted, but it might require a portage. Rae Basin is a protected anchorage.

Hesquiat Point

South of Rondeault Point there are some beautiful beaches, though they can be exposed to surf. At Hesquiat Point a line of reefs extends southward and can make travel difficult, though it's possible in most circumstances to carefully pass through the reefs on the shore side. The kelp beds around the point are extensive.

Hot Springs Cove

This deep and narrow inlet is well protected from the worst of the west coast weather and home to a thriving native community called Refuge Cove. It's also home to the world-famous Ramsay Hot Spring. There's a beautiful sand beach on the west side of the inlet as you enter, but it's on reserve property. Well down McNeil Peninsula is a government dock and the main park entrance to the hot spring. A rough beach allows kayak landings next to the dock. A 2-km (1.2-mile) boardwalk trail leads to the spring.

Ramsay Hot Spring

This geothermal spring tumbles down a waterfall into three tiers of pools set within steep and quite jagged black rocks. The spring is a warming 50°C (122°F). The lower pools can be subject to swell from the ocean, which can be either refreshing to offset the heat or surprisingly cold, especially if a large wave washes into the pool. This usually occurs only at higher tides. The trail leading to the spring from the dock is along a scenic boardwalk, but

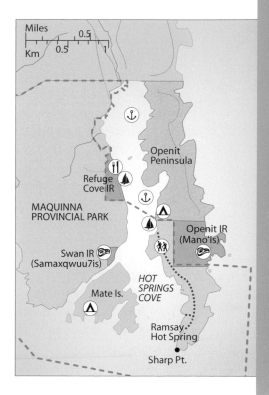

Visitors quickly fill various pools at Hot Springs Cove.

distance and many stairs can be difficult for some visitors. The water runs from the spring at the rate of 450 litres (100 gallons) per minute. If you're travelling to the hot spring by kayak, you can avoid the long walk by landing at a small beach immediately north of the hot spring. The beach is fairly rough rock. Look for the large logs above the high tide line. One log has a section cut out to make way for a trail that leads to the main boardwalk.

The hot spring has become an international travel destination, and this can mean visits by tour boats, Zodiacs and floatplanes every few minutes (yes, minutes) during peak tourism season, seven days a week. The pools can be brimming over with people, with little room to move in the water. The best time to visit is before 10 a.m. or after 6 p.m., though as the hot spring grows in popularity, tour operators are extending their hours to accommodate more visitors.

Hot Springs Cove was and is Ahousaht territory. The native name for the hot spring is Mok-se-kla-chuk, which means 'smoking water.' This area once had a general store in the 1940s, built by Ivan Clarke. He donated the land for a park in 1954.

Camping: A campsite is operated by the Refuge Cove band immediately north of the park. A fee applies. This is the only camping allowed on Openit Peninsula. Campers found trying to camp elsewhere on the peninsula will be asked to move. If you want to stay near Hot Springs Cove and prefer wilderness camping, consider a very small and well-protected wilderness site on the outer shore of Mate Islands. The surrounding water is thick with reefs and kelp, which drastically reduces the swell at the outside of Mate Islands. To find the beach, watch the shore and you'll see a beautiful but narrow beach between two rock ledges. There are no amenities. This is the closest free camping option near the hot springs without trespassing. Other wilderness camping options near Hot Springs Cove are on Flores Island immediately east of Openit Peninsula (see page 247).

Refuge Cove

This native community, located across the inlet from the hot springs dock, has a store located in the basement of a home on the reserve. The store keeps unusual hours and stocks snacks, refrigerated drinks and frozen meats. To get there, your best bet is to land at the north public dock and ask for directions. Someone is sure to point you the way. A new motel has opened at Refuge Cove across the inlet from the park's dock. Several rooms are available for rent. A large 1920s boat, the InnChanter, offers summer accommodation in the harbour. Call **250-670-1149** or visit **www.innchanter.com**.

Sharp Point

The outer point of Openit Peninsula is prone to rough conditions. Swell, tide, wind waves and clashing currents can make the water here miserable. Use caution. Beware that conditions can deteriorate as the winds pick up, so a calm arrival isn't a guarantee of calm conditions when leaving. Sharp Point was a traditional native diving spot and a training place for players of *lehal*, a gambling stick game.

THE NORTHERN INLETS

Composed of Sydney Inlet and its associated waterways, plus Shelter Inlet, these waterways are among the more secluded and protected of the various inlets on the west coast of Vancouver Island. That translates into some phenomenal exploration, especially by kayak. Three provincial parks are located here, protecting entire watersheds, breathtaking waterfalls, intriguing islands and pristine channels.

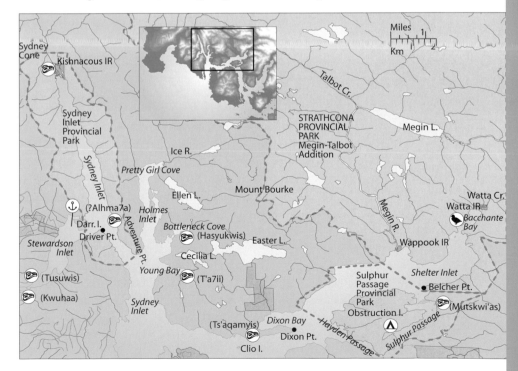

Shelter Inlet meanders deep into the mountainous heart of Vancouver Island.

Sydney Inlet Provincial Park: Created in 1995, the park protects 2,774 hectares (6,854 acres) in an unlogged and undeveloped wilderness setting. It's a near-perfect west coast fjord in its entirety—an increasingly rare feature on the coast. To be found here are Nuu-chah-nulth heritage sites, a mountainous skyline, old-growth Sitka spruce and Douglas-fir forests and the Sydney River estuary, which supports four species of salmon, including a notable population of chinook.

Because they're farther afield with no land access closer than Tofino, they're less likely to be visited than the more southerly channels in Clayoquot Sound. The result is a fantastic wilderness setting.

Sydney Inlet

Now a provincial park, Sydney Inlet is one of the few almost perfectly intact fjords on the west coast of Vancouver Island. Several channels branch off the main inlet. Steep shorelines make for beautiful views but provide few rest areas beyond the occasional cobble beach that's invariably unsuitable for camping. The inlet ends in a drying mudflat. The watershed is estimated to be 98.5 percent old-growth forest (over 141 years of age is considered old-growth). That factor increases the biological diversity of the watershed, as old-growth forests attract a range of species not associated with younger forests. In Sydney Inlet, .8 km (half a mile) north of Young Bay, is a mystery wreck. It's a designated provincial heritage site.

Between Sydney and Matilda inlets, six pilchard reduction plants were temporarily located in Clayoquot Sound. Their presence was the result of a short-lived environmental anomaly. The warm-water

Japanese current normally passes hundreds of miles off Vancouver Island, but during the 1920s it shifted to the Vancouver Island shoreline. This brought schools of pilchard into the sound. Pilchard, similar to herring and sardines, is prized for its high oil content. Many of the factory sites are still visible today.

Stewardson Inlet

This long waterway stretches southwest from Sydney Inlet toward Hesquiat Peninsula. It's most popular for the anchorage located behind Darr Island. The most impressive physical feature about this region is the huge cliff face immediately northeast of Darr Island. Otherwise the shorelines are quite steep along most of its 8-km (5-mile) length.

Two native villages were located in the inlet; the residents of both villages were wiped out by smallpox. Indian Chief Mine on Stewardson Inlet would become the most significant mine in Clayoquot Sound. Between 1904 and 1935, 72,000 tons of ore would be removed, yielding 2.4 million pounds of copper, 5,500 ounces of silver and 722 ounces of gold.

Holmes Inlet

This waterway heads north from Sydney Inlet at Adventure Point. It splits again where two islands lie mid-channel. The inlet ends in a gravel shoal at the Ice River estuary. More of a lagoon than a cove, Bottleneck Cove, at the sound end of the inlet, is occasionally used as an anchorage. Though pretty enough, it's quite small. Hasyukwis, a village used for carving canoes, was located here.

Young Bay is a pretty bay that ends at Cecilia Creek. Fresh water is available at the creek's mouth, where there's a rough trail. Young Bay was the site of an Ahousaht village meaning 'a lot of creeks come in.' If you visit here on the north shore you'll notice a set of concrete foundations, the remains of a pilchard reduction plant.

Camping: While there are no recognized campsites in this area, the north shore of Young Bay near the pilchard reduction plant ruin is probably the best bet for pitching a tent. Otherwise spots in Sydney Inlet and its neighbouring waterways are almost nonexistent.

Shelter Inlet

This pretty inlet is almost entirely protected parkland from Obstruction Island eastward. Rarely visited, it's one of the prettiest inlets in Clayoquot Sound.

Megin River

This inviting river on Shelter Inlet is accessible by paddle at higher tides and can be navigated (with some difficulty) to Megin Lake, a beautiful inland recreation lake. The elevation rises just 20 m (65 feet) along the river's 10-km (6-mile) length. The whole area is protected as part of the Strathcona Provincial Park Megin-Talbot Addition. The Megin River is significant for spawning sockeye, chinook, coho, pink and chum salmon. Just east of the river is a waterfall that plunges into a deep pool very close to Shelter Inlet. It's possible to paddle up a short river to the main pool. This is best done at higher tides. Once inside, you can nose right up to the waterfall—or stop at the nearby beach and walk to the pool for a view.

Camping: While there are no official or even unofficial campsites here, there are a number of beach-like areas that could serve in a pinch. One is at the waterfall. Other beaches are located farther northeast in Shelter Inlet. Just be sure the site you choose is above high tide.

Bacchante Bay

Accessible through a narrow passage on the northeastern end of Shelter Inlet, Bacchante Bay is considered the best all-weather anchorage in the area. The bay ends in a drying mudflat. It's backed by breathtaking mountain scenery. Watta Creek leads up a valley to Lone Wolf Mountain, which peaks at about 1,460 m (4,790 feet). Several other mountains surround the bay, with the highest visible peak being Splendour Mountain at 1,680 m (5,511 feet).

Obstruction Island

This beautiful and intact island is another of the protected attractions in Clayoquot Sound. Sulphur Passage, to the island's southeast, is a narrow, twisting waterway through a maze of reefs and islets.

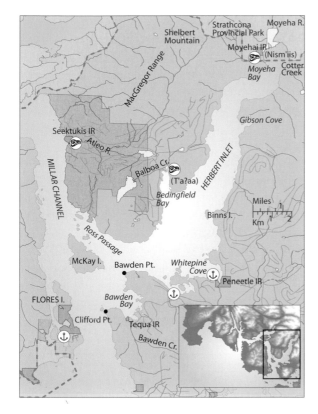

Sulphur Passage Provincial Park: The park is named after the passage, but it also includes Obstruction Island and Hayden Passage to the west, plus a significant portion of the Vancouver Island upland fronting Sulphur Passage. The park protects an old-growth Sitka spruce forest and a rich intertidal estuary. The park, like many across Vancouver Island, was established in 1995, and protects 2,298 hectares (5,678 acres).

Current can run as high as 4 knots, though turbulence is minimal. The area is ecologically very rich, including the small cove set into the south side of Obstruction Island. If you're there at low tide, be sure to take the time to explore the rich subtidal environment. Keep your eyes open for sea cucumbers. Sulphur Passage can be very difficult for boats to navigate due to the many rocks and shoals. That, however, makes it perfect for exploration by paddle.

Camping: A good site is on the islet at the entrance to the southern cove on the island. The access is from the inside of the cove. A rough beach leads to clear areas on the islet suitable for tents. Watch for the sensitive mosses on the bluff. Tread lightly!

Millar Channel

Millar Channel is the sheltered route alongside Flores Island. Much of the upland on Vancouver Island fronting Millar Channel is privately owned. There are few rest spots except for McNeil Peninsula (see Flores Island, page 249) and rough beaches at the various creeks along the channel. Given a choice of the two routes, the outer side of Flores Island is prone to swell and exposure to the weather, but is a far more exotic and appealing environment.

Atleo River, once an Otsosat fall fishing village, was taken over by the Ahousaht after an Ahousaht-Otsosat war.

Herbert Inlet

Herbert Inlet is filled with various pocket coves and bays used occasionally as anchorages. At its head is Moyeha Bay, which ends in the estuary of Moyeha River. The bay is within the southern boundary of Strathcona Provincial Park. No trails lead into the park from this inlet. That opportunity is at Bedwell Sound in south Clayoquot Sound (see page 269).

Native communities once dotted this inlet. One at Moyeha Bay, Nism'iis, is believed to be a site used by the Otsosat for winter ceremonies known as Ts'aayiqa, the Power Dance. It was also an important Otsosat fishery location that evolved into an Ahousaht village.

FLORES ISLAND

Flores Island is the second-largest island on the outer coast of Vancouver Island (the largest is Nootka). Mount Flores rises to an impressive 880 m (2,887 feet). Shores range from the beautiful beaches of Cow Bay and Whitesand Cove to the wave-battered rocks of Rafael Point or the more protected waters of Shelter Inlet and Millar Channel.

Place names: Flores Island can trace its name to the Spanish explorer Capt. Eliza in 1791, who named it after Don Manuel Antonio Flores, the viceroy of Mexico from 1787 to 1789.

Rafael Point

This is the most rugged, exposed and wave-battered of the many faces of Flores Island. The outer coast on both sides of Rafael Point is a feeding ground for gray whales and one of the best places, bar none, to see gray whales on the Vancouver Island coast. Unfortunately tour operators have discovered this as well, so it's likely to be among the busiest spots on the coast for tour vessels. Even so, it's well worth the trip to see the whales. To avoid most of the tour groups, be on the water near here before 9 a.m.

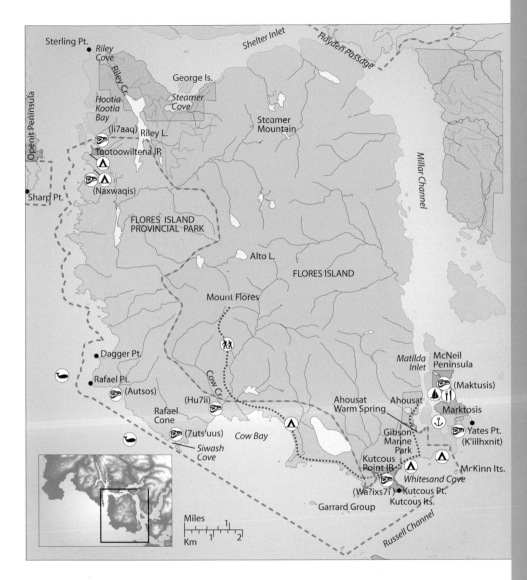

Rafael Point to Sterling Point

This stretch of Flores Island has a multitude of bays and islets along the shore. Hidden in various locations are beautiful pocket beaches. Opposite Openit Peninsula is a highly visible sandy beach, a former First Nations summer and winter village site.

Camping: Several beaches along the coast are useful as a staging ground for kayakers visiting Hot Springs Cove. The nicest is slightly northeast and across the inlet from Sharp Point. Here the beach is slightly exposed to westerly winds. This also tends to be a popular camping area. There are no amenities. A more protected alternative is slightly farther north, tucked into a bay south of an unnamed island (look for the elevation marker "65" on Clayoquot chart 3674 to identify the island). This beautiful crushed-shell beach faces north and has space for several tents above the high tide line. It's next to the Ahousaht Tootoowiltena reserve.

Riley Cove

This pretty cove is popular as an anchorage. The sand, shell and cobble beach looks inviting for a campsite, but the high tide line reaches the understorey, meaning the entire beach disappears at high tide. If you do wish to camp here, there's a tiny cleared area underneath some bushes on the southwestern end of the beach. It's very small and not recommended.

A pilchard reduction plant was once located here. The foundations of the wharf can still be seen in the cove, as can bricks from the ruined structure.

Travel notes: During a stop here, while my partner snoozed on the beach, I explored the bushes in search of more ruins. The growth made moving around difficult, but eventually I came across an empty wine bottle and a full, unopened bottle of Orange Crush with the orange drink still inside. The glass bottle was marked with the year 1929.

Steamer Cove

Despite several pretty islands and a cove, it was heavily logged recently with industrial traces all too visible, making it a rather unattractive spot. The name is a nod to the cove's usefulness as a safe and sheltered anchorage for passing steamers in days past.

Matilda Inlet

This deep, narrow inlet on the southwest side of Flores has numerous coves and an island in its centre. It ends in a drying mudflat. The east side is Marktosis, a First Nation Ahousaht community. The inlet is used regularly by boaters seeking a secluded and sheltered anchorage.

Not quite rivalling Hot Springs Cove for popularity—or warmth— is Ahousat Warm Spring. The spring is fed from the same geothermal style of spring that heats Ramsay Hot Spring. It just doesn't do it as well. It was described to me by a couple from Alberta as "tepid," and that seems appropriate. The spring flows into a concrete pool that has been constructed to make the most of the water, and indeed it's a pleasant enough dip. Maybe four or five people could enjoy the pool at a time without it being overly crowded, but don't worry, there won't be many crowds. The spring can be hard to locate. It's a 20-minute hike from either Whitesand Cove or Ahousat. It's located on the southern end of Matilda Inlet next to the shore, just off the main path. If you're near the head of the inlet keep an eye open for the pool, for it's easily passed by. It's about 3 m (10 feet) off the main trail and largely hidden from view by bushes.

Flores Island Provincial Park: The park includes 7,113 hectares (17,782 acres) of shoreline on the island's exposed south and west coasts. It protects three complete watersheds and a stand of old-growth Sitka spruce. The shoreline is a varied mixture of sandstone reefs, beaches and sandbars. Gray whales are year-round residents of the shore here. The park was created in 1995.

Marktosis

This community on the east side of Matilda Inlet is home to about 550 people. The smaller community of Ahousat is located slightly north across the inlet. Ahousat has a public dock, gas, a store and a café. Hummingbird Hostel is open from March to October. Dormitory rooms are available. A sea bus, *Ahousaht Pride*, leaves from the First Street dock in Tofino each day at 10:30 a.m. and 4 p.m. It returns from Ahousat at 8:30 a.m. and 1 p.m. The cost is reasonable—about $14 each way.

Marktosis means 'moving from one side to the other.' A former winter village of the Otsosat, the territory was lost to the Ahousaht through war.

Matilda Inlet was the site of a bloody incident in 1864. A Clayoquot sub-chief named Cap-Chap ordered an attack on the schooner *Kingfisher* anchored in the inlet. The captain and crew were killed. In retaliation, the British Royal Navy sent the ships *Sutlej* and *Devastation* from Victoria. Several local villages were destroyed, 15 natives were killed and several others arrested. Cap-Chap, however, was never found. Shells fired during the incident were still being found fairly recently. Some are on display at the Maritime Museum of B.C. in Victoria. The Kingfisher was burned down to the waterline, then sunk by loading the hull with rocks. The remains have been the subject of fairly recent archeological investigations.

A storm passes through Clayoquot Sound—a perfect time to stroll the beach at Whitesand Cove.

Whitesand Cove

Part of Gibson Marine Park, Whitesand Cove is one of the more scenic and protected beaches off Vancouver Island. It lives up to its name with a series of sweeping white sand beaches in a cove well protected from the westerly weather. The westernmost stretch is an Indian Reserve and consequently off-limits to campers. Camping is possible at any of the other beaches. All portions of the beach are joined by short trails that traverse the headlands.

Caution: Wolves frequent the beaches on Flores Island and through contact can become conditioned to humans. Stow gear and food carefully and under no circumstances attempt to feed or socialize with the wolves (see page 267).

Gibson Provincial Marine Park: This park, located on the southeast end of Flores Island, is a small adjunct to Flores Island Provincial Park. Established in 1967, the park includes Whitesand Cove, which shelters one of the finest beaches in Clayoquot Sound. Attractions include Ahousat Warm Spring on Matilda Inlet and some rarely hiked trails. It's most popular among kayakers, who use the beach as a base for explorations of Clayoquot Sound, and mariners, who anchor in Matilda Inlet. It protects 143 hectares (353 acres).

Hiking: There are two trails worth following. One leads from the centre of Whitesand Cove to Ahousat Warm Spring and the village of Ahousat. To find it from Whitesand Cove, look for the floats on the bushes. Another trail, the Wild Side Trail, leads to the west and is a much longer hike to Cow Bay. It's about four hours, one way. Another challenging leg leads to the top of Mount Flores.

Camping: Whitesand Cove is one of the more popular stretches to camp in Clayoquot Sound.

A waterfall in Shelter Inlet can be reached by kayak after a short paddle upriver to the waterfall's lagoon.

With several beaches to choose from, you're still likely to find some privacy. There are no amenities. Surf tends to be light in the more sheltered portions to moderate in the more exposed stretches.

Kutcous Point

This pretty point is characterized by a volcanic rock shoreline, numerous offshore reefs and thick kelp beds. West of the point is an exposed beach. A former Otsosat village located near Kutcous Point was strategic for defence, and the location of a major battle between the Otsosat and Ahousaht. Southwest of Kutcous Point was Qatqwuuwis, once an Otsosat summer camp. During the Ahousaht-Otsosat war, captives were beheaded here. A sign near the entrance of the Wild Side Trail commemorates the bloody battle.

Cow Bay

This sweeping beach stretches for miles. Potentially more exposed to surf than Whitesand Cove, watch for numerous submerged and semi-submerged rocks that dot the bay. East of Cow Bay is another long stretch of beach. It's rarely visited except by the few hikers trudging from Ahousat to Cow Bay.

At Siwash Cove just west of Cow Bay was the main summer village of the Otsosat. The village name means 'water gets into bay.' Several longhouses were located at a midden mound still visible today.

Hiking: The Wild Side Trail connects Cow Bay with Ahousat. A 4-km (2.5-mile) extension leads to the summit of Mount Flores for a breathtaking view around Clayoquot Sound. The trail is quite difficult, with sections of slippery boardwalk. Mud and puddles are to be expected after rain.

Camping: Cow Bay is a beautiful stretch of beach for wilderness camping. There are no amenities.

Caution: As with Whitesand Cove, wolves are known to visit the beaches here (see page 267). Avoid leaving food open, and avoid close contact.

The beach at Whitesand Cove makes for a picturesque place to pitch a tent for a weekend.

South Clayoquot Sound

FOR MANY PEOPLE, CLAYOQUOT SOUND PERSONIFIES THE WEST COAST OF Vancouver Island with its sweeping beaches, wave-battered headlands, mountainous backdrops, old-growth forests and marine wildlife ranging from birds in the estuaries to land mammals in the open sea. South Clayoquot differs from many other coastal areas in that there are two very different worlds to explore: protected inner waterways that meander through mountain-bordered inlets, and the more dramatic and exposed outer shorelines where high seas batter exposed rock and wildlife ranges from tufted puffins to whales. South Clayoquot is also brimming with history, from the remnants of Fort Defiance on Meares Inlet to memories of Chief Wickaninnish and the days when the Tla-o-qui-aht ruled.

When I paddled down the coast from Port Hardy in 2003, I reached Tofino after more than a month since the last stop at a town. Tofino was like an oasis of civilization. I cleared the grocery store of Power Bars; I ate breakfast in a restaurant; I washed my laundry in a machine and had a hot shower. I even bought souvenirs. It was grand—for a short time.

Fortunately civilization doesn't extend far beyond the town limits. As I paddled back to my campsite on the south end of Vargas Island—a strategic location to continue down the coast to Ucluelet the next day—I was back in wilderness within minutes.

I had spent the previous few days exploring the inner channels. There's recreational traffic, the occasional resort or fish farm and even the high possibility of tour groups of kayaks as neighbours at the campsite. But the wilderness remains as magnificent as ever. Clayoquot may be discovered, but it hasn't been tamed.

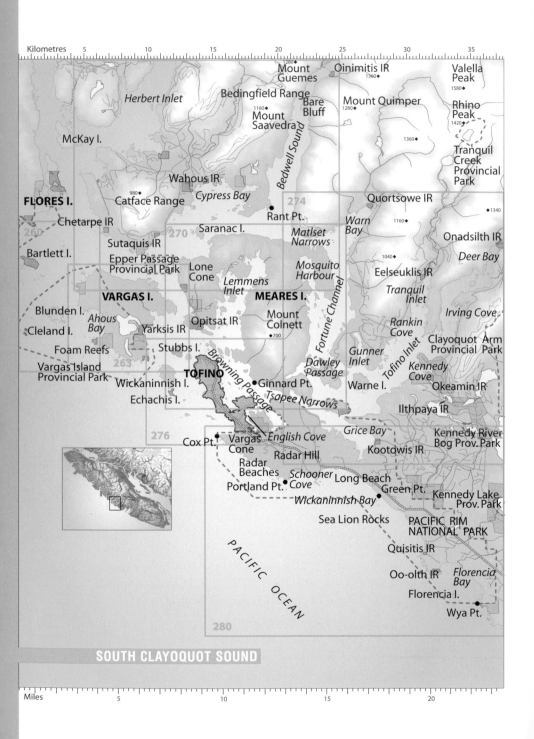

Kilometres 5 10 15 20 25 30 35

Mount Guemes 1280♦
Oinimitis IR 1360♦
Valella Peak 1580♦

Herbert Inlet
Bedingfield Range
Bare Bluff
Mount Quimper 1280♦
Rhino Peak 1420♦

Mount Saavedra 1160♦
McKay I.
1360♦
Tranquil Creek Provincial Park

Wahous IR
Cypress Bay
Bedwell Sound

FLORES I.
Catface Range 980♦
Rant Pt.
274
Quortsowe IR

Chetarpe IR
Saranac I.
Warn Bay
1160♦
♦1340

260
270
Matlset Narrows
Onadsilth IR

Sutaquis IR
Deer Bay

Bartlett I.
Epper Passage Provincial Park
Lone Cone
Mosquito Harbour
1040♦
Eelseuklis IR

Lemmens Inlet
Tranquil Inlet
Irving Cove

VARGAS I.
MEARES I.

Blunden I.
Ahous Bay
Opitsat IR
Mount Colnett 700♦
Rankin Cove
Clayoquot Arm Provincial Park

Cleland I.
Yarksis IR
Fortune Channel

Foam Reefs
Stubbs I.
Gunner Inlet
Kennedy Cove

Vargas Island Provincial Park
263
TOFINO
Browning Passage
Dawley Passage
Tofino Inlet
Okeamin IR

Wickaninnish I.
Ginnard Pt.
Warne I.

Echachis I.
Tsapee Narrows
Ilthpaya IR

276
Cox Pt.
Vargas Cone
English Cove
Grice Bay
Kennedy River Bog Prov. Park

Radar Hill
Kootowis IR

Radar Beaches
Schooner Cove
Long Beach
Kennedy Lake Prov. Park

Portland Pt.
Green Pt.

Wickaninnish Bay

Sea Lion Rocks
PACIFIC RIM NATIONAL PARK

Quisitis IR

PACIFIC
Oo-olth IR
Florencia Bay

OCEAN
Florencia I.

280
Wya Pt.

SOUTH CLAYOQUOT SOUND

Miles 5 10 15 20

254   The Wild Coast

GETTING HERE

Clayoquot Sound is blessed with a paved highway leading directly to Tofino. It's a 320-km drive (200 miles) from Victoria and will take about 4 hours (3 from the ferry at Nanaimo). For all practical purposes, Tofino is the only access point for both north and south Clayoquot Sound.

EXPLORING BY KAYAK

South Clayoquot Sound is one of the major gateways to the west coast, and Tofino attracts about 250,000 visitors each year. Kayakers run the gamut from absolute beginners touring Lemmens Inlet to veterans visiting the outer shores of Vargas and Bartlett islands.

Recommended short trips

- *If you have a day:* Since the best launch is at Tofino, Tofino is the logical starting point for any day trip into Clayoquot. For beginners, Lemmens Inlet, Maurus Channel and Browning Passage provide suitable areas. More advanced paddlers will find drama and wildlife at Vargas. Hardy kayakers might possibly circumnavigate Vargas Island in a day (a distance of about 32 km/20 miles), or get as far as Cleland Island (recommended, but with a caution for open water).

- *If you have two days:* Most of the campsites in South Clayoquot can be paddled in a day, making any one of them suitable for an overnight journey. Recommended are the beaches at Ahous Bay, north Vargas Island or even Whaler Islets. Circumnavigating Vargas Island over the two days will give a magnificent introduction to Clayoquot Sound.

- *If you have three days:* Stay for two nights at any of the locations above (Ahous Bay is recommended), and consider using the middle day for exploring the outer channels and islands, such as Cleland Island, or even Flores Island in north Clayoquot Sound.

- *If you have five days:* If you have this much time you could travel most of the inner waters around Meares Island and still have time to explore Vargas Island and the outer islands. I recommend heading out to Vargas Island and using the extra time to explore into north Clayoquot Sound.

If carefully navigated, a crushed-shell beach on Florencia Island makes a perfect campsite on the outer coast.

- *If you have a week:* To really uncover south Clayoquot Sound take the time to round Meares Island through Fortune Channel, then head north into Millar Channel. Spend some time exploring north Clayoquot Sound and its various attractions, such as Shelter Inlet and Hot Springs Cove. Don't forget Maquinna Provincial Park. Consider returning via the outside coast along Flores and Vargas islands.

- *The ideal trip:* Any longer trip into Clayoquot should involve its northern waters. Vargas Island and its surrounding islands and islets are without a doubt the highlight of the southern section. But the northern side is so much more isolated and generally more wild. Ideally, an exploration of Clayoquot would take in the outer coast from Vargas Island to Hesquiat Peninsula. For the really adventurous—assuming the transportation details can be worked out—a trip from Tahsis or Zeballos in Nootka Sound and down the outer coast to Tofino would make an incredible journey.

THE BASICS

Geology and ecology

Clayoquot Sound comprises about 350,000 hectares (864,869 acres) in total, with rainforests composing about 93 percent of the land. Many of the region's large forested valleys remain untouched by logging.

Like most of the west coast of Vancouver Island, Clayoquot Sound's various inlets and passages were carved by glaciers thousands of years ago. Exposed granite rock shows evidence of volcanic activity long ago, while conglomerate rock, a compressed mixture of sand and gravel, was formed during the Cretaceous period. As the volcanic rock eroded, it was washed into deep water and compressed into cemented rock. Glacial outwash from the last ice age left sand and rubble in various waterways of the sound, creating shallows that have formed large sandbanks. One significant sandbar is between the Catface Range and the southeast shore of Flores Island. Here water rises from a depth of 10 m (33 feet) to 40 m (130 feet) in about a mile. Silt from the various bays and inlets has settled on the shallows, creating extensive intertidal mudflats around Esowista Peninsula, Browning Passage, Templar Channel and Lemmens Inlet. This is one of the key bird areas of southern Vancouver Island. The mudflats are critical habitat for western sandpipers, each year attracting an estimated 2.5 percent of the global population, as well as a significant number of great blue herons and many other species of birds.

Opitsat is a historic native community on Meares Island that still thrives today.

The rainforests house a diverse range of wildlife; fresh waterways are salmon spawning areas. The narrow passages in the sound are rich with intertidal life, from eelgrass to sea squirts, and sea lions, harbour seals, gray whales, killer whales and humpback whales are common.

Weather

Weather in Clayoquot Sound is characterized, like most of the coast, by mild temperatures year-round. Tofino's average temperatures are a low of 4.2°C (39°F) in January and a high of 14.6°C (58°F) in July. Tofino also receives about 3,300 mm (130 inches) per year of precipitation, with significantly less (about 100 mm per month, or 4 inches) in July and August. As much as 450 mm (18 inches) can fall in November.

Native overview

Clayoquot Sound is part of the traditional land of the Nuu-chah-nulth, a people linked largely by their common language. Nine distinct tribes made use of Clayoquot Sound, with six of those in the southern portion. One of the major tribes was the Ahousaht, a people who lived mainly on western Vargas, Calmus Passage and Cypress Bay. They would absorb various independent groups over the years to rise in power. Those included the Owinmitisaht of Bedwell Sound, the Quatsweaht of the Warn Bay area and Meares Island, and the Keltsomaht, who lived on the eastern side of Vargas Island and on Meares Island. They amalgamated after losing a high number of men at sea during a sealing expedition in the late 1880s.

The Tla-o-qui-aht (formerly known as the Clayoquot) would rise as the other most powerful tribe in Clayoquot Sound. The Tla-o-qui-aht once lived in the Kennedy Lake area but expanded their territory to include Tofino Inlet, Esowista Peninsula and portions of Meares Island. They absorbed the Puneetlaht of Mosquito Harbour on Meares Island. The name is derived from the native word *tla7uukwi*, which means 'different' or 'changing.' It has also been interpreted as 'people of other tribes.'

Like other Nuu-chah-nulth groups, the Clayoquot Sound bands comprised a variety of local and family groups that collectively formed each tribe. Each local group was centred upon a group of chiefs who owned territorial rights and inherited privileges. Village sites were seasonal, beginning in March with the move to meet the arriving herring. Summer villages were more permanent here than on other areas of the coast; cedar plank houses were built in some locations. Whaling was highly esteemed, and was limited to chiefs who travelled with six paddlers and a steersman in a canoe.

THE SHORELINES

THE OUTER ISLANDS

The outer islands of Clayoquot Sound are an enchanting mixture of isolated sand beaches and wave-battered rocks. The main islands are Bartlett Island and Blunden Island, part of Vargas Island Provincial Park. The ecological highlight is Cleland Island, a collection of remote rocks that are a major bird nesting area.

Bartlett Island

Bartlett Island is an Indian Reserve and is surrounded by reefs and islets. Recreationally, Whaler Islets are the most impressive. The main islet is a long, thin wedge with perfectly white sand on two sides visible for miles.

Once an Otsosat Village, an Ahousaht war party attacked Bartlett Island one night, allowing the Ahousaht chief to extend his territory from here to Herbert Inlet. Seal hunting and salmon and halibut fishing took place here.

Camping: Whaler Islets offer an exceptionally fine, though small beach. It has the disadvantage of being both remote and exposed. The long stretch of beach is set between two headlands on the east and

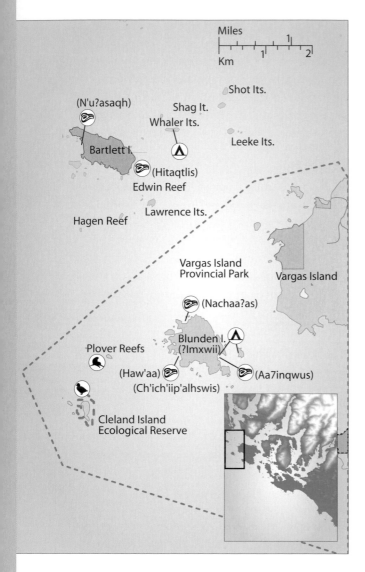

west sides. The headlands offer some protection, and campers usually like to set up under their cover rather than in the exposed middle portion. The surf can be moderate to even high here, and neither side is usually completely protected. The reward is incredible views.

Blunden Island

Blunden Island is a fairly large island midway between Cleland and Vargas islands in the exposed waters off Clayoquot Sound. Numerous small coves and passages break up the sheer rock shoreline. Five ancient native villages were located here; known names are marked on the map. One, Aa7inqwus, was an Ahousaht summer village site. The island was used for fishing halibut, fur sealing, whaling and gathering sea urchins. Deer and mink were also hunted here.

Camping: Two pleasant and protected beaches are suitable for camping. A beach on the east side of Blunden Island faces an islet. A second option is a beach on the west side of the islet. The islet is perhaps the prettiest spot. A flat clearing, suitable for a few tents, is set above the beach. The cove between the beaches is well protected.

Cleland Island

Set in the waters outside of Clayoquot Sound, Cleland Island is a glimpse of life on the edge—an exposed rock rich in wildlife. By jumping from Tofino to Blunden Island, the stretch of open water is surprisingly short (it's about a 15-km/9-mile paddle from Tofino). An interesting area to explore is the cove on the island's east side. Watch for seals and sea lions on the rocks. Landing is prohibited.

Place names: Originally Cleland Island was called Bare Island on the British Admiralty Chart of 1863, and the name was officially adopted in 1934. It didn't last long. To avoid confusion with another Bare Island, it was renamed Cleland Island later that year. It's named after F. H. Cleland, who bought a property on the west side of Vargas Island in 1912.

Cleland Island Ecological Reserve: The island is a treeless basalt rock rising only to 10 m (33 feet) above sea level at its tallest point. Salmonberry, wild (Nootka) rose and grasses grow above the rock shore. The island was made an ecological reserve in 1971 to protect the breeding populations of seabirds. Cleland Island has one of the highest populations of seabirds in comparison to its size on the coast. It's particularly significant as important habitat for four species of breeding birds. As many as 57 pairs of black oystercatchers have been recorded here—about 1 percent of the global population. About 5,700 pairs of nesting Leach's storm-petrels have been recorded, about 1 percent of the Canadian eastern Pacific population. About 1,700 pairs of glaucous-winged gulls nest here, or 1 percent of the North American population. Pigeon guillemots number about 200 pairs, 2 percent of the Canadian population.

Also found here are fork-tailed storm-petrels, tufted puffins, rhinoceros auklets and Cassin's auklets, which tunnel into the sandy soil. Look on the bare rocks and beach logs for pelagic cormorants and common murres. Black Brants enjoy the eelgrass, though their numbers appear to be in decline. About 4,000 were recorded here in 1970; that has since dropped to as low as 480. In early spring migrating white-winged scoters and surf scoters can be seen molting. About 10,000 waterfowl are believed to congregate here in the spring. Clouded salamanders are also found here and northern sea lions haul out on the nearby reefs, as do seals.

Numerous rocks surround Cleland Island, providing habitat for seabirds.

Marbled Murrelet: This area of Clayoquot Sound, particularly the southeast of Vargas and Flores islands, is host to a substantial number of marbled murrelets during the summer. They can often be seen in protected waters such as inlets, bays, lagoons and harbours foraging for food. They also like tidal rips and shallow banks. These small seabirds are related to auks, murres and puffins. During the winter they're black and white with easily recognized wing patches; while breeding they're a mottled brown.

They need old-growth forests for their nests, which are built high in trees. Their needs are quite particular—cover above the nests but small gaps in the canopy to reach them. The nests are usually on a large limb covered with deep moss. They don't actually construct the nests; a single egg is simply laid in a depression in the moss.

The Clayoquot marbled murrelets represent about 5 percent of the national population. They're considered a nationally threatened species in rapid decline. In 1982, 4,500 birds were recorded in this area; the population has since dropped to below 3,000. There are two theories for the decline: one is a natural shift in the climate, making it a short-term population change (a situation that held true for tufted puffins at Triangle Island). The other theory—one that seems more likely given their nesting needs—is the loss of old-growth forests through logging. That would mean a permanent population decline.

Their range is from Alaska to northern California. Globally significant populations are found in Brooks Peninsula, Clayoquot Sound and Barkley Sound. The marbled murrelet is protected by the new Canadian Species at Risk Act, and a recovery initiative is underway. One problem is that so little is understood about them; the first two nests weren't discovered in Canada until 1990 and 1991 (in the Walbran Valley near Juan de Fuca Strait). Knowledge about the species is increasing thanks to monitoring and a banding program involving more than 1,000 birds. Interim habitat protection measures are in effect for known nest sites, and forest companies on Vancouver Island are helping by voluntarily deferring harvesting some old-growth habitats used by marbled murrelets. A particularly significant step was taken by Interfor in 2004 when it announced a five-year moratorium on harvesting virgin forests in the Sydney River and Pretty Girl Lakes valleys in northern Clayoquot Sound. The moratorium will allow the completion of watershed studies and protects the birds until at least 2009. Meanwhile, two-thirds of Clayoquot Sound remains available for logging, which is proceeding in areas such as Sulphur Pass in north Clayoquot Sound and Satchie Creek on Hesquiat Peninsula.

VARGAS ISLAND

Vargas Island has a multitude of white sand beaches to choose from on the outer shores and numerous sheltered areas around the island, as well as challenging stretches around the La Croix Group. It's very close to Tofino, making it an outstanding coastal setting that's easily accessible.

Place names: The island was first named in 1791 by Lt. Commander Eliza as Isla de Feran, and was reflected in the Spanish charts that year. In 1792 Commanders Galiano and Valdes changed it to Isla de Vargas, reputedly for the Spanish governor who reconquered New

Mexico in 1693. Vancouver's chart of 1798 called it Feran Island, and it wasn't until the 1861 survey by Hecate that Capt. Richards adopted the named Vargas Island.

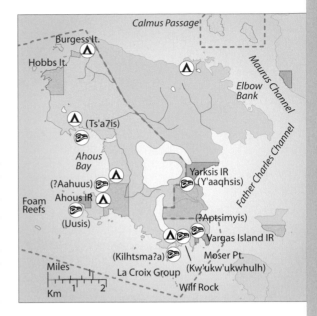

The south coast

Definitely the most rugged portion of Vargas Island, rocky headlands and reef-strewn waters are interspersed with inviting beaches. Three Keltsomaht villages were used in the spring and summer for sealing, whaling, halibut fishing and collecting beach foods such as Indian rhubarb.

Caution: While the south shore of Vargas Island between Ahous Bay and Moser Point can be an impressive place to explore the reefs, the La Croix Group is a sometimes dangerous barrier. The shallow ocean floor around the reefs tends to exaggerate the swell, which can pile up over submerged and semi-submerged reefs. Swell of 3 to 4 m (10 to 14 feet) isn't uncommon. In rough seas this is an area best avoided. In even moderate swell give the La Croix Group a wide berth to avoid the hazardous rocks. The good news is, the problem is localized. If you move away from shore and around the outside of the reefs, conditions will quickly change.

Camping: The nicest and most easily accessible beach is the third bay west of Moser Point, where a deep sand beach stretches well back from the ocean. Expect some surf.

Ahous Bay

This is one of the prettiest and most accessible beaches in Clayoquot Sound, and as a result one of the most popular. A long, sweeping beach makes for pleasant strolls at sunset—or any other time of day, for that matter. The central beach can be exposed to high surf and wind, but pockets to the north and south provide protection.

A number of native sites were located along Ahous Bay, but the major village site, Uusis, was located south of Ahous Point at the

The fine white sand beaches of Vargas Island stretch along the outer coast.

west-facing bay. Here the Ahousaht spent the summer whaling, seal hunting and fishing for cod, salmon and halibut.

Camping: Ahous Bay is a popular destination for kayakers and other recreational users, and wilderness campsites of various quality dot the shoreline. The busiest and most sheltered locations are immediately to the north and south of the bay. One particularly nice beach is to the north between two rock outcroppings that isolate it from the main beach. The most sheltered spot to the south is near a small creek that drains into the bay. Camping can be on the beach or you may find a clearing to your liking. The clearings have often been modified with scavenged tables and shelters and are often used by tour groups. The central portion of the beach is prone to surf (which can be anywhere from low to high) and is also open to high westerly winds, which can make for unpleasant camping on exposed beach areas.

Vargas Island Provincial Park: Vargas Island is another of the many provincial parks in Clayoquot Sound created in 1995. It protects 5,788 hectares (14,300 acres) of the western side of the island. The park includes the many islets of the La Croix Group plus Blunden Island and its associated reefs and islets. Cleland Island Ecological Reserve, a significant bird sanctuary, is within the park boundaries. The most popular feature of the park is the sweeping white sand beach of Ahous Bay.

North Vargas Island

Unbroken beach continues north of Ahous Bay until the rock bluffs near Hobbs and Burgess islets. While this entire stretch of beach is impressive white sand, it's also quite exposed, so is rarely visited by campers. Instead, two beaches on the island's north shore are favoured. One is to the west of

Burgess Islet past some private property; a few houses are located here but fortunately aren't visible from the camping area. The second recreational beach is located well along Calmus Passage. For those who prefer shelter, Maurus Channel is a pretty stretch of Vargas Island characterized by reefs and islets. Elbow Bank is a shallow bar set along Maurus Channel. Here the Vargas shoreline is dotted with small coves to explore. Novice paddlers will enjoy this stretch. It's protected, in close proximity to Tofino and will allow a break at the beaches on the island's north end.

Camping: The beach east of Burgess Islet is long and deep with pockets in the driftwood for sheltered camping. The beach farther east is the more sheltered of the two. The only amenity is an outhouse where an illegal cabin was built.

Yarksis
The southeast side of Vargas Island fronting Father Charles Channel is part private property and part reserve land. The reserve was the former principal village of the Keltsomaht, known as Y'aaqhsis. It would be abandoned in favour of a village on western Meares Island. A scattering of homes line the private property along the shorefront. One is the Vargas Island Inn, a pretty and affordable location. Call **250-725-3309**.

BEDWELL SOUND

The waterways north of Vargas and Meares islands begin with Calmus Passage, which runs south of the captivating Catface Range. Once within the cover of the Catface, the water is well protected. Two islands make up Epper Passage Provincial Park. Bedwell Sound, pretty and largely unvisited, extends north well into the tall mountains of Vancouver Island. It's the only way to enter Strathcona Provincial Park by foot from the West Coast. Though it's named Bedwell Sound, the sixth sound on the west coast of Vancouver Island, the waterway is more like an inlet.

Catface Range
The Catface Range isn't so much a range as a mountain of a very distinct shape due to its many highly visible cliffs. It was named Catface in 1861 due to a large mineral deposit that gives it a cat-like appearance. The range has been logged heavily in recent years but is starting to recover.

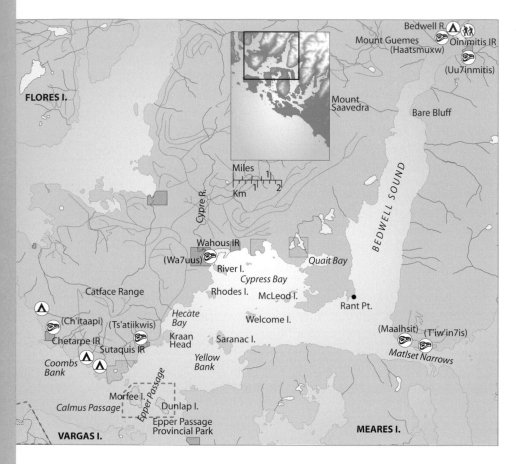

On the west side, at the Chetarpe reserve, was an Ahousaht village used in the spring for dogfish, halibut, cod, seal, sea urchin and herring spawn. The village name, Ch'itaapi, was also the name for the Catface Range. To the south, at Sutaquis reserve, was a major winter village of the Ahousaht and Keltsomaht.

Camping: The Catface Range shoreline is ringed with very pleasant sand beaches that extend far north of Chetarpe reserve and east into Calmus Passage. All locations are wilderness camping. Be sure to avoid camping at the reserves and at the private property immediately north of Morfee Island. Camping on Vargas Island or at Whitesand Cove on Flores Island is generally more popular, but the Catface beaches can be just as pretty and are visited less often. A few pocket beaches are particularly pleasant north of Chetarpe.

A word about wolves: Vargas Island was the site of a particularly vicious wolf attack. It's significant because wolf attacks are generally rare. And as remarkable as the attack was, it's the conditioning of the wolves, not the attack itself, that should be the lesson learned.

The attack took place in June 2000. A group of 18 kayakers arrived to camp at Ahous Bay, and all but two slept in tents. The two men slept outside in their sleeping bags near a campfire. At 1:30 a.m. one of the men awoke to find a wolf sitting on the end of his sleeping bag. He yelled to scare it away, but it didn't move until another camper discharged a noisemaker to scare it. One of the men moved into a tent, but the other stayed outside. He awoke at roughly 2 a.m. to find a wolf pulling on his sleeping bag. It had dragged him several yards before he awoke. The wolf released its grip on the sleeping bag then moved back a step. The man shouted to scare the wolf off, but instead it moved forward and attacked the man on his upper body. The wolf caused serious cuts and lifted part of his scalp. Eventually other campers drove the wolf away. The man had to be transported to Victoria for treatment that included more than 50 stitches to his scalp.

The next morning two young wolves near the campsite were killed by conservation officers—a young male and a young female. Both wolves were found to be healthy, rabies-free and had no evidence of feeding on human food or garbage.

Both wolves, unfortunately, had apparently been well-conditioned to human contact and food. They weren't alone, either. Wolves would continue to pillage campsites on Vargas Island after the attack, stealing shoes, camping gear and clothing from tents. A few days before the attack one visiting kayaker found the wolves even slept near her tent, stole clothing, pulled a water jug from beneath a log and ran circles around her then crouched, as if looking to play. At one time they seemed to approach her threateningly. Eventually her group drove the wolves away by throwing rocks. She had been told the wolves had been hand-fed as pups.

The case is an important reminder that as cute and accessible as wildlife may seem, it's still wild and still dangerous. Attempting to help animals, especially by feeding them, is perilous for both people and the animals. Food should always be properly cached and wild animals should never be fed. While it's nice to see wildlife up close, a healthy distant respect should always be maintained.

Bedwell Sound is an area rarely explored, with trail access deep into the heart of Vancouver Island.

Cypress Bay

Cypress Bay is blessed with numerous nooks and crannies to explore, but fish farms and a large floating resort make it one of the more developed of the wilderness areas. Quait Bay is favoured as an all-weather anchorage. Clayoquot Wilderness Resort is a huge luxury barge permanently moored in the northwest corner of the sheltered cove of Quait Bay. The floating resort has 16 rooms, with an on-shore Healing Grounds Spa and a cedar longhouse/ conference facility. Call **1-888-333-5405** or visit **www.wildretreat.com**. The most appealing area for kayaking is the headland west of Rant Point.

Fish farms are located at Hecate Cove, Saranac Island, Mussel Rock and Rant Point. The David Suzuki Foundation came out swinging against them, citing a disregard for federal legislation in allowing netcage salmon farms in the bay. The Ahousaht First Nation has also lodged many complaints against the fish farms. One of the items in dispute was a briefing note from the government that reads: "Because the Guidelines are believed not to be scientifically based, they tend not to be rigidly adhered to by officers responsible for licensing and tenuring; and the approach to date, in order to avoid triggering CEAA [Canadian Environmental Assessment Agency], has been to site farms in locations where there will not be habitat alteration, disturbance or destruction" ("FO Officials Disregarding Federal Legislation on Acquaculture—Minister Must Act Immediately in Public Interest," News Release, David Suzuki Foundation, 8 Feb. 2000). The David Suzuki Foundation is questioning how the latter can be achieved if the guidelines aren't scientific, and why it would be public policy to approve licenses in a way that avoids triggering an environmental assessment.

Wahous reserve at Cypre River was the main Ahousaht salmon fishing location and winter village. Cypress Bay was once a British West Indies station for repairing and repainting vessels after rounding Cape Horn before sailing to Esquimalt Harbour.

Matlset Narrows

This pretty stretch of waterway is prone to strong tidal currents, which run as high as 4 knots in spring. A village site here, Maalhsit, is believed to have been wiped out by smallpox. It later became a hunting and trapping site.

Bedwell Sound

Bedwell Sound is home to numerous aquaculture operations, but is otherwise undeveloped. It heads deep into the Vancouver Island mountains, with views toward Mariner Mountain, which tops 1,785 m (5,856 feet).

In 1856 the Bedwell River valley was explored by John Buttle, who found gold, prompting a gold rush. By the end of World War Two the area, known as Bear City, had boomed and busted three times. Nine prospects were listed in 1898. Overgrown ruins and abandoned mines can still be seen. The head of the sound was known as Port Hughes. It once boasted its own taxi service, brothel and store. The Port Hughes Hotel was built by Moses McGregor in 1899. Two miles farther upstream on Penny Creek was a copper-iron prospect. It was the focus of much early activity, but no mine at the prospect went into production.

Clayoquot Wilderness Resort, located in Cypress Bay, has a safari-style tent wilderness outpost in the Bedwell River valley. The 10 luxury tents are set on wooden platforms and include sleeping, dining, lounge and massage tents. The outpost sleeps up to 24 guests. Yes, there's even hot and cold running water.

Hiking: Bedwell Sound presents a fantastic opportunity for veteran wilderness hikers. The trail at the head of the inlet is the only direct access to Strathcona Provincial Park from the West Coast. Hikers dropped off by water taxi at Bedwell Sound can hike the Bedwell Valley Trail and travel along adjoining trails to the east side of the island at Courtenay. The Bedwell Sound Trail is considered a "route," not a trail, and could be very overgrown. It's estimated to be a five-day hike. The Central Westcoast Forest Society is attempting to upgrade 26 km (16 miles) of trail.

Camping: Wilderness camping is possible at the trailhead at the head of Bedwell Sound.

Meares Island is now a Tla-o-qui-aht tribal park, created after a logging controversy that served as a precursor for the massive protests that rocked Clayoquot in 1993. It's an impressively tall island, with Mount Colnett topping 700 m (2,300 feet). Lemmens Inlet is often an introduction to novice kayakers taking tours from Tofino. While pleasant, Meares lacks the drama and beaches of many of the other islands in Clayoquot Sound.

The tribal park can be traced back to a decision by the logging company MacMillan Bloedel (now Weyerhaeuser) in the early 1980s to log 90 percent of the island, holding back the remaining 10 percent for 20 years (which would have been about 2003). To make matters worse, Tofino gets its fresh water from Meares Island, and logging and spraying near the watershed were a concern for the town's residents. The Ahousaht First Nation made several declarations to turn Meares Island into a tribal park, the most significant being April 21, 1984. In November of that year MacMillan Bloedel tried to begin logging Meares, but protesters blocked the attempt. In 1985 a B.C. Supreme Court ruling recognized aboriginal rights to the area's resources in an undisturbed state, and urged a negotiation with the province for native rights and title. It's a best-case scenario for the preservation of the island. The Tla-o-qui-aht and Ahousaht First Nations are vowing to preserve the island, with traditional uses only and recreational access for all, plus water protection for Tofino. For water taxi or

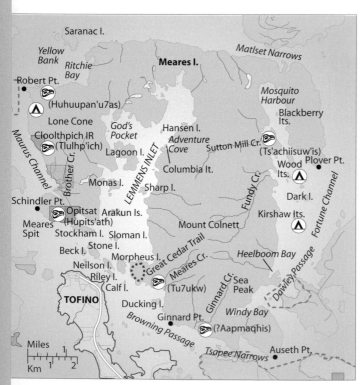

A stream of mist begins to disperse along Maurus Channel on Meares Island.

guided tour information, call the Nuu-chah-nulth Booking and Info
Centre at **1-800-665-9425** or the Tla-o-qui-aht First Nations office at
250-725-3233.

Lemmens Inlet

The inlet is a deep tidal bay with many drying tidal flats and shallow
eelgrass beds, particularly on the southeast side (which is known as
Ducking Mud Flats). Due to tidal flats, the mouth of the inlet is a mile
wide at high tide, but can drop to just a few hundred feet when the
tide is low. The inlet is a significant corridor for boaters, fishing boats
and kayakers. While the shores might look like beach, they're generally rough and intertidal, and not suitable for camping. There are five
tenured shellfish farms in Lemmens Inlet. In 2000 they were allowed
to expand their operations from 22 hectares to 40 hectares (60 to
100 acres).

Fort Defiance was built here by Robert Gray, an American trader
and skipper of the *Columbia*, while he wintered here in 1791–92. He
made the decision to stay rather than return with only a partial load
of furs to Macao, the Portuguese trading post in China. Fort Defiance
was built on the eastern shore of the inlet. The fort's site and its remnants are a provincial historic landmark. They were partially excavated
in the 1960s after its discovery, but a full investigation has never
been done.

That winter Gray also built a small schooner from the cedars of Meares Island and named it *Adventure*. The strip of rocks moved aside for its launch is still visible. The first task of the *Adventure* was a mission of destruction. An attack against Fort Defiance was revealed by a Hawaiian member of Robert Gray's crew. The attack never materialized, but Gray decided nonetheless to destroy Opitsat in retaliation by cannon fire from the *Adventure*, on February 23, 1792. The ship was used for just six months before being sold to Capt. Quadra at Nootka Sound for 70 sea otter skins.

Lemmens Inlet was also notable for its early mining operations. One, known as the Iron Cap prospect at the head of Lemmens Inlet, would produce 19 tons of ore yielding 30 ounces of gold. Another mine on the east side of the inlet would ship 1,500 tons of ore yielding 60,000 pounds of copper, 569 ounces of gold and 3,544 ounces of silver.

Hiking: The Meares Island Big Cedar Trail runs for 3 km (2 miles) in a loop. Access is tucked in behind Morpheus Island at the southeastern entrance to Lemmens Inlet. Features along the trail include the Hanging Garden Tree, an ancient tree believed to be about 2,000 years old. It's ranked as the fourth-largest western redcedar in B.C., with a circumference of 18.3 m (60 feet) and a height of 42.7 m (140 feet). Water taxis are available from Tofino to take hikers on the five-minute crossing. The trail takes about two hours, with some boardwalk that can be slippery.

Opitsat

This thriving Tla-o-qui-aht community is home to about 230 residents, most of whom live alongside a sandy beach facing Tofino. A dock and marina are located in the sheltered bay northwest of Stockham Island.

Opitsat was originally Chief Wickaninnish's principal winter village, occupied from mid-December to the end of March. Opitsat was visited in 1791 by a Boston trader, John Kendrick, who was given a small island nearby in exchange for an American flag and some other objects. He fortified it as "Fort Washington." The Catholic Church built a mission and residential school here in 1899. It was Father A. J. Brabant's proudest accomplishment—the Christie Indian Residential School. It was designed to house 50 children. The building still stands, but it's no longer a school.

Maurus Channel to Matlset Narrows

The shore along Maurus Channel is a pretty stretch with a few pocket beaches but an otherwise rugged shoreline. The same general description applies to the north end of the island through Matlset Narrows. The intertidal area in Maurus Channel is quite rich. At lower tides be sure to look for the many subtidal creatures near Robert Point. Some homes are located on private property facing Maurus Channel.

Camping: The best beach for camping is just south of Robert Point. It's well sheltered, but most of the beach will disappear at high tide. It's a wilderness site with no amenities. Alternatives with larger beaches and nicer views can be found nearby on north Vargas Island and below the Catface Range.

Mosquito Harbour

Yes, this area can live up to its name. In fact, most of the interior sounds and inlets are far more bug-ridden than the exposed ocean sites. However, Mosquito Harbour has many nice beaches and numerous islets and coves perfect for novice paddlers to explore.

Mosquito Harbour was known as Paniitl and was home to two Puneetlaht villages. A sawmill began operation here in 1906. The Sutton Lumber and Trading Company would grow to have up to 400 employees. Its success was aided by a harbour deep enough to accommodate ocean-going vessels.

Camping: There are numerous small beaches along Mosquito Harbour for a rough wilderness camping experience, but a nice spot is on the southernmost Wood Islets. Here you'll find a rough beach with a grassy area suitable for pitching a tent. Another rough campsite is located in the middle of Kirshaw Islets. The beach is rough but sheltered, and flat areas suitable for tents can be found on grassy banks. These spots are a far cry from the beautiful beaches along the outer coast, but they can be a good base for exploring the inner waterways.

Windy Bay

This pretty stretch includes Dawley Passage, a provincial park covered in more detail below. North of Dawley Passage is a small cove, Heelboom Bay, where a sign proclaims Meares Island Tribal Park. A small beach provides access to a rough but well-made cabin originally built as base for the Meares Island logging protest.

Tsapee Narrows

This idyllic stretch is best enjoyed when travelling with the current. Otherwise you're looking at fighting as much as 5 knots. It's a mariner's nightmare with the many rocks and shoals, but a kayaker's paradise. There are numerous nice beaches for breaks along the narrows.

THE INNER WATERWAYS

The inner waters of Clayoquot Sound include a variety of passageways for sheltered exploration, but at the cost of fewer attractions than the outer islands.

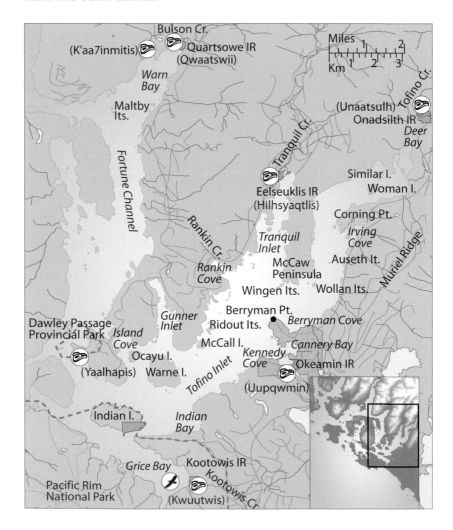

A view through Dawley Passage toward the mountainous backdrop of Fortune Channel.

Warn Bay

This bay is used as a fish farm, with much of the shoreline recently logged. Tidal rips can appear around Maltby Islets due to the current from Matlset Narrows. A village site at the mouth of Bulson Creek was Qwaatswii, a place used for fishing chum, coho, sockeye, spring salmon and steelhead.

Dawley Passage

The passage is a pretty, twisting and narrow channel with Dawley Passage Provincial Park protecting a significant portion. Logging has taken place recently over much of the headland, including the northern portion of the provincial park's upland. Creative Salmon Company Ltd. has a salmon farm operation in Dawley Passage and Fortune Channel. Be aware of currents here, which can run as high as 3 knots. The beach immediately east from Lane Islet was Yaalhapis, a winter village.

Tofino Inlet

This deep inlet runs northwest from its namesake town of Tofino east of Tsapee Narrows. There are several aquaculture operations here, and a fair amount of recreational traffic. Kennedy Cove is backed by extensive private property, though Gunner Inlet and Tranquil Inlet provide sheltered and isolated areas to explore.

Dawley Passage Provincial Park: This marine park was created in 1995 out of the Clayoquot Sound Land Use Decision. It protects 154 hectares (380 acres), and most of that is foreshore. The tidal narrows is a rich marine environment, prompting the park's designation. Much of the upland has been recently clearcut. There are no facilities.

Numerous native villages were located along the inlet. Tidal fish traps were constructed at the narrowest portion of the entrance to lower Kennedy River. Cedar for canoes was collected at the head of Deer Bay, where chum and coho were also fished. At Grice Bay the bullrushes were used for basketry.

Ruins of the Kennedy River Cannery are still visible. It opened in 1892, and would operate for the next 40 years.

Grice Bay

Grice Bay is a tidal mudflat that makes it prime bird habitat.

Launches: Parking here involves paying the national park fee—about $8 per day. Overnight parking is prohibited. A more popular alternative, and more practical for longer trips, is the launch at downtown Tofino.

ESOWISTA PENINSULA AND OUTLYING ISLANDS

Esowista Peninsula is the end of the highway to Clayoquot Sound. The peninsula is dominated by the village of Tofino. Most development is on the sheltered eastern shore, although resorts dot the west side.

Most significant for the ecology here are the Tofino Mudflats, which run along both sides of Browning Passage near Tofino. There

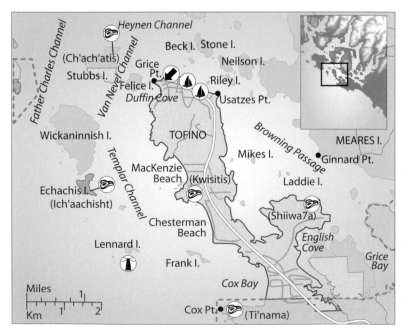

are six mudflats in all: Arakan Flats, Ducking Flats, Doug Bank's Flats, Maltly Slough, South Bay and Grice Bay. The flats encompass 32 square km (12.3 square miles) during low tide. They're covered by eelgrass and algae, with the upper limit lined by salt marshes. They're a critical stopping point for migrating western sandpipers, second only to the Fraser Valley. About 164,000 are estimated to use the mudflats each fall, making it home to 2.5 percent of the global population. Also to be found here are dowitchers, dunlins, least sandpipers, black-bellied plovers, greater yellowlegs, sanderlings, whimbrels and black oystercatchers. Adjacent areas attract wintering waterfowl, such as trumpeter swans, mallards, northern pintails, American wigeons, surf scoters, buffleheads, loons and grebes. It's also a late summer feeding area for great blue herons, with as many as 100 inhabiting the mudflats each August—about 1 percent of the global population. The mudflats can be a problem for kayakers during low tide. It's easy to run aground.

Surrounding the peninsula are a number of islands, many of which are developed, such as Stubbs and Wickaninnish islands. They're generally pleasant places to paddle past on the way to wilderness locations, but their colourful histories are worth noting.

Tofino

This is the cultural, economic and tourist centre of the west coast of Vancouver Island. It was first settled in 1888 by a Mr. Grice; by 1900 Tofino had a school and a post office. Today the population is about 1,500. It has a burgeoning tourist and artistic economy, including an incredible gallery of works by native artist Roy Henry Vickers. Whale-watching tours and Zodiac boat trips to Hot Springs Cove whiz in and out of Tofino. Tofino is a full-service community with banks and grocery stores on First Street. A laundromat is located behind a popular café near Fourth and Campbell Street.

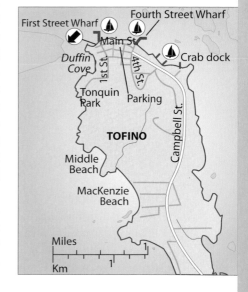

Tofino Sea Kayaking Co. offers rentals, tours, gear sales and accommodation at the Paddler's Inn. The associated Tofino Kayaking School offers all levels of classes.

Call **250-725-4222**. Pacific Kayak offers instruction and equipment. Call **250-725-3232**. Paddle West Kayaking offers guided daytrips. Call **250-726-2868**. Rainforest Kayak Adventures offers instructional courses or guided tours. Call **1-877-422-9453**.

Launches: Tofino is unique for having the only designated municipal kayak launch on Vancouver Island. It's located at the end of First Street next to the government dock. It isn't ideal for launching; the beach is rough and rocky and disappears to the concrete seawall at high tide. Access is down a concrete ramp. For some reason, the ramp has a 1-metre (3-foot) drop to the beach, making carrying kayaks and gear difficult. Parking is limited to loading and unloading only. A parking lot is located off Campbell Street toward Third Street.

Stubbs Island

This is a pretty island with mostly sandy beaches on all sides. A few appear very tempting, especially to the north, but the island advertises itself, through a liberal use of signs, as private property.

Several native villages were located here; the island was popular for digging butter clams in the fall. The Tla-o-qui-aht from Kennedy Lake summered here.

A Danish man, Frederick Thornberg, would open a one-man trading post on Stubbs Island in the 1870s, buying seals, furs and dogfish oil from the natives. This was the first settlement on the west coast of Vancouver Island. In 1889 Walter Danby and Thomas Stockham built a store and hotel here. Ewan McLeod, the first policeman on the coast, built his jail on Stubbs Island.

Place names: The island is named after Capt. Napoleon Fitz Stubbs, who sailed up the coast in 1861 on a naval vessel.

Wickaninnish Island

This is one of the larger of the many islands scattered around Esowista Peninsula. There are a few nice sand beaches, with the nicest on the north side. The island is developed residentially.

Echachis Island

This small island south of Wickaninnish Island has a long history of native occupation and is reserve land. A small bay to the southeast side of Echachis was Ich'aachisht, one of the principal villages of Chief Wickaninnish, the hereditary great chief of the Tla-o-qui-aht

(Clayoquot) tribe in the days of the sea otter trade from 1785 to 1810. His name rivaled Maquinna in Nootka. Whales hunted during the northern migration were sometimes towed to Ich'aachisht to be butchered. If the story is true, an insult by Capt. Jonathan Thorn of the trade ship *Tonquin* against Chief Wickaninnish led to one of the largest bloodbaths on the Vancouver Island coast. Wickaninnish had the *Tonquin* attacked, killing the crew, including those who survived and tried to leave the next day in a longboat. While the ship was being swarmed, the *Tonquin* exploded and sank. One theory is that an injured sailor (named as a Mr. Lewis) ignited the ship's ammunition stores rather than face being captured or killed. Estimates place as many as 50 crew and 200 to 300 Tla-o-qui-aht killed. The source for the information was an interpreter captured by the Tla-o-qui-aht. The *Tonquin* went down somewhere between Lennard Island and Echachis Island, but its exact location is unknown.

Lennard Island

The lighthouse here was built in 1904—a white, wooden, 25-m (82-foot) octagonal building with sloping sides and a red metal circular lantern. It has since been replaced by a cylindrical tower. Other wooden buildings include a residence.

Cox Bay

The west side of Esowista Peninsula is home to numerous resorts. The rocky headland north of Chesterman Beach, for instance, is dominated by the world-famous Wickaninnish Inn. Inside Cox Bay is Frank Island, which is connected to Vancouver Island by a sand tombolo at low tide. Chesterman Beach is an important roosting area for western sandpipers. The autumn population reaches 35,000, one of the highest numbers on the west coast of Canada.

Near Cox Point was Ti'nama, the traditional home of a local group of the Tla-o-qui-aht. At a small bay just to the east of today's Wickaninnish Inn was the main village of the K'inaxamis?ath, the 'Long Beach People.' The village's name, Kwisitis, means 'other end of the beach.' It was used for whale, sea lion and seal hunting as well as halibut fishing. The K'inaxamis?ath were master canoe builders, but were decimated by the combined forces of the Opitsat and Ahousaht.

There are three distinct portions of Pacific Rim National Park—the Long Beach unit, the Broken Islands Group and the West Coast Trail south of Bamfield. (See chapters 10 and 11 for the Broken Group and West Coast Trail.) The Long Beach unit is a popular gateway to the coast, with a reservation campground, trails and many popular sand and surf beaches. This portion of the park attracts almost a half-million visitors a year thanks in large part to the paved highway access.

Kayaking this stretch means travelling through unprotected open ocean for a considerable distance with no all-weather shelters. The distance from the south beaches on Vargas Island (the closest campsite in Clayoquot Sound) to Florencia Islet is 30 km (18.6 miles). Add another 15 km (9 miles) to make the entrance of Ucluth Inlet and the next all-weather shelter at Francis Island. This coast is recommended for veteran paddlers only, but it's a necessary, achievable and ultimately intriguing paddle for anyone making their way down the Vancouver Island coast.

Radar Hill

This 126-m (413-foot) cone provides views north over Clayoquot Sound and south to the many beautiful sand beaches. Radar Hill is

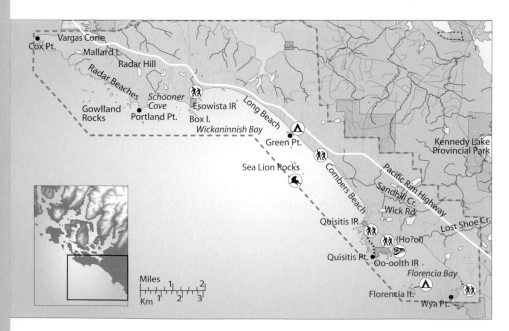

open to vehicle access during the day for sweeping views with minimal effort. A 10-minute trail leads from the parking lot to the summit. Radar Beaches are set between rocky headlands and are generally very exposed.

Schooner Cove

This cove is a beautiful white sand beach located between the rocky headland of Portland Point and Box Island. It tends to be far less visited than most of the other beaches due to less convenient access. Camping used to be allowed here, but it's now prohibited.

Hiking: The Schooner Cove Trail parking lot north of Long Beach is the start for a 1-km (.6-mile) trail to the north end of Long Beach. From there hikers can cross at low tide to Schooner Cove or take a rough trail behind the headland.

Long Beach

Long Beach has the distinction of being the longest beach on Vancouver Island. It stretches from Box Island to Quisitis Point and covers all of Wickaninnish Bay. Though the area southeast of Green Point is usually referred to as Combers Beach, it's one and the same. Surfing and beachcombing are the most popular activities. Parking is available at a number of locations off the highway. Midway along its length is Green Point, the park's main campground.

Long Beach is a popular surf and recreation beach, aided by paved road access.

The surf tends to be very high on Long Beach, making landing by kayak extremely hazardous. You'll get dumped. Sea Lion Rocks are the aptly named reefs located in Wickaninnish Bay south of Green Point. The rocks are used as a year-round haulout, and attract hundreds of sea lions annually.

Green Point was Chaw'in?is, meaning 'rock in centre,' and was the boundary between the Tla-o-qui-aht and Ucluelet. Sea Lion Rocks were often fought over due to the high number of seals and sea lions.

Wickaninnish Interpretive Centre is located in a former inn on the shoreline at the end of Wick Road, off the Pacific Rim Highway. The centre includes interpretive displays, a gift shop, a restaurant, films and other occasional events including guided tours. An all-terrain wheelchair is available for use. It's open mid-March to mid-October. Call **250-726-7333**.

Camping: The Green Point Campground is accessible by road via the Pacific Rim Highway, and has 94 drive-in sites for tents, trailers and RVs. An additional 20 walk-in sites are located in a forested area, while 33 more walk-in sites are located on the beach. Amenities include water, garbage collection, washrooms, food caches and an interpretive centre with hosted programs throughout the summer season.

Hiking: As well as strolling the beaches, Long Beach has a number of trails, including the South Beach Trail that starts at Wickaninnish Centre. The trail leads to several secluded beaches south of the centre through a forest trail, including Lismer Beach (named after Group of Seven artist Arthur Lismer who spent his summers here from 1951 to his death in 1969). A highlight is a double sea arch and surge channels. Another popular hike is the Spruce Fringe Trail, south of the Combers Beach day-use area, and the Rain Forest Trail, a 1.2-km (.75 mile) trail located on the north side of the highway. It leads through a variety of forest types.

Florencia Bay

Florencia Bay, known locally as Wreck Bay, is set back between two headlands: Quisitis Point and Wya Point. The long, curving beach is another in the series of white sand beaches located in Pacific Rim National Park. Steep sand bluffs line the shore.

Two Ucluelet villages were located in Florencia Bay. Wya reserve was a fishing station and defensive site. Its name, Wa:ya, means 'rock bluff.' A family lived here to oversee T'ok'wa:?ath drift rights. The mouth of Lost Shoe Creek was the home of the Ho?ol?ath, which means 'flock place people' or 'cormorant nesting place.' It was known as a good fishing location, as the waters around Florencia Islet used to teem with halibut.

Hiking: The north side of Florencia Bay is accessible by a trail from the parking lot near the Wickaninnish Centre. This trail is on an old route between Tofino and Ucluelet, and some of the original corduroy road is still visible. Access to the south of Florencia Bay is possible from the Willowbrae and Half-Moon Bay Trail. To get there, turn off the highway to Ucluelet onto Willowbrae Road and follow it to the parking lot. More portions of the corduroy road are visible here.

Place names: Florencia Bay is named after a Peruvian brigantine that wrecked near here on December 31, 1860. It was travelling from Washington to Callao, Peru, when it ran into a storm at Cape Flattery, Washington. Thrown onto her beams she was able to right herself, but lost all her masts and drifted into Nootka Sound, where she anchored and was pumped out. The gunboat *Forward* attempted to tow her to Victoria, but a problem with the *Forward* required setting the *Florencia* adrift, and the ship was wrecked at what was first known as Wreck Bay. It was renamed by Capt. Richards during his 1861 survey.

Florencia Islet

Set in among a series of rocks and reefs, Florencia Islet is a tiny refuge along the otherwise open stretch of water between Tofino and Ucluelet. The islet had the misfortune of being used for aerial bomb target practice during World War Two by the air force. Several undetonated bombs were discovered here in the 1970s. They were safely defused.

Camping: Florencia Islet offers relatively sheltered camping. Two small crushed-shell beaches are located on the northeast side facing Florencia Bay. Note that at lower tides the beach becomes landlocked by rocks. Caution is necessary when landing or launching here. A nearby alternative is Francis Island, just off the south end of Ucluth Peninsula in Barkley Sound.

A rock pillar lies in the sheltered inner harbour of Benson Island in the Broken Group.

Barkley Sound

BARKLEY SOUND ISN'T THE LARGEST OF THE FIVE MAJOR SOUNDS ON Vancouver Island's west coast, but it's the most open. At 32 km wide (20 miles) and 22 km deep (14 miles), it's sprinkled liberally with distinct archipelagos separated by wide channels. On the leeward side of these islands, conditions can be remarkably calm. Serene passages are rich in intertidal life; protected bays, lagoons and long inlets meander deep into the tallest peaks of Vancouver Island. On exposed shorelines the constant battering of waves has created sea caves, arches and surge channels.

There are two distinct sides to Barkley Sound—the Broken Group and the Deer Group—separated by Imperial Eagle Channel. The Broken Group is a maze of more than 100 islands, islets and rocks scattered over a wide area with a reputation as one of the world's most desirable kayaking locations. The Deer Group is also becoming a top tourist destination; visitors are drawn to its rugged shores, with numerous sea caves and a scattering of inviting beaches. Only two communities are located alongside Barkley Sound: Ucluelet to the west and Bamfield to the east. Port Alberni is at the head of Alberni Inlet, deep in central Vancouver Island.

Place names: Barkley Sound was first discovered by Capt. Charles William Barkley of the trading ship *Imperial Eagle*, and named after himself. The ship left the Thames in 1786, arriving in Nootka in June, 1787. Travelling with Capt. Barkley was his young wife, 17-year-old Frances Hornby Barkley, the first European woman to see the northwest coast of America.

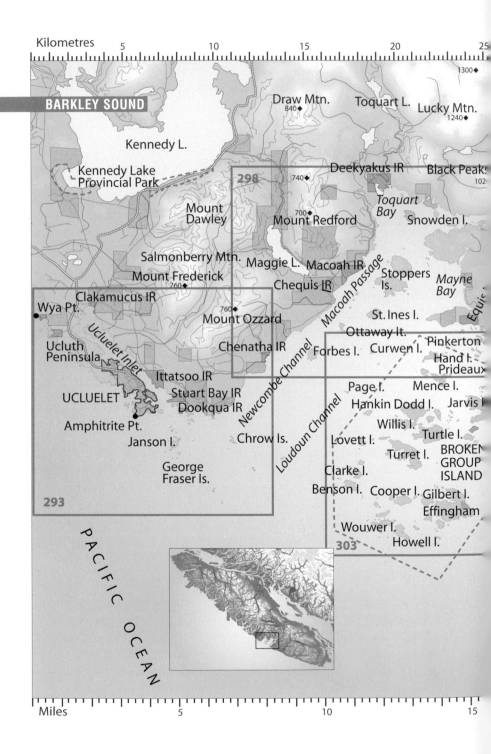

Kilometres

Draw Mtn.
840◆

Toquart L.

Lucky Mtn.
1240◆

1300◆

Kennedy L.

Kennedy Lake
Provincial Park

298

Deekyakus IR

Black Peak

740◆

102

Mount
Dawley

700◆
Mount Redford

Toquart
Bay

Snowden I.

Salmonberry Mtn.

Maggie L.

Macoah IR

Stoppers
Is.

Mayne
Bay

Mount Frederick
760◆

Chequis IR

Clakamucus IR

Wya Pt.

Mount Ozzard
760◆

St. Ines I.

Ottaway It.

Equi

Ucluth
Peninsula

Chenatha IR

Forbes I.

Curwen I.

Pinkerton

Hand I.
Prideaux

Ittatsoo IR

Page I.

Mence I.

UCLUELET

Stuart Bay IR
Dookqua IR

Hankin Dodd I.

Jarvis I

Amphitrite Pt.

Chrow Is.

Willis I.

Turtle I.

Janson I.

Lovett I.

Turret I.

BROKEN
GROUP
ISLAND

George
Fraser Is.

Clarke I.

293

Benson I.

Cooper I.

Gilbert I.

Effingham

Wouwer I.

303

Howell I.

PACIFIC OCEAN

Miles

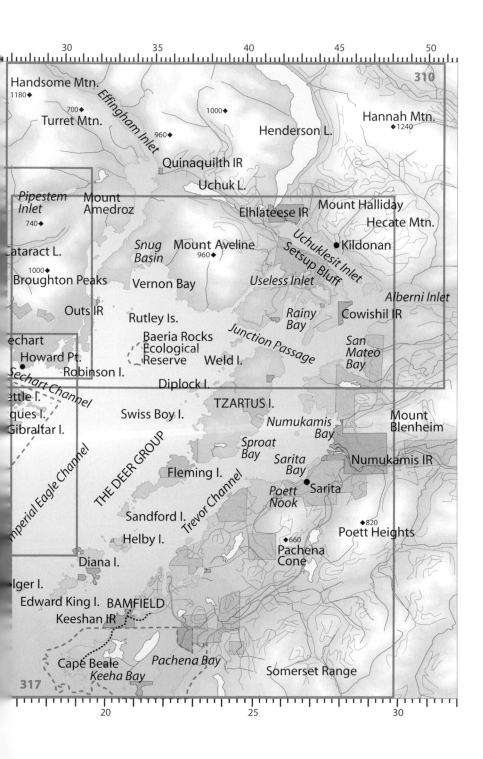

30 35 40 45 50

Handsome Mtn.
1180◆

Turret Mtn.
700◆

Effingham Inlet

960◆

1000◆

Henderson L.

Hannah Mtn.
◆1240

Quinaquilth IR

Uchuk L.

Pipestem Inlet
740◆

Mount Amedroz

Elhlateese IR

Mount Halliday

Hecate Mtn.

Uchuklesit Inlet

●Kildonan

Cataract L.
1000◆

Broughton Peaks

Snug Basin

Mount Aveline
960◆

Setsup Bluff

Useless Inlet

Vernon Bay

Alberni Inlet

Outs IR

Rutley Is.

Rainy Bay

Cowishil IR

echart

Howard Pt.●

Robinson I.

Sechart Channel

Baeria Rocks Ecological Reserve

Junction Passage

Weld I.

San Mateo Bay

Diplock I.

ettle I.

ques I.

Gibraltar I.

Swiss Boy I.

TZARTUS I.

Numukamis Bay

Mount Blenheim

Imperial Eagle Channel

THE DEER GROUP

Fleming I.

Sproat Bay

Sarita Bay

Numukamis IR

Sandford I.

Trevor Channel

Poett Nook

Sarita●
Sarita

Helby I.

◆660
Pachena Cone

◆820
Poett Heights

Diana I.

Iger I.

Edward King I.

BAMFIELD

Keeshan IR

Cape Beale

Pachena Bay

Keeha Bay

Somerset Range

GETTING HERE

Barkley Sound has three major access points: Ucluelet, Toquart Bay and Bamfield. Ucluelet has the advantage of being the only route of the three with an entirely paved road. To get there, follow the Island Highway north of Parksville and turn west onto Highway 4. It will end at a junction to Tofino and Ucluelet (the Pacific Rim Highway). Turn south to Ucluelet. Unfortunately, a launch from Ucluelet means a large open water crossing to get to the Broken Island Group (it's 12 km/7.5 miles from Francis Island to Clark Island). A more popular entry point is Toquart Bay. On Highway 4 about 12 km (7.5 miles) before the Ucluelet-Tofino intersection there will be a very poorly marked logging road leading south. You'll know you're close when you're parallel to Kennedy Lake. There are three progressively better views of Kennedy Lake as the road descends downhill. The third view is the best and follows the lake's shoreline for several miles. This is your cue to watch for the turnoff. It's about 12 km (7.5 miles) from the first stretch of road alongside Kennedy Lake. The launch is located about 16 km (10 miles) down the logging road.

The other option—by far the most convenient for the Deer Group—is Bamfield. Unfortunately, the logging road from the outskirts of Port Alberni to Bamfield is quite active. From Highway 4 at the east entrance to Port Alberni, take the circuitous route through the town following the signs for Bamfield. You'll reach a logging road. Once on the dirt road there will be a major junction. Keep to the right. Bamfield Road is wide and well-groomed, but the traffic—and the dust—can make it a gruelling 80 km (50 miles). This portion of the trip might take just a little over an hour, but you could age a year or two.

Another route to Bamfield, ideal for people coming from Victoria, is via Lake Cowichan. Take the Island Highway north from Victoria and turn off on the Lake Cowichan road. Continue west on the Nitinat Main and the South Main until it leads to Bamfield Road. The route is well marked. The Poett Nook launch is also located along Bamfield Road.

A good way to avoid all this is the *Lady Rose*, a commercial vessel that takes passengers, complete with kayaks, to the edge of the Broken Group. For many, the trip on the *Lady Rose* is as enjoyable as the kayaking.

Clarke Island in the Broken Group.

EXPLORING BY KAYAK

The largest draw in Barkley Sound is the Broken Group, ideal for its sheltered waters and breathtaking beauty. Second place belongs to the Deer Group. Add to this menu interesting side trips, such as Pipestem and Useless inlets, and you have a great range of options.

Recommended short trips

- *If you have a day:* Day trips are limited by the launch sites. Options include explorations of Ucluelet Inlet and George Fraser Islands from Ucluelet; Pipestem Inlet or Stopper Islands from Toquart Bay; Numukamis Bay from Poett Nook; or the waters near Bamfield. All these trips are markedly different and none will bedisappointing. Recommended is a launch from Poett Nook and an exploration of the sea caves on the far side of Tzartus Island through Robbers Passage.

- *If you have a weekend:* For an overnight trip, consider Ross Islets in the Deer Group, launching from Bamfield. It's a pleasant crossing across Trevor Channel and the islets are magical.

- *If you have three days:* Consider a short visit to the Broken Group, spending the middle day exploring. Or travel to Ross Islets, Diana Island or even Stud Islets in the Deer Group. Camp for two nights and take the middle day to enjoy the attractions.

A sea arch on Effingham Island is one of the larger in the group.

- *If you have five days:* Go to the Broken Group and relax. Camp at a central place and explore all the islands or jump from camp to camp.

- *If you have a week:* With this much time you could explore both the Broken Group and the Deer Group. A week could be spent exploring the Broken Group, but the Deer Group is fundamentally different, and you'll have a wider appreciation of Barkley Sound.

- *The ideal trip:* Take the MV *Lady Rose* from Port Alberni, jumping ship at Sechart near the Pinkerton Islands. Explore the Pinkerton Islands and stop the first night at Gibraltar Island. Then head to Alma Russell Islands, with an overnight rest at the beautiful beach at Vernon Bay. Next day scoot into Useless Inlet with an exit via Rainy Bay to overnight at Stud Islets (to shorten the trip omit the break at Vernon Bay). The next day explore the caves of Tzartus and Robbers Passage, making your way to Diana Island. Maybe take an extra day to explore Edward King Island and Folger Island. The next day cross Imperial Eagle Channel to overnight at Turret, Benson or Clark islands. Use the camp as a base to explore the Broken Group to your heart's content (or as your time allows). Return to Sechart to meet up with the MV *Lady Rose* and a relaxing trip back to Port Alberni. This trip would probably take 10 days to do well and would be an unforgettable experience, taking in most of the main attractions of Barkley Sound. The *Lady Rose* is simply an interesting luxury; to avoid the cost or trouble, launch from Toquart Bay.

THE BASICS

Geology and ecology

Set on the exposed southwest coast of Vancouver Island, Barkley Sound is characterized by low-lying rocky headlands interspersed with occasional beaches. The forests are largely Sitka spruce, western hemlock and western redcedar. Sea lions bask on the rocks on the outer and most exposed areas. Whales are also frequent visitors; Barkley Sound is on the annual migration route of the gray whale in spring and fall. Some gray whales can be seen year-round on the outer coast or in Imperial Eagle Channel. Six-gill sharks are found at Renate Reef, a popular diving location amid Imperial Eagle Channel north of Fleming Island.

Birds, however, are what make Barkley Sound stand out. Six species that breed here are considered globally important, and two are of national significance. A 1982 survey found 3,400 marbled murrelets, in the sound, which is 1 percent of the North American population (see page 263). A later count showed that number had decreased by 41 percent. The marbled murrelets will spend summers in both inshore and outer channels, particularly in the Broken Group and Trevor Channel.

In the spring, numerous bird species congregate here, including as many as 52,000 surf scoters. Mew gulls and western grebes are also prominent. About 4 percent of the global population of western grebes can be found here in the spring. Surfbirds, surf scoters, gulls and grebes gather to feed on the herring spawn. Barkley Sound is also the major breeding site for Canadian Brandt's cormorants, another species in decline. In late summer as many as 1,200 birds stage here, or about 1 percent of the global population. Black oystercatchers nest on 13 islets; these 42 pairs account for 4 percent of the Canadian population. The Barkley Sound population of glaucous-winged gulls, at 728 pairs, is about 3 percent of the Canadian population.

Weather

Regional weather is compiled at Bamfield, and reflects a rainy, mild climate—an average of about 2,870 mm (darn close to 10 feet) of rain per year and a balmy average temperature of 9.4°C (49°F), with average temperatures of over 14°C (57°C) in both July and August. Highs rarely exceed 18°C (64°F). July and August also have the year's least rain—just 61 and 75 mm respectively (2.4 and 3 inches).

The Broken Group, like many other areas of the West Coast, is prone to morning fog during summer, particularly in August. It can roll in at dawn and not dissipate until the winds begin to rise later in the morning. This can hamper navigation, especially in the maze of islands.

Native overview

The natives of Barkley Sound are part of the Nuu-chah-nulth linguistic and cultural group, and were once among the most prominent tribes on the west coast. When Jose Maria Narvaez first visited Barkley Sound in 1791, he noted five major villages and believed they contained more residents than Nootka and Clayoquot. Another visitor a century later, ethnologist George Blenkinsop, would write, "The numerous old village sites, some of them several hundred yards in length, now overgrown in some instances with gigantic maple trees of a noble appearance, prove incontestably that the population of Barkley Sound must have been at no very remote period ten times its present number. War in former years and disease… in later years have wrought this change."

Five native bands have traditional territory within Barkley Sound: the Tseshaht, Toquaht, Ucluelet, Huu-ay-aht and Uchucklesaht. The Tseshaht would absorb two other significant tribes: the Hiko:l?ath in the 1800s and the Hach'a:?ath in the 1700s.

War characterized the history of Barkley Sound First Nations during the 1800s. The Ucluelet captured Hi:kwis, the winter village of the Tseshaht in the early 1800s. A so-called Long War followed in the mid-19th century.

THE SHORELINES

UCLUTH PENINSULA

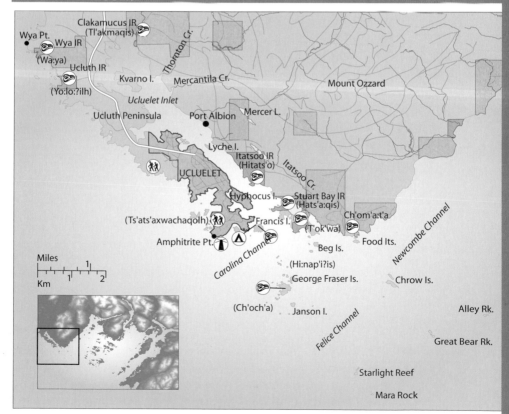

Ucluelet tends to be overlooked by many kayakers entering Barkley Sound, most of whom launch from Toquart Bay. While Ucluelet Inlet can be sheltered, the outer waters are exposed to Pacific swell. For those who brave the elements, the rewards are numerous islands and islets and some very rugged shore.

Outer Ucluth Peninsula

Many small coves and islets among rocky headlands characterize this shoreline. Most coves are inaccessible due to the open conditions. Past Amphitrite Point the entrance to Carolina Channel is strewn with rocks, so careful navigation is required. In swell, kayakers might want to follow the navigation buoys meant for larger boats. A trail skirts this portion of the coast. Off Ucluth Peninsula is a key abalone area.

South of Wya Point, at Ucluth reserve, was a major Ucluelet village. The name Yo:lo:?ilh was derived from a word meaning 'landing place for canoe.' As the only possible landing spot in a storm on the out-side coast between Tofino and Ucluelet, it was a choice location. Northwest of Amphitrite Point is a cove that contains a group of small islands. The westernmost, outer islet was known as 'harpooning place.' Gray whales would come so close that whalers were able to stand on shore and harpoon them. The Ucluelet would only use their canoes to retrieve the whales.

The Amphitrite Point Lighthouse guards the northern entrance to Barkley Sound. It began operating on March 23, 1915, after troubles with a Wigham lamp maintained by the Ucluelet lifeboat operator. A tidal wave washed it away on January 2, 1914, prompting the construction of a proper tower. In 1919 the keeper was James Frazer. For $10 per month he hiked one mile to light the wick, again at midnight to wind the machinery and trim the wick, and again at sunrise to put the light out—no matter the weather.

One of Canada's species at risk is a little-known lichen by the name of seaside centipede. It's only found in undisturbed forests and in only two places on the west coast of Vancouver Island: Ucluth Peninsula, north of Ucluelet, and Schooner Cove, northwest of Long Beach. A lichen is a plant made up of both a fungus and an alga.

Hiking: The Wild Pacific Trail is being built in phases. The first phase covers 2.7 km (1.7 miles) of the outer end of Ucluth Peninsula in a large loop that can be walked in about 30 to 40 minutes. It visits Amphitrite Point Lighthouse, skirts the rugged coast and uses part of the He-Tin-Kis Park boardwalk. Access points are off Peninsula Road at either He-Tin-Kis Park or at a rough parking lot at Coast Guard Road. The eventual goal is a route to Halfmoon Bay along 14 km (9 miles) of the outer coast. Other stretches are also complete; see the map of Ucluelet below for a better look.

A trail in He-Tin-Kis Park leads to Terrace Beach, a sheltered recreational beach. The cove is protected by a multitude of reefs and islets near the entrance. Though the beach in the park is nicely sheltered, the reefs make it difficult to reach by water without local knowledge.

Place names: Amphitrite Point is named for the 24-gun, 1,064-ton frigate that served here from 1851 to 1857. Amphitrite is the Greek Goddess of the Seas and the wife of Poseidon.

Ucluelet Inlet

This long, narrow inlet is a marine route for the village of Ucluelet, Port Albion and a residential Indian Reserve. Pretty areas are Stuart Bay and the outer stretch toward Beg Islands. Ucluelet's harbour is a significant squid area, the only one in Barkley Sound.

Numerous native villages once lined the inlet, with names like 'lodgepole pine,' 'inside the inlet,' 'wide beach,' 'having beaches on both sides'

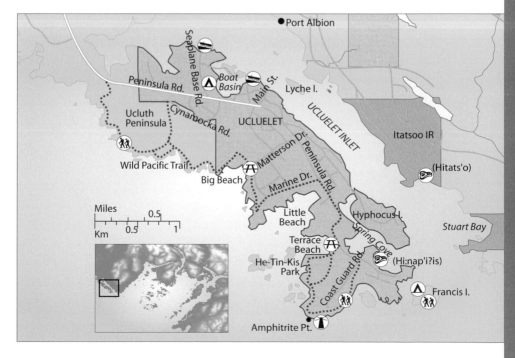

and 'people living on the beach where there are rocks sticking out of the sand.' T'ok'wa, the main Toquaht summer village, was set on the small bay at the eastern entrance to Ucluelet Inlet. The name means 'narrow beach.' The village was used for sea mammal hunting. The residents moved to Toquart in late summer for the coho and spring salmon.

Port Albion is the location of an abandoned pilchard processing plant that became a herring processing plant when the pilchard disappeared in the 1930s. The deserted buildings are still visible. A telegraph station and clam cannery were also located here.

Ucluelet

Ucluelet is a full-service community located on the south end of Ucluth Peninsula. Most of the development faces Ucluelet Harbour. Over the past decades it has missed out on much of the tourism and cultural development that has boosted Tofino, but it has developed its own charm, with cottage artisans, bed and breakfasts, resorts and marinas facing the pretty shoreline. Most of the commercial retail sector is located along Peninsula Road (the extension of the Pacific Rim Highway through town) near Main Street. The information centre is at the base of Main Street by the government wharf. A selection of coffee shops, restaurants and stores are located nearby.

Launches: There are two boat launches right within Ucluelet. One is at the end of Seaplane Base Road. Follow the private property signs. The other is at the end of Bay Street.

The Wild Pacific Trail is one of the easiest ways to get to see the rugged outer shore of Vancouver Island.

Camping: Ucluelet Campground is a combination of 85 waterfront or forested sites with hookups or tent sites. Amenities include washrooms, showers and boat trailer storage. It's located along Seaplane Base Road up from the launch site. Call **250-726-4355**.

Francis Island

This small island is located in the western mouth of Ucluelet Inlet. The north side connects with Ucluth Peninsula at lower tides via a sand and crushed-shell tombolo. The island is Crown land, and very pretty. A choice of trails criss-cross the island and can be reached from the beach at the tombolo. One ends at a pretty cove on the outer side of the island, but many others are dead ends.

Camping: The tombolo on the north end of the island may disappear at higher tides, but a beach on the island doesn't. Camping is possible near the point facing the tombolo. The beach tends to become rock-strewn at lower tides. Keep to the Fraser Island side of the tombolo; the Vancouver Island side is private property.

George Fraser Islands

Numerous small islands lie in the waters outside Ucluelet Inlet, creating a hazard for mariners but a host of exploration opportunities for kayakers. The George Fraser Islands are a natural jump for a trip from Ucluelet to the Broken Group. Between George Fraser Islands and Chrow Island to the east is an important sea urchin area.

Port Albion and Ittatsoo reserve hug the shore of Ucluelet Inlet in this view from Francis Island.

Ch'och'a was the native name for the George Fraser Islands. A summer whaling village was located here. It was also used for salmon and halibut fishing on the nearby banks. It's said that one great whaler, Wi:hswisan'ap, tried to fill up the channel between the two islands with the bones of his whales.

Place names: The islands are named after an early Scots settler who grew azaleas, rhododendrons and heather, much to the surprise of visitors not expecting to see such exotic and colourful plants in this remote area.

THE NORTHWEST SHORE

The shore along Newcombe Channel and Macoah Passage is fronted by numerous beaches and uninhabited islands. Toquart Bay is the main entry point to the Broken Islands for many boaters and kayakers, while Pipestem Inlet meanders deep into Vancouver Island.

Salmon Beach

There are various sandy beaches along the northwest shore of Barkley Sound; most are undeveloped except for the stretch facing Forbes Island. Here a reserve houses a variety of campsites and trailers, while its neighbour, Salmon Beach, is a recent urban-style development of

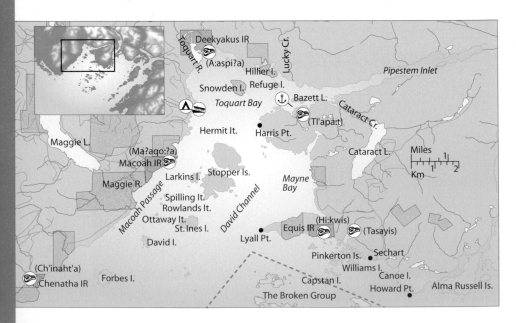

homes facing the waterfront. Forbes Island has a rocky foreshore and is difficult to access.

A number of village sites were located along the coast of Newcombe Channel. Nearby is a cave, A:a:aytl'a, where wolves, both natural and supernatural, were said to appear. The other end of the cave was at the top of Mount Ozzard. At Chenatha reserve there was a village used for fishing chum, coho and sockeye salmon.

Stopper Islands

These islands are the largest of a multitude on the outside of Toquart Bay. The southernmost island has several pretty coves with moderately rough beaches that can make for a pleasant break. A large aquaculture operation is located on the northernmost side. The Maggie River shore west of Stopper Islands is one of only two notable geoduck areas in Barkley Sound. The other is at Mills Peninsula. Macoah Passage is also an important crab area, probably the largest in Barkley Sound.

On the Macoah reserve was the residence of the head chief of the Toquaht, and this was their winter village. The village name means 'house on the point.' A stockade was built around the village during the wars in Barkley Sound during the early 19th century. A village at Maggie River was named Kohats'o, a reference to a type of trap built here. It featured wide planks and walls of stone. The trap had a door that tripped when contacted, preventing the escape of seals and sea otters. Keep your eyes open for remnants of these traps if you visit here.

A gray whale flukes while passing Dixon Island in the Broken Group.

Toquart Bay

Toquart Bay is the recreational hub for the area, due to a large and popular forest service campground and a busy boat launch. This is a calm and protected entry point to Barkley Sound. It's about a 10-km (6-mile) paddle to the nearest Broken Group campsite at Hand Island.

Most traditional native activity in Toquart Bay was centred around the Toquart River, the main fall salmon fishery of the Toquaht. The name comes from *t'I:kwa*, which means 'dig for plant roots.' Other villages were located around the bay with names like 'wide area between eyebrows.' Upstream from the mouth of the Toquart River was a major Toquaht fishing encampment. The village used fish traps that worked with the rising and falling tides. Upriver two miles from Toquart Lake is a set of falls where basket traps were used to catch salmon. It was known as Hayots'aqapi, meaning 'ten peaks,' a name that also referred to the mountain visible in the background.

A trading post was built at Toquart Bay in 1860. A cannery was also built here, but was abandoned in 1940. A mine and wharf sent thousands of tons of crushed iron concentrate to Japan. The ruins of a cone-shaped shed and a conveyor system can still be seen.

Caution: Toquart Bay contains the ore magnetite. This creates magnetic anomalies that prevent compasses from reading accurately. This can be a problem in fog. Fortunately the effect is fairly localized.

Camping: Toquart Bay is a large, maintained, forest service campsite facility. It's supervised, and a fee for camping and parking applies.

Launches: There's a boat ramp, but kayakers will probably prefer to park temporarily at the day use picnic area and head over the low concrete seawall to the sandy beach.

Pipestem Inlet

This pretty inlet disappears between the steep mountain slopes of Broughton Peaks to the south and Black Peaks to the north. The peaks, over 1000 m (3,280 feet) in height, are even more impressive because the inlet is so narrow. A wonderful waterfall flows into the north side of the inlet at Lucky Creek. A trail leads up the west side of the waterfall. Pipestem Inlet is remarkable for its warm water. It has about the warmest recorded surface temperature (above 21°C/70°F) on the west coast of Vancouver Island—one of the few areas in B.C. warm enough to allow a natural oyster spawn. Pipestem Inlet is used by growers to collect oyster seed (spat).

Local First Nations found the inlet south of Baett Island attractive for two reasons: the chum salmon in the creek and the wild cherry bark. A Toquart village was located here.

Mayne Bay
This bay is filled with interesting nooks and crannies; a lagoon on the northeast corner is a popular protected anchorage. The Canadian Navy has used Mayne Bay on occasion for exercise. A large orange mooring buoy in the bay belongs to them.

Pinkerton Islands
Not part of the Broken Group, the Pinkerton Islands lie to the north of Sechart Channel. The group is an archipelago in its own right with shallow, narrow, river-like waterways. It makes for very secluded paddling, with a few cottages that can be avoided by staying to the inner channels. The bay southeast of the islands is Sechart, a developed area.

Now uninhabited, Equis reserve was the Tseshaht's main winter village at the start of the 1800s. It was used for the Wolf Ritual—a Nuu-cha-nulth initiation for young men performed over a period of days. As the Tseshaht expanded their territory, Equis dropped in status and was used only as a seasonal camp for herring, shellfish, seals, salmon and dogfish. A defensive stockade in a bay behind the Pinkerton Islands was used during the Long War to ward off raids.

Near Equis was a small cove called To:xpo:lit, meaning 'bullhead on rocks.' Here the Toquaht and a neighbouring tribe, the Hach'a:?ath, would hold a jumping contest to

Pinkerton Islands aren't normally a destination but make for interesting sheltered paddling.

determine their boundaries. The winner gained rights to the cove, but it wasn't a foolproof system—a dispute with the contest eventually led to war.

The Sechart Whaling Station, the only whaling operation in Barkley Sound, opened at Sechart in 1905. A mining site operated there starting in 1892 with claims for iron ore, marble and mercury. A pilchard reduction plant was the industry here in the 1930s. Remnants of these operations can still be found. A midden indicates the site was an ancient village. The area was also a cause for superstition. Canoe Island, near Sechart, was said to be inhabited by the spirits of the newly deceased, and anyone seeing the spirits would die.

Sechart is a stop-off point for the MV *Lady Rose*. The ship's captain created Sechart Lodge at the Sechart Whaling Station site. He used MacMillan Bloedel's old office building, transporting it from Port Alberni 56 km (35 miles) away. The lodge has bedrooms, washrooms, shower rooms, a dining room and a sunroom. For information call **1-800-663-7192** in season or **250-723-8313**.

Place names: James H. Pinkerton was a homesteader who resided here beginning in 1891.

THE BROKEN GROUP

The Broken Group is one of three sections that make up Pacific Rim National Park (the others are the Long Beach unit, page 280, and the West Coast Trail, page 342). The dozens of islands and reefs in the Broken Group have become world-class kayaking destinations. Despite the popularity, their charm remains intact. First-time kayakers can explore the sheltered waters amid a maze of islands; veteran kayakers can venture to the rugged outer islands with their sea caves and array of wildlife. In all, more than 100 islands and islets are located within the park's boundary, with eight campgrounds. The area attracts an incredible 230 species of birds. A special treat is the abundance of chanterelle mushrooms in the fall.

Hand Island

This pretty island is the closest campsite for people kayaking out of Toquart Bay. Most of the shoreline is rough rock except for the lagoon and beach on the north side of the island. A short trail leads from the central beach to a composting toilet and the northeast point of the island.

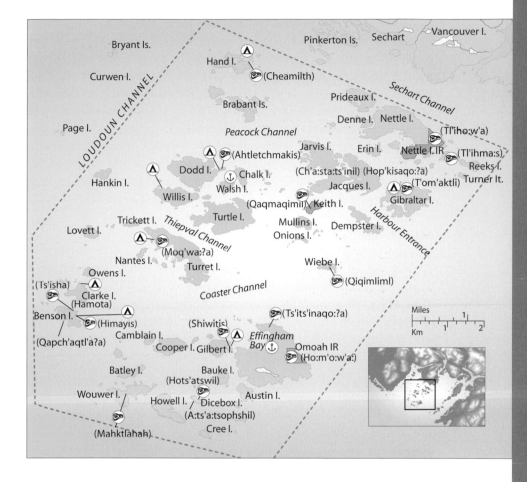

A long midden on the small island off the northeast corner of Hand Island is from a former village site. A circular ring of rocks in the bay is a native fish trap (another is at Jacques Island; see page 305). A homestead for a family of early settlers and a small summer trading post were located here in the late 1800s. A rusting donkey engine is located along a rough trail leading through the centre of the island.

Camping: There are a few cleared tent sites, but most of the camping will be on the beach facing north. A nice site on the northwest point is above an inviting beach that becomes a rocky jumble at lower tides.

Brabant Islands
A rock shoreline makes landing on these islands impractical.

Place names: Brabant Islands were labelled Pender Islands in 1865. The name was changed in 1924 to avoid confusion with the other Pender Islands off southeastern Vancouver Island. The islands are named after Rev. Augustus Joseph Brabant, a Roman Catholic missionary who first came to the coast in 1869. He was born in Courtrai, Belgium. In April and September of 1874 he made preliminary visits to the natives of the coast with Bishop Charles John Seghers. On May 6, 1875, he became the first missionary on the coast at Hesquiat Peninsula. He was appointed administrator of the Diocese of Vancouver Island in 1907. In 1911 he returned to Hesquiat to complete a dictionary of the Nuu-chah-nulth language. He died on July 4, 1912.

Nettle Island

This island is the largest of a group that includes Prideaux, Reeks and Erin islands plus numerous smaller islets and rocks. The southeast corner of Nettle Island is Indian Reserve with a residence above a very pretty, off-limits beach. The reserve was once the sight of a large Tseshaht village used in February and March until the 1940s for the spring salmon, cod and shellfish. The name Tl'iho:w'a means 'redface rocks.' Houses spilled over onto nearby Reeks Island.

Gibraltar Island

This is a popular island with a pretty beach connected to a small headland. The outer shore is battered by the open water of Imperial

Serene channels amid picturesque islands with mountainous backdrops characterize the Broken Group.

Eagle Channel, resulting in wonderful sea caves and arches. More caves are located on the south side of nearby Dempster Island.

An unusual development in 2003 was the arrival of a family of wolves on Gibraltar Island—a mother and two cubs. Park officials were worried by the mother's unusual behaviour and closed the campsite on Gibraltar Island for the summer, believing the mother's strange conduct was related to the young age of the offspring. The wolves hunted on other islands, and footprints were found as far away as Turret Island.

This island was home to an independent native group that was wiped out by war before European contact.

Camping: The campground is on the northwest corner of the island. The choice spot, with views both east and west, is on the headland. Other spots are in the forest along a winding trail. Most are accessible from the beach, though a few sites are set on the far side of the trail. All are very pretty, and some are quite private.

Jacques Island

Together with Jarvis Island, this cluster protects one of the most interesting waterways in the Broken Islands Group—a beautiful and sheltered lagoon rich in intertidal life. The lagoon, called Ch'a:sta:ts'inil, contains a number of tidal fish traps formed by rings of stones. Fish would become marooned in the rings by the falling tide. The traps here are among the best-preserved relics in the sound, with numerous tiers still visible.

Keith Island

This small island is part of a cluster, including the Tiny Group and Wiebe Island, scattered along the central portion of the Broken Group. Keith Island is an Indian Reserve. The island was called Qaqmaqimil, meaning 'alder tree.' From the early 1800s until World War Two it was used by the Tseshaht in early spring for gathering cod, salmon and sea mammals. The island's valued timber was used for planks and canoes. Nearby Wiebe Island (Qiqimliml: 'lots of things drifting ashore') was used year-round for seal hunting. Cod fishing was also good here.

Dodd Island

This cluster of islands has created a pretty series of channels. Dodd and Turtle islands form a relatively sheltered cove popular as an anchorage. A large midden near the campground was once a major village site, Ahtletchmakis. Tseshaht Wolf Rituals were held here in historic times; later it would be the site of potlatch ceremonies. It was a valued clamming location.

Back in the 1960s Joe Wilkowski moved to Dodd Island and tried to eke out a living. Known as Salal Joe, he planted a garden still visible today among the huge old-growth trees near the campsites. In 1980 his skiff was found washed ashore. He hasn't been seen since.

Camping: Dodd Island's campsite faces Turtle Island. The beach is well protected. There are a few sites by the central section of the beach near Salal Joe's Garden, set among magnificent old-growth forest. More sites extending north along a bit of a peninsula face out over both the east and west sides of the peninsula.

Willis Island

The outer side tends to be exposed to westerly weather, but tucked into the northwest side is a pleasant and protected beach. The inner channels are generally very peaceful.

Thiepval Channel, to the south of Willis Island, got its name from the 40-metre (130-foot) minesweeper HMCS *Thiepval* that hit an uncharted rock in the centre of the channel on February 23, 1930. The crew was rescued. *Thiepval*, however, was never salvaged and lies in about 12 m (40 feet) of water. It's now a popular diving site.

Camping: A large campground is on the northwest corner, with many sites in the forest behind an expansive beach.

Turret Island

This long, thin island is quite beautiful, particularly on the south side, where various coves are filled with islets and reefs. A chain of islands extends westward and includes Trickett and Lovett islands. The ridge becomes a landlocked bar at lower tides. Turret Island has many old-growth Sitka spruce trees; look for one particularly huge tree on the southern end.

Camping: The campground on Turret Island is in a small cove on the southwestern shore. It might be tricky to find. It's south of the elevation marker "(8)" on the Barkley Sound chart 3671 and behind what appears to be an island. The beach is pleasant but small for the number of campsites. Numerous sites are above a steep embankment. It's charming enough, but the sites aren't very private.

Clarke Island

This beautiful island has one of the finer sand beaches in the Broken Group. A trail crosses the island from the beach.

Camping: The camping area is behind the sandy beach on the island's northwest side. There's a lot of room in the clearing behind the beach, though some campers pitch tents on the beach. A second beach, not quite so large, is located on the west side of the island and attracts a few tents.

Benson Island

The south and west shores of Benson are exposed to the full brunt of the open Pacific. This has created some incredible features, including a blowhole. Waves rush up the submerged tunnel and explode out the top. This beach was known as 'blowing sound beach.' The blowhole was used by natives to predict weather; when the sound of blowing could be heard, bad weather was about to follow. According to the Tseshaht, their origins are here, at Ts'isha, where the first Tseshaht man and woman were created. The island was originally occupied year-round, but by the early 1800s it was simply one summer village among many and was replaced by Hi:kwis, near the Pinkerton Islands, as the main Tseshaht winter village. The channel between Clarke and Benson islands was called Hamota, meaning 'bones.' Great whalers among the Tseshaht tried to fill this pass with the bones of their whales.

A hotel, built by Capt. John Benson, a sealer, operated here from 1893 to 1922.

Camping: This island tends to be one of the least visited due to its distance from Toquart Bay. There are two pretty camping areas to choose from on the north side of the island. The eastern of the two is probably the nicest. A wonderful sand beach backs a cove dotted with reefs and sea stacks. Camping sites are located in the trees along the shoreline. The other beach is located to the west and separated by a rock bluff. A trail joins the two.

Gilbert Island

To the north an islet with a navigation beacon has a nice sand beach—a popular rest spot for kayakers. A large midden on Gilbert Island is an indication of an ancient village (called Shiwitis). Keep an eye open for culturally modified trees—that is, cedar trees that have had their bark stripped off. In the late 1800s a store was located here that traded with the natives of Barkley Sound.

Camping: A campsite on Gilbert Island is located in the trees behind a beach facing Effingham Island. The beach is a bit rough. The sites are in a clearing in the forest floor behind the beach; they're rather enclosed and lack privacy.

Effingham Island

This is the largest of the islands in the Broken Group and arguably the most interesting to explore. The outer shore has steep bluffs with numerous surge channels and sea caves. The cliffs are as high as 100 m (330 feet) at Meares Bluff. Below the bluff is a long paddle-through sea arch. On the west side is a cove with the best anchorage in the Broken Group. On the south shore look for a particularly large sea cave that can be paddled into when the swell is light. Bring a flashlight. A 20-minute trail leads across the island from the eastern end of Effingham Bay.

Today a reserve, the central eastern portion of the island was once a large village, as indicated by a sizable midden. Wars for control of this location date back to the late 1700s, but the Tseshaht would eventually win control through amalgamations, not bloodshed. The village was a defensive site during wars in the early 1800s, and as a result it became the main summer village of the Tseshaht. A large battle between the Tseshaht and Ahousaht was fought in the waters near a small island north of Effingham Bay; the Tseshaht were victorious. In the late 1800s during the fur trade, the village, Ho:m'o:w'a, became a sealing station. Effingham Bay, across the island, became a popular anchorage for trading ships during the fur trade, and natives used the bay when storms made landing at Ho:m'o:w'a too rough.

On March 14, 1972, the 8,500-ton freighter *Vanlene* ran into trouble near here. The ship was en route from Japan with a shipment of automobiles when the captain reported trouble with his gyrocompass. He estimated he was 100 km (60 miles) west of Cape Flattery. Moments later the ship struck a rock just south of Austin Island and became impaled on the rock. The crew and eventually the cargo were rescued by helicopter. The ship was left to rot and sink. It's a popular diving site.

Dicebox Island

This small but interesting island has a pleasant, north-facing beach with a very high bluff to the east. It was named Hots'atswil for a cave

The isthmus at the campsite at Gilbraltar Island is a fine place for a marshmallow roast.

in the island's middle where waves splash during storms (the name means 'drift back'). Two archaeological sites are here. A large village site below the bluff was used for hunting and fishing during the summer. There's evidence of nine longhouses. The other is the steep 30-m (100-foot) bluff, a Tseshaht defensive site once used to defeat an Ahousaht attack by rolling logs down the cliffs. The bluff was also a valuable lookout for spotting whales and seals. The beach on the west side was called A:ts'a:tsophshil, meaning 'when you're there it's so beautiful that you don't want to leave.'

Wouwer Island

Ruggedly beautiful, Wouwer Island lies on the exposed outer limits of the Broken Group. The inside is a protected channel abutting Batley Island. The exposed side is a wild and wave-battered rock shoreline. Two beaches opposite one another on the north and south sides of the island are connected by a five-minute trail. Kayakers can stop on the sheltered beach to the north and walk across to a cove that looks out onto the open Pacific. The rocks around Wouwer Island's north and west shores are a sea lion haulout. Hundreds can be found here and around Batley Island; their barking is clearly audible even from Turret Island.

Wouwer Island was a year-round village site before the resident group amalgamated with the Tseshaht. After that it became one of many summer villages used by the Tseshaht from May to August.

Howell Island

This island and Cree Island are the southernmost of the Broken Group, with rugged outer shores. A pocket beach is to the northeast of Howell Island.

If you keep your eyes peeled during lower tides, in the intertidal area you may see a spongy plant with thin encrustations and a colour ranging from beige to bright green. It won't smell nice. It's probably *Halichondria panicea*, a sponge. It has been found in only a few locations on the coast of Vancouver Island: Howell Island; Gilbert Island and Charles Island in Barkley Sound; and Whiffen Spit in Sooke Harbour.

THE INNER WATERS

The interior waterways of Barkley Sound offer an interesting mix of islands and inlets, including the often ignored Alma Russell Islands.

Alma Russell Islands

This group's passages and inlets are worth paddling, particularly the cove between the two islands. The opening between the two islands

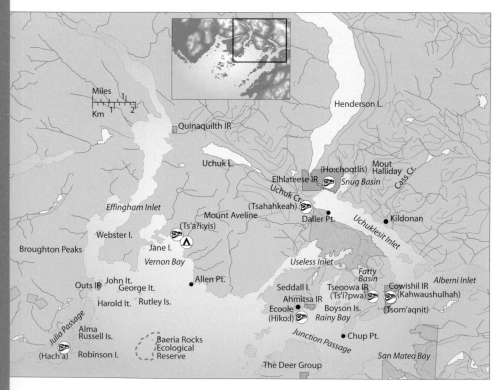

can become landlocked at lower tides. Numerous houseboats line Julia Passage.

A major village site was once located here, protected by a defensive fortress on a steep-sided bluff. It would fail in its purpose, however; a Ucluelet and Tla-o-qui-aht attack would decimate the population, forcing the survivors to join the Tseshaht. A steep-sided hill on the south end of the Alma Russell Islands was believed to be haunted by spirits, the *ma:tsayoxwin*, that would spear passersby.

Camping: A few locations might make campsites in a pinch (not recommended). A few wilderness sites are set on the east side of the islands at small beaches. Unfortunately, like many unregulated and unmaintained sites they can become trashy. The best spot I managed to find had a large fire pit built right where a tent should go. If you do try to camp here, note that several of the inviting grassy areas are actually intertidal.

Effingham Inlet

This long, narrow inlet ends in a drying mudflat. There are two shellfish operations, one near the mouth and one near the head. The most dramatic feature of the inlet is the surrounding countryside, which rises dramatically to over 900 m (2,950 feet) on either side. While the resident orca pods of southern Georgia and Juan de Fuca straits generally stay farther south, pods J, K and L do travel through Trevor Channel into Effingham Inlet.

Vernon Bay

Vernon Bay is a deep, pretty bay with an unnamed interior cove and a resort overlooking the peninsula. There's a pleasant sand beach on the bay's northeast shore. Eagle Nook Ocean Wilderness Resort occupies 30 hectares (75 acres) on the peninsula overlooking Vernon Bay. It offers four-star accommodation plus fishing, touring and kayaking. Call **1-800-760-2777**.

Camping: The expansive beach at Vernon Bay could serve as a wilderness camping area. The beach can be exposed to surf.

Useless Inlet

This pretty inlet was probably given its unflattering name because it could not be used as a port. It is, however, one of the best environments on the coast for shellfish harvesting and is home to about five

Baeria Rocks Ecological Reserve:
This seemingly innocuous collection
of rocks and rock islands is actually
teeming with nesting seabirds and
rich intertidal and subtidal ecolo-
gies. The only vascular plant is hairy
goldfields (Baeria maritima), a rare
plant in B.C. Otherwise lichens are
the only vegetation. The rocks are
significant for the nesting seabirds,
which include pelagic cormorants,
glaucous-winged gulls, black oystercatchers and pigeon guillemots.
It's also used by harbour seals as a
haulout. Fish to be found here
include yellowtail, quillback and
China rockfish. The rocks were
declared an ecological reserve in
1971; it's closed to the public and
vulnerable to disturbance.

shellfish operations. A meandering, river-like entrance gives access to Fatty Basin and Rainy Bay. Mount Aveline to the northwest soars to almost 1000 m (3,300 feet).

It was here that Fisheries and Oceans first discovered European green crab in B.C. waters. Introduced first to San Francisco Bay in about 1989, the crab has slowly been making its way northward. It took eight years to reach Coos Bay, halfway to B.C., but strong north-ward El Nino currents in 1997 and 1998 sped its arrival here. The green crab feeds on juve-nile clams, oysters and intertidal organisms, and accidental transportation to other areas of B.C., particularly the Strait of Georgia, is a con-cern. By 2004 there were eight official reports of green crabs off the Vancouver Island coast. The most disturbing was at Espinosa Inlet in Nootka Sound—the first report of a probable breeding colony. The green crab has five easily identified spines on the top front of each side of the shell. The rear legs are somewhat flat-tened. The colour isn't a particularly good clue, as some native species are green.

If you've ever wondered why the East Coast can have lobsters but the West Coast can't, look no farther than Useless Inlet. An experi-ment to raise Atlantic lobster on the West Coast failed miserably. Keep your eyes open for the concrete foundations and hatchery pens that are a testament to this failure.

Rainy Bay

This bay is filled with reefs and coves, but the best part is the passage to Fatty Basin, a narrow, river-like route that's prone to fairly strong tidal currents. It's very scenic and runs under a picturesque log bridge. Fatty Basin has a narrow passage leading to Useless Inlet.

The cove west of the modern Ahmitsa Indian Reserve was a major village whose name means 'overhanging face,' a reference to trees overhanging the point. Unfortunately, the land was pre-empted for settlement in the 1860s and made into a trading store. When it came time for reserves to be assigned in the 1880s, the commissioner instead assigned Ahmitsa, the present-day reserve location. It was a poor trade. The land was rocky and steep and only ever used during the dogfish season. Ahmitsa means 'maple tree ridge.'

The pre-empted land became a settlement known as Ecoole. A fish reduction plant operated in 1910 and again in 1926, lasting until the late 1930s. As many as 20 people lived here, with a post office, general store and school. The ruins are marked on the chart. Dogfish oil collected from Rainy Bay after European intervention was

The channel between Rainy Bay and Fatty Basin is capped by a log bridge.

stored in drums and traded for blankets at places like Ecoole. Before drums became common, the oil was stored in seal stomachs.

Uchucklesit Inlet

This inlet is quite developed, with cottages and houseboats along much of the shoreline, but it has interesting elements, such as the possibility of heading upriver to Henderson Lake. Many native villages were located here, including the principal year-round village of the Uchucklesaht at today's Cowishil Indian Reserve. Just to the south-west is a distinctive cliff. It marked the extent of the Uchucklesaht territory. The cliff was called Ho:p'asoqo:?a, meaning 'person watching the moon,' and was used to watch the moon's cycle and determine solstices. The Elhlateese reserve became the main fall village of the Uchucklesaht in the 1900s, then the main village. It's still a residential reserve—one of the few.

On the north central shore of Uchucklesit Inlet was Kildonan, the site of a thriving cannery and small village that once housed 300 people.

The cannery, which operated from 1903 to 1960, was apparently the first on the coast. The operation was named Kildonan by the Scottish owners after their hometown. It was once a Uchucklesaht village; its name translates to 'thistle place.'

ALBERNI INLET

Alberni Inlet is one of the longest on Vancouver Island, stretching 42 km (26 miles) and averaging 1.3 km (.8 mile) in width. It's a major marine navigation corridor, well used both recreationally and commercially, but its length is a detraction for kayakers. The inlet is subject to more pollution than just about any other waterway on Vancouver Island, with input from pulp mills, sewage and marina outfalls. Oxygen readings are usually below average.

A 1975 ecological survey showed human habitation in the Alberni Valley dates back more than 5,000 years. Numerous villages lined Alberni Inlet (the names are shown on the map), with many dogfish camps or camps where tyee salmon was fished, including by torchlight. The Nahmint River was valued for its spring and chinook salmon, leading the Ucluelet to decimate another tribe to earn the territory.

Caution: What makes Alberni Inlet popular for sailboarders might make it unattractive for paddlers. Winds can funnel down the inlet, creating adverse conditions.

Place names: In 1790 Lt. Eliza named the inlet after Don Pedro Alberni, a captain of infantry in the Spanish Army. Alberni was also in charge of the soldiers when Eliza sailed to reoccupy the coast at Nootka Sound in 1789.

Map labels:
Sproat Lake
Fossil Provincial Park
(Amits'a:as)
Hoik I.
(Wahta:k)
Cous Cr. Main
(No:pts'ikapis)
PORT ALBERNI
(Qalqmakok)
(Tlokwatqo:?is)
Alberni IR (T'i:pis)
Stamp Narrows
Cous IR (Tl'athalts'is)
(Wa'itnit)
(Ts'aqowipt)
(Tlo:shtlo:shok)
Macktush Access
Dunsmuir Pt.
China Creek Regional Park
Arden Creek Rec. Site
Mount Underwood
Sproat Narrows
Iwachia IR (?A:wa:chis)
Hocking Pt.
Chuckakacook IR
Kleykleyhous IR
Hiwatchas Mtn.
(Nam'int)
(Ch'isnoqnit)
Bamfield Road
Miles
Km
Pocahontas Pt.
Alberni Inlet
(Yashitqo:?a)
Coleman Cr.
(Kaqo:?a)
(T'a:xmitaqol)
Pelham Range

Alberni Inlet stretches 26 miles north, deep into Central Vancouver Island.

Camping: The Arden Creek Recreation Site is accessible by an industrial logging road from Port Alberni. It's most popular during July and August during the salmon fishing season. It's a forested site with a picnic area and a view along a short trail. China Creek Regional Park, across the inlet, also has camping facilities and is a popular summer location.

Launches: There's a launch for small cartop boats and kayaks at Arden Creek Recreation Site. Another launch, at China Creek Regional Park, is accessible from Bamfield Road. This is a very busy and supervised launch site. Fees apply.

Port Alberni

This full-service community is the gateway to Pacific Rim National Park and communities like Tofino, Bamfield and Ucluelet. It's primarily a mill town, with industrialization fronting the inlet's northeast head. Port Alberni offers hotels, restaurants, tours, rentals and supplies. For kayaking rentals, accessories, tours and lessons, visit Alberni Outpost at 5161 River Road. Call **1-800-325-3921**.

The area is rich in native history, much of it of a morbid kind. Much activity focused on the mouth of Somass River, at the head of Alberni Inlet. Many salmon weirs and harbour seal traps were located here, as was the main Tseshaht village. The area was important for winter ceremonies, including Tlokwana, the Wolf Ritual. That led to the village's name, which means 'Wolf Ritual Beach.' What is now the Alberni Indian Reserve, on the south end of Port Alberni, was used in late September for trapping waterfowl and picking roots of wild onion, cinqefoil, ladyfern and other vegetation. Just south was Ts'aqowipt, a place used for washing the heads of executed war captives. After a ceremonial washing, the heads were placed on poles set along the Somass River.

Anderson sawmill, the first mill built at the head of Alberni Inlet, began operating on May 22, 1861. It was the first major sawmill on Vancouver Island and was run using 65 oxen. By 1865, however, the mill closed—the nearby first-rate timber was gone—and it was destroyed by fire in 1869. A farm next door, on the right bank of the Somass River, was the first farm on the coast between the Alaskan peninsula and Sooke.

The MV *Lady Rose* leaves from downtown Port Alberni next to the Alberni Harbour Quay. Passengers can be transported by the working freight vessel and dropped off at Sechart (see page 302). For information, call **1-800-663-7192** April to September or **250-723-8313**.

THE DEER GROUP

As the Broken Group grows in popularity, the Deer Group has become an attractive alternative for paddlers. The islands are strung southwest to northeast, leaving fewer protected channels than the Broken Group. There are also fewer campgrounds, but features such as large paddle-through sea caves make the Deer Group a worthwhile alternative. No islands are protected as parkland.

Tzartus Island

This is the largest island in the group, but it's easily circumnavigated in a day (a distance of 20 km/12 miles). Many interesting islands are located nearby, most notably Stud Islets on the exposed western shore. Robbers Passage, while developed, is picturesque and worth exploring. North of Robbers Passage, in Marble Cove, is an elegant new resort, Canadian King Lodge (call **250-728-2357**). Along Robbers Passage is evidence of the island's mining past, plus a derelict Greenpeace freighter.

Formidable caves are located along the outer coast of Tzartus Island and on Weld Island, but the grandest is at the north end of Marble

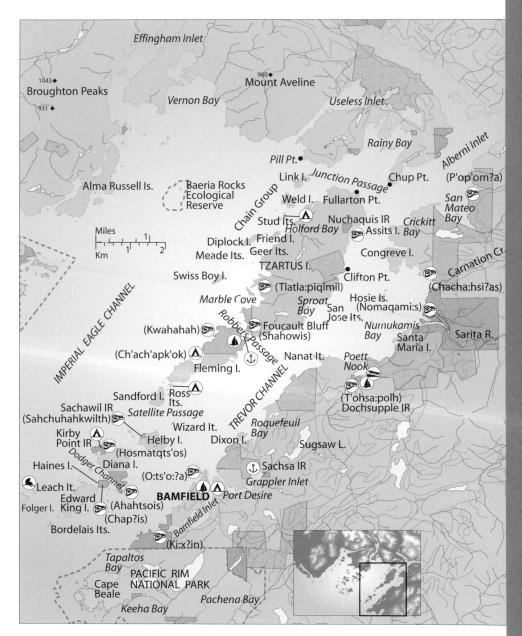

Effingham Inlet

1043 ◆
Broughton Peaks

931 ◆

960 ◆
Mount Aveline

Vernon Bay

Useless Inlet

Rainy Bay

Alberni Inlet

Pill Pt. ●

Link I. Junction Passage

Chup Pt. ●

(P'op'om?a)

Alma Russell Is.

Baeria Rocks
Ecological
Reserve

Chain Group

Weld I. Fullarton Pt. ●

San
Mateo
Bay

Stud Its.

Nuchaquis IR

Crickitt
Assits I. Bay

Miles

Diplock I. Friend I.
Meade Its. Geer Its.

Holford Bay

Congreve I.

Km

TZARTUS I.

Swiss Boy I.

Clifton Pt. ●

(Chacha:hsi?as)

Carnation Cr.

Marble Cove

(Tlatla:piqimil)

Sproat
Bay
San
Jose Its.

Hosie Is.
(Nomaqami:s)

(Kwahahah)

Robbers Passage

Foucault Bluff
(Shahowis)

Numukamis
Bay

Santa
Maria I.

Sarita R.

(Ch'ach'apk'ok)

Fleming I.

Nanat It.

Poett
Nook

Sandford I. Ross
Its.

TREVOR CHANNEL

(T'ohsa:polh)
Dochsupple IR

IMPERIAL EAGLE CHANNEL

Sachawil IR
(Sahchuhahkwilth)

Satellite Passage

Wizard It.

Roquefeuil
Bay

Kirby
Point IR

Helby I.
(Hosmatqts'os)

Dixon I.

Sugsaw L.

Dodger Channel

Haines I.

Diana I.

(O:ts'o:?a)

Sachsa IR

Leach It.

Edward
King I.
Folger I.

(Ahahtsois)
(Chap?is)

BAMFIELD

Port Desire

Grappler Inlet

Bordelais Its.

Bamfield Inlet

(Ki:x?in)

Tapaltos
Bay

PACIFIC RIM
Cape NATIONAL PARK
Beale

Pachena Bay

Keeha Bay

Cove. You can paddle through this cave, or elongated arch, if you pay
attention to converging swells (not recommended for novice paddlers).

Tzartus Island is currently being logged over a 5- to 10-year term
that began in 2000. About 75,000 cubic metres of wood are expected
to be culled from the island.

Tzartus Island's shore is pocked with caves.

Three large native villages were located on Tzartus Island. The present-day Huu-ay-aht reserve was Nu-cha-quis, a dogfish camp meaning 'seagull egg place.' Tzartus means 'place of seasonal or intermittent waterfall' in Nuu-chah-nulth. In the 1850s a trading store was located at Clifton Point.

Place names: Swiss Boy Island, to the west of Tzartus, is named for the brig that was travelling from Port Orchard to San Francisco with a load of lumber on February 1, 1859. It stopped in Barkley Sound to fix a leak. The vessel was boarded by natives, who were said to have cut the masts, rigging and sails. The story of destruction, however, was exaggerated by the crew. A later inspection found it mostly intact and the load undisturbed. The vessel, however, was found to be rotten, and it was abandoned in Barkley Sound.

Camping: By far the best camping opportunity in this area is at Stud Islets. A west-facing crushed-shell beach is protected from the worst of the weather by reefs. A number of very pretty sites are set back from the beach with wonderful views down Imperial Eagle Channel. There are no amenities. The beach is steep and prone to crashing waves, complicating the minimal surf. Another camping opportunity is at Holford Bay. It does have an inviting beach, but few sites are cleared. The beach is protected, but the understorey is thick and grows to the high tide line. There's a tent site, located in the forest on the beach's north end up a steep and dirty embankment. It's prone to bugs and is dark. Until someone creates better sites, Stud Islets are preferable.

Fleming Island

The north end of the island, along Robbers Passage, is privately owned. A huge cave is on the exposed western side in the middle of the island. The Port Alberni Yacht Club owns 3 hectares (7.5 acres) on Fleming Island for use as an outstation. A floating cabin and 90 m (300 feet) of dock are tucked behind an isthmus on the south end of Robbers Passage.

Camping: The beach on the bay in the middle of the northwest side of Fleming Island is suitable for wilderness camping. There's a campsite located on the northeast side of Sandford Island behind a pretty beach, but it has been heavily modified for use as a fishing camp, with makeshift buildings and personal trash. Far more inviting are two of the more northerly Ross Islets, where a beautiful crushed-shell beach offers wonderful sites in the trees. About a half-dozen sites have been cleared, many with driftwood shelving provided. Unfortunately, sometimes the better sites can be occupied for long periods as fishing camps.

Diana Island

This is the largest and most recreationally used of the outer islands, thanks in part to many inviting beaches. The north and south ends of the island are Indian Reserves, but recreational use of the reserve at Kirby Point, including camping, is welcome if you pre-register with the Huu-ay-aht First Nation office.

Archeological evidence indicates an expansive village was located here for several centuries. It was called Ooheh, from which the Huu-ay-aht took their name.

At Dodger Cove was the native village Ahahtsois. A trading store and church would be built here in the late 1800s. This and the sea otter fur trade would make Ahahtsois rise in Huu-ay-aht prominence.

On nearby Helby Island, in a little bay called Sauchuhahkwitth, 'stranded in the bay,' perch was caught in a falling tide by blocking the mouth of the bay with branches. Paddlers would form a line of

Ross Islets provide one of the most pleasant locations for pitching a tent.

canoes across the mouth and, holding fir boughs weighted with stones, would work them toward shore until the fish were packed tightly enough to be scooped out with nets or rakes.

Caution: While all the Deer Group islands can be exposed, Satellite Passage tends to be an unofficial line. If you cross from Fleming Island to Helby, the conditions tend to be worse, and they will continue to worsen the closer you get to Edward King Island. Conditions can be particularly brutal in Dodger Channel where large swells can break on the numerous reefs and submerged rocks.

Place names: Diana Island is named after the 87-ton steam schooner *Diana*. Built in 1860, it was operated by Alberni Sawmill. Voss Point honours Capt. Voss, who stopped here in 1902 on his voyage around the world in an Indian dugout canoe.

Camping: The Huu-ay-aht reserve at Kirby Point is available for recreational use. Fees are payable to the band in advance. Two beaches on either side of a narrow isthmus are sheltered, but the eastern beach has the best camping and avoids tumultuous Dodger Channel. A half-dozen large, private sites are set among the trees. A variety of benches, seats and tables have been constructed at various locations. A pit toilet with a canvas cover is located slightly to the north. The east beach has space for a tent or two; more than two tents and you'll be searching for a flat area off the clearing and in among the trees. A trail leads between the beaches. Just off the short trail is a pioneer graveyard, with the tombstones enclosed by a fence. For information about the reserve's sites or to make arrangements to camp here, call 250-728-3414. Other beaches east of the reserve are also suitable for camping and are free.

Edward King Island

Edward King Island is among the most beautiful of the Deer Group islands, with numerous sea caves, sea pillars and an awe-inspiring rock shoreline. It's quite exposed to the open weather of the Pacific, so expect swell. Another sea cave is located on Seppings Island. A village at Haines Island was used during the sealing season, in April and May.

Place names: It's not King Edward, but Edward King after the captain who founded two newspapers: the *New Westminster Times* and the *Victoria Gazette*. He died on his namesake island during a deer-hunting expedition in 1861.

Folger Island

The outermost of the Deer Group islands, Folger Island is exposed and wind-battered. If conditions are right you'll be treated to a spectacular sea cave, a rugged rock shoreline and a sea lion haulout.

Numukamis Bay

The shores on the Vancouver Island side of Trevor Channel are largely forgotten as kayakers scoot across to the Deer Group, but there are numerous bays to explore. Numukamis is a deep, pleasant bay fronted by numerous islands and backed by either reserve or private property. Poett Nook is a protected cove with a recreation site and launch that are now a private marina.

Numerous former village sites dot this stretch, including at Carnation Creek ('reefs in front'), at Poett Nook and at Sarita River. The latter was the major winter village called Nomaqami:s, meaning 'taboo beach.' When the Clallam attacked the fortress at Ki:x?in, the surviving Huu-ay-aht relocated up the Sarita River, only much later returning to live along the ocean. The Sarita River was an important source of spawning salmon and was occupied from September to January.

Superstition weighed heavily in the names of a few areas here. Between Cricket Bay and San Mateo Bay was a place meaning 'many ghosts,' the site where Makah were massacred by the Huu-ay-aht. The pass between Dixon Island and Vancouver Island in Roquefeuil

Bay was called K'wak'walqo:?is, and was considered taboo. Anyone swimming here was believed at risk of being pulled underwater and drowned by an octopus.

Nomaqami:s was the site of the second Roman Catholic mission on the coast (after Hesquiat). Father Nicolaye operated the mission until it was abandoned after 1886.

Place names: Poett Nook is a tribute to a physician from San Francisco who held copper claims on Tzartus Island. Roquefeuil Bay is named for Camile de Roqefeuil, a French commander who arrived here in 1817 on the 200-ton ship *Bordelais*. Seeking new French markets, Roquefeuil stayed about two weeks on his two-year around-the-world trip. His adventures led to a book that described Barkley Sound and stories of native life.

Launches: Formerly a forest recreation site, the Poett Nook launch is now subject to a fee for parking and launching. The nook is well protected from wind. The marina has camping, but it's open and RV-oriented. The marina's gate is closed overnight, so if you're hoping to arrive at the crack of dawn to launch you may have to wait till opening hours. Call **250-720-9572**.

BAMFIELD

The small community of Bamfield is the commercial centre for southeastern Barkley Sound and is the western terminus of the West Coast Trail. It has many tourist-related amenities, including a hostel, campgrounds, a store, a pub, hotels, bed and breakfasts and water taxis.

Bamfield West is across Bamfield Inlet on Mills Peninsula, and isn't accessible by road. A water taxi is available to make the crossing. A phone to call for the service is available at the government dock.

Bamfield Marine Sciences Centre is located on the outermost point of the peninsula between Grappler and Bamfield inlets. It's a year-round research facility serving five western Canadian universities, plus visiting scientists. It offers graduate and undergraduate courses in marine sciences, and a public education program and tours for schools and tourists. A popular program is the volunteer work experience and training for young scientists.

On the Keeshan reserve is the site of a Huu-ay-aht village and fortress with significant architectural remains, including crumbling longhouses. In 2002 it was named the Kiix?in Village and Fortress

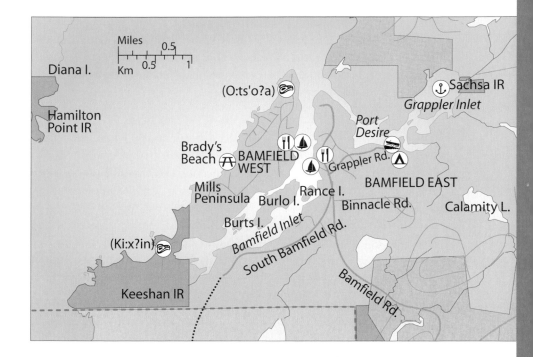

National Historic Site. Mostly hidden in among tangled rainforest and thick undergrowth, plans include making the ruins accessible to the public. A large headland next to the village, a 35-metre-high (120-foot) rock pinnacle jutting into the ocean, known as Execution Rock, protected the village from the elements and provided a defensive fortress with views over the ocean to watch for both approaching vessels and wildlife. Once a key village, it was abandoned in the late 1800s for Dodger Cove on Haines Island.

Bamfield's modern claim to fame was its position at the end of the trans-Pacific telegraph cable. Completed in 1902, it linked Australia and North America. The longest link was 5,692 km (3,537 miles) from Bamfield to Fanning Island. The cable station closed in 1959. The landmark structure now houses the Bamfield Marine Sciences Centre.

One early visitor to Bamfield was Camille de Roquefeuil. He first entered Barkley Sound in 1817 and anchored in Bamfield Inlet, but a sudden wind forced the crew to cut the anchor to escape being dashed on shore. The ship then moved to a sheltered spot he called Port Desire. After five days of dragging Bamfield Inlet to find the lost anchor, the crew gave up—meaning the anchor must still be down there somewhere.

Hiking: One of the most popular trails starts at South Bamfield Road and leads to Keeha Beach; another leads to Cape Beale (see page 334 for more on these trails). From West Bamfield a short trail leads to Brady's Beach, a popular recreation area, where a picturesque stone pillar is situated.

Place names: The name is in honour of William Eddy Banfield. Unfortunately, the British Admiralty Charts in 1863 and 1865 misspelled it. It was corrected on later charts, but the error was duplicated by the post office when it opened in 1903, and the name has stuck ever since. For 50 years Bamfield was located on Banfield Inlet, but in 1951 historical accuracy took a back seat to common usage and all references were changed to Bamfield. Banfield came to the coast aboard HMS *Constance* in 1846 and later traded with the natives on the west coast of Vancouver Island. By 1861 he was named Indian agent, but lost his life in 1862. An Huu-ay-aht was charged with his murder but was not convicted due to lack of evidence.

Camping: A municipal campground, Centennial Park Campground, is located near the launch site in Bamfield. The sites are open and charmless. A prettier nearby alternative is the campground at Pachena Bay (see page 336).

Launches: Kayakers and boaters alike can launch at Centennial Park. A fee applies for both the launch and the parking. You must pay at the information centre, which can be an annoyance for those who arrive early. It has limited hours of operation.

Juan de Fuca Strait

JUAN DE FUCA STRAIT IS A DESTINATION LIKE NO OTHER ON VANCOUVER Island: miles upon miles of exposed rock shoreline with few breaks, no islands and almost no protection from the open weather. The weather can be rough. Juan de Fuca Strait is among the worst areas of the island for high winds. This means the outer coast from Cape Beale to Victoria is often passed over by all but the most adventurous travellers. It's unfortunate, for while conditions can be harsh, with care they're manageable and the rewards are incredible. Huge rock arches, sea caves, some of the most spectacular seashore in the world, secluded sand beaches and wildlife including year-round gray whales—it's a kayaker's paradise. People from all over the world arrive at either Port Renfrew or Bamfield to hike the West Coast Trail, an arduous journey skirting 78 km (48 miles) of shoreline that takes five days or more to walk. Kayakers, on the other hand, get all the best scenery, are free from cumbersome backpacks and can easily complete the length of the trail in two days (it's 67 km/42 miles by water). Trail use fees and restrictions that hikers must abide by aren't enforced for kayakers, though policy changes may come.

South of Port Renfrew explorers will find protected parkland along the shoreline until near Sooke Harbour. Once at Sooke Harbour things change. Toward Victoria the shore is a combination of waterfront mansions, protected regional parks, jails and industrial development. The wild coast ends.

GETTING HERE

Juan de Fuca Strait is accessible from Pachena Bay, Port Renfrew and locations around Sooke including as far north as Jordan River.

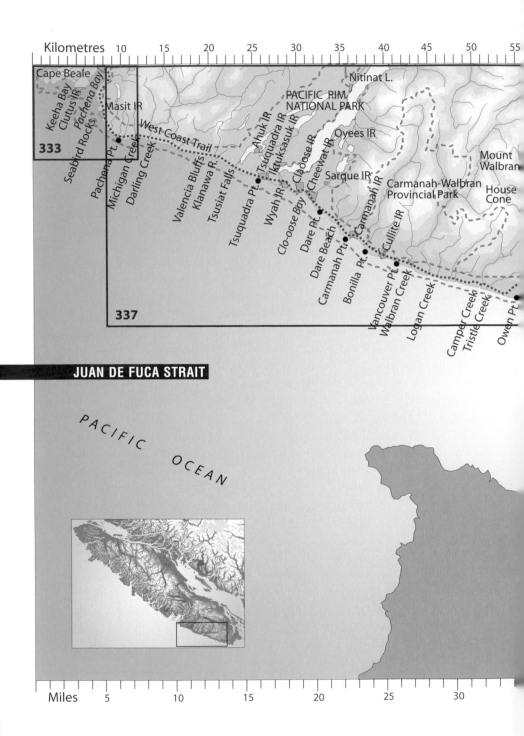

Kilometres 10 15 20 25 30 35 40 45 50 55

Cape Beale

Keeha Bay
Clutus IR
Pachena Bay
Seabird Rocks

Masit IR

Pachena Pt.
Michigan Creek
Darling Creek

West Coast Trail

333

337

Nitinat L.

PACIFIC RIM
NATIONAL PARK

Ahuk IR
Tsuquadra IR
Iktuksasuk IR

Oyees IR

Claoose IR
Cheewat IR

Sarque IR

Mount
Walbran

Carmanah-Walbran
Provincial Park

House
Cone

Valencia Bluffs
Klanawa R.
Tsusiat Falls

Tsuquadra Pt.

Wyah IR

Clo-oose Bay

Dare Pt.
Dare Beach

Carmanah Pt.

Bonilla Pt.

Carmanah IR

Cullite IR

Vancouver Pt.
Walbran Creek

Logan Creek

Camper Creek
Tristle Creek

Owen Pt.

JUAN DE FUCA STRAIT

PACIFIC

OCEAN

Miles 5 10 15 20 25 30

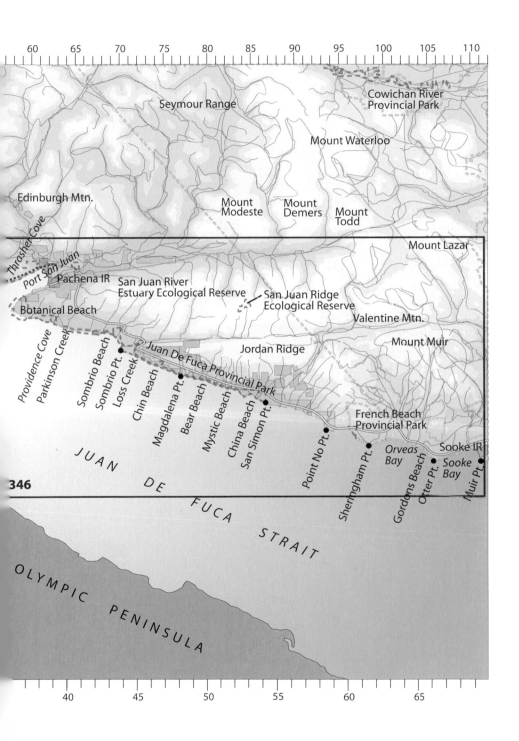

Pachena Bay is the most difficult to drive to, as it means taking Bamfield Road (see page 288 for directions). The turnoff for the Pachena Bay Campground is just before Bamfield and just after the West Coast Trail trailhead. Port Renfrew is easily accessible from Victoria; simply follow Highway 14 to its terminus. It's also accessible by well-marked and well-groomed logging roads from Lake Cowichan. This is a more direct route if you're coming from Nanaimo. From the Island Highway, take the Lake Cowichan Road, South Shore Road then the Gordon River Main (there are actually two routes, and both are well marked). The Highway 14 route has the advantage of being paved the entire way. For launches in Sooke, see the information offered at the individual launch sites.

EXPLORING BY KAYAK

Juan de Fuca Strait is probably the most intimidating stretch of coast along Vancouver Island for its length, exposure and lack of protected shore. Casual visitors will have considerably fewer options than hardy explorers ready for a lengthy expedition.

Recommended short trips

- *If you have a day:* A good day trip by paddle would be an exploration of Port San Juan to Owen Point or Pachena Bay to Keeha Beach. Numerous nice day trips are possible by foot, including Cape Beale, Keeha Bay, Botanical Beach, Sombrio Beach, China Beach, French Beach and East Sooke Regional Park. Flatwater paddlers might like Sooke Basin, while the outer waters of East Sooke Regional Park from Whiffen Spit would be a pleasant day trip.

- *If you have a weekend:* Few reasonable overnight trips are possible along this stretch. My advice to people wanting to explore by paddle would be to find a nice campsite, the best being Pachena Bay, and paddle during the day. The only reasonable overnight trip would be from Port Renfrew to Thrasher Cove or from Pachena Bay to Keeha Bay. Thrasher Cove can become very crowded with hikers during the summer.

- *If you have a week:* This much time would allow the ideal trip: a run down Juan de Fuca Strait. Launch at either Pachena Bay or Bamfield and consider ending the trip at Sooke or even Victoria. A possible itinerary would be Bamfield, Pachena Bay, Clo-oose, Thrasher Cove, Jordan River, Sooke, Pedder Bay then Victoria.

Rugged shore along the West Coast Trail.

A mythical sea monster is carved into the rock at East Sooke Regional Park.

Some paddlers may want to arrange for bed and breakfasts in Sooke and/or Metchosin. Experience with surf landings is a necessity. Arrangements must be made for transportation at either end.

THE BASICS

Geology and ecology

Juan de Fuca Strait is characterized by few major indentations in the coast, with exceptions being Pachena Bay, Port San Juan and Sooke Harbour. Otherwise the shoreline is largely rocky intertidal platforms rich in kelp, interspersed with small beaches, only a few of which are sand. During flood tide deep ocean water moves eastward along the bottom of the strait, mixing with the water of Georgia Strait, which is comparatively brackish due to the influence of the Fraser River and many other large estuaries. Some of this new mixture of water will escape into the Pacific. The result is relatively warm water rich in nutrients.

A submarine mountain about 500 km (310 miles) offshore is known as the Juan de Fuca Ridge. Here young volcanoes, hot springs and lava flows are formed when the plates of the ocean floor separate. This contributes to the region's susceptibility to earthquakes; hundreds occur every year off the coast of Vancouver Island, Puget Sound and the Olympic Peninsula.

Weather

The weather systems of Juan de Fuca Strait aren't significantly different from the rest of the south coast, but it does have its own particular facet—wind. The strait has its own marine weather forecast quite separate from south Vancouver Island. Daily wind warnings can continue for weeks on end, with Race Rocks being a significant trouble spot. Winds, sandwiched by Vancouver Island and the Olympic Peninsula, funnel down the strait. Typically, they rise in the early afternoon. As with the rest of the coast, there's a lot of rain. Port Renfrew receives 3,670 mm (144 inches) of it each year. November and December are the wettest months, each receiving over 500 mm (20 inches) of rain. July receives just 64 mm (2.5 inches) of rain.

Native overview

This stretch of coast includes the southern extent of the Nuu-chah-nulth and the beginning of Coast Salish territory. Huu-ay-aht territory extended south along the coast to Pachena Point or possibly as far as Tsusiat River. The groups who lived on the outer coast were great whalers who relied on sea mammals to survive.

Farther south the coast is home to the Ditidaht, once known as the Nitinaht, a group that includes the remnants of the Clo-oose and Carmanah. Together with the Pacheedaht of Port San Juan, they were known as the southern Nootka. The Clo-oose, Carmanah and Nitinaht banded together in the mid-20th century, taking the Ditidaht name in 1984. The coalition was not a decision on the part of the bands; it was a decision by the Canadian government.

A short totem stands guard over the San Juan River at Pachena.

The Qwa-Ba-Diwa (Carmanah) hereditary family still claims sovereignty over their Carmanah-Walbran territories. The Ditidaht are claiming those territories as well.

Most of the Ditidaht population lives on Malachan reserve on the northern end of Nitinat Lake. The Pacheedaht occupy four reserves at Port Renfrew. The Huu-ay-aht live at Pachena Bay.

Historically the southern Nootka population was much larger. In 1790 John Meares estimated the number at 25,900. By 1924 it was 1,500, cut down largely by epidemics. As whalers and sea travellers, the southern Nootka had frequent contact with the Makah on the U.S. side of the strait. They were also initially friendly to the Tsou-ke of Sooke, but hostilities arose in the 1800s.

All these bands were users of marine resources—shellfish, halibut, cod, snapper, seals, sea otters and whales.

East of Port San Juan the land of the Nootka ends, and the traditional territory of the Coast Salish begins. Linguistically and culturally distinct, the Coast Salish lived along the southeastern coast of Vancouver Island and the British Columbia mainland. European settlement and heavy development of this area affected the Coast Salish particularly harshly. Traditional lands and sites were often commandeered for development and homesteading. This has hastened the destruction of historic remnants, from village sites to middens.

The Scia'new (Becher Bay) and T'Sou-ke First Nations still inhabit small portions of the outer coast.

THE SHORELINES

CAPE BEALE AND PACHENA BAY

This stretch of the outer coast is one of the most accessible, thanks to launch sites in Bamfield and Pachena Bay. Both kayakers and hikers can access beautiful sand beaches and wave-battered rocky headlands, getting a taste of the wilder sections of the coast. Gray whales are regular visitors to the waters outside Pachena Bay.

Cape Beale

This rugged headland is a rock bluff with exposed pocket beaches and is protected as part of the Pacific Rim National Park Reserve. The lighthouse can be reached by a difficult trail, if the tide is low. The light began operating July 1, 1874. The present structure, a white square with a skeletal framework and a red lantern, was installed in

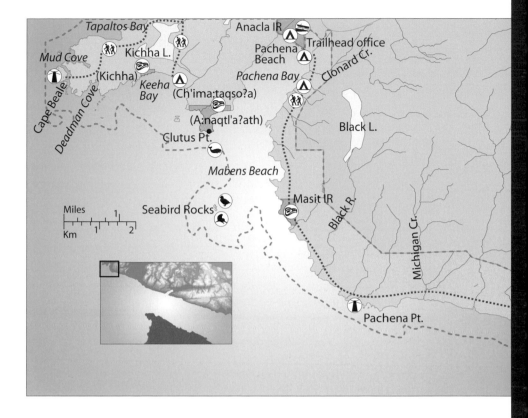

1958. The headland is surrounded by numerous reefs and exemplifies the outer coast of Vancouver Island—at once breathtakingly beautiful and dauntingly untamed.

On a point on the north end of the cape was a place known as 'rock standing up from the water.' It was believed to be the entrance to a mythical underground river full of spring salmon.

Caution: Cape Beale is one of the trouble spots on the outer coast of Vancouver Island. The waters of Barkley Sound and Juan de Fuca Strait meet the open Pacific here. Add to that wind and a shallow shelf around the cape and the result is a potentially dangerous sea. The best time to cross is at or near slack tide in the morning, before the seas have a chance to build. Even then the swell can be high, and steep in the shallowest portions. Numerous reefs extending outward from the cape can be hidden due to the steep swell—and what appears to be simply steep swell can suddenly turn into a breaking wave. If unsure, give the cape and its reefs a wide berth.

Place names: John Beale was the *Imperial Eagle*'s purser. He did not live long to enjoy the honour of being the cape's namesake. He was killed a few weeks later by natives at Destruction Island near Cape Flattery (U.S.).

Hiking: A rough and muddy trail leads from road access to the Cape Beale Lighthouse. Some stretches go through swampy areas, so dress appropriately. The trailhead is at the end of South Bamfield Road. Parks Canada provides a parking lot 400 m (1,312 feet) from the road's end. At about 1.5 km (1 mile) along the trail, you'll reach the junction to Keeha Bay. Turn right for Cape Beale. (Note: the junction can be difficult to find. A good backup plan is a trip to Keeha Bay instead.) The Cape Beale trail will take you to Tapaltos Bay, then will turn inland past Lawton Point. The last stretch of the 7-km (4.3-mile) trail is largely mud flats passable only at tides 1.8 m (6 feet) or lower. Just past a bridge at the south end of Bamfield Inlet is a sign for Tapaltos Bay. This leads along mud flats and is passable at tides below 1.8 m (6 feet). It's not recommended, as it's easy to get lost.

Keeha Bay

This bay's sweeping beach is hemmed in by a multitude of reefs. It can be reached by paddle or a hike from South Bamfield Road. The Kichha reserve on the west side of the bay was a summer village for sealing, whaling and halibut.

Hiking: To get to the Keeha Beach Trail take the Cape Beale Trail (see above). The Keeha Beach Trail is much shorter, at just 3.5 km (2.2 miles), but it has some interesting challenges. It skirts the outside of Kichha Lake, where a floating bridge must be crossed on the southeast corner. From there it crosses a steep hill to the beach.

Camping: Keeha Beach is a pretty and relatively protected stretch suitable for camping from a kayak or backpack. It's part of Pacific Rim National Park and as such subject to restriction and fees, while the western portion is a First Nation reserve. Kayakers may be enticed by a crushed-shell beach on an islet in the bay facing toward Clutus Point. It's indeed a picturesque place to visit and stay, but the beach becomes rimmed with large rocks in all but high tides. Launching is next to impossible in lower tides, but if the tides work for your schedule, camping is possible on the spit. It's one of the few places where you can watch the sun set from your campsite in the evening and watch it rise from the same spot in the morning. The beach next to Clutus Point is also inviting, but it's reserve land and is off-limits.

Pachena Bay

This deep bay provides access to the outer coast. There are pocket beaches all along the eastern shore of the bay, but the best, Pachena Beach, is on the north end. This is a popular recreation area, with numerous families making use of the surf and sand on any given summer day. It's mostly Huu-ay-aht reserve, with a band-owned campground behind the beach. The trailhead and information office for the West Coast Trail are on the eastern end. A short trail leads from the park office to the beach. A shuttle from the West Coast Trail trailhead to Bamfield takes hikers from the trail to the town. The staff at the trailhead office will call for the shuttle if asked.

Gray whales can often be seen feeding near the kelp at the mouth of the bay near Clutus Point. Seabird Rocks, off the mouth of Pachena Bay, are rugged and exposed but home to a nesting seabird population. The rocks house a high population of endangered rhinoceros auklets, and sea lions use the rocks as a year-round haulout.

Launches: An option is from the Pachena Bay Campground. From a beach-front campsite, simply trudge down to the beach with your kayak and launch into the surf, which is generally light to moderate. Another option is to launch into the Pachena River from the dirt boat

Pachena Beach is a popular recreation area, campsite and gateway to the West Coast Trail.

launch within the Huu-ay-aht reserve (near the short totem). The river is free from surf. Parking is available next to the launch. As of 2004 the Huu-ay-aht had no restrictions on use of the launch or parking.

Camping: Pachena Bay Campground is set in a forested area next to the beach. Amenities are washrooms, pay showers, fire pits, firewood and running water. The fee is $18 a night. Call **250-728-1287**. For those arriving by kayak, there are many small beaches along Pachena Bay's east shoreline on Pacific Rim parkland. Hikers are discouraged from using the beach, but kayakers are generally tolerated.

Pachena Point

Pachena Point should be a point of no return for kayakers; at 10 km (6 miles) from the launch site at Pachena Beach, if you travel much farther east you run the risk of not being able to return the same day. The coast along here is spectacularly rugged and exposed. If you're paddling, don't expect a casual rest on a beach along this stretch.

Pachena Point was called Satsnit, which means 'place of many large spring salmon.' This was believed to be the division between Ditidaht and Huu-ay-aht territories. A few miles northwest is Masit, a Huu-ay-aht reserve. The name means 'cool water.' It was a summer village site used for halibut fishing and sea mammal hunting.

The Pachena Point Lighthouse began operating in July 1908, and is now the last original wood lighthouse on Canada's west coast. The tower is octagonal with a red lantern on top. The current keepers offer brownies to visitors who ring the bell at the information kiosk. The grounds are well groomed, a slice of suburbia in the midst of untamed wilderness.

Hiking: Hiking the full West Coast Trail from Pachena Bay to Port Renfrew requires a permit and reservations, but a day hike is possible anytime. A good destination is the Pachena Point Lighthouse. Just 10 km (6 miles) from the trailhead, it's along the most pleasant and leisurely section. The lighthouse offers views of the rugged coast. A short side trail west of the lighthouse leads to a scenic lookout.

THE OUTER COAST (PACHENA POINT TO OWEN POINT)

This is one of the longest stretches of unbroken coast on the west coast of Vancouver Island—wave-battered and reef-strewn shore with little to no shelter for marine travellers for the 50 km (30 miles)

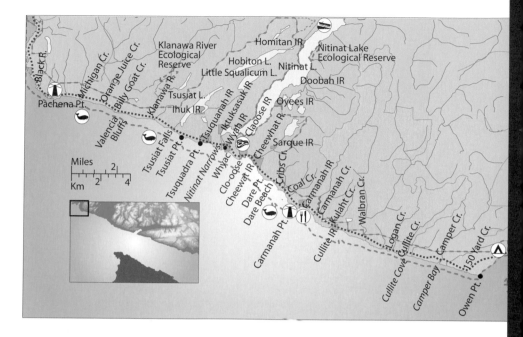

from Pachena Point to Owen Point. For kayakers it represents a potentially dangerous but stunningly dramatic journey, with gray whales, sea caves and unforgettable scenery.

This area in the entrance to Juan de Fuca Strait claimed 137 major shipping vessels in the days of sail between 1830 and 1925, earning it the title Graveyard of the Pacific. Those lucky enough to survive the earlier shipwrecks were often rescued by natives and taken to Fort Victoria by canoe. The numerous tragedies prompted the construction of a life-saving trail, later reborn as the recreational West Coast Trail.

Caution: The wind and swell will be your greatest concern, but current can also be a factor. It runs southeast at 1.5 knots in the summer and northwest at 2 knots in the winter. While it won't stop you, it can delay (or speed) your journey.

Valencia Bluffs

Creeks are the most significant checkpoints for hikers along this portion of coast. Between Pachena Point and Valencia Bluffs are Michigan Creek, Darling River, Orange Juice Creek and Tsocowis Creek. Valencia Bluffs, steep cliffs overlooking the ocean, are a significant landmark for kayakers.

A sea arch near Tsusiat Point is one of the largest on the Vancouver Island coast.

The worst wreck on this stretch of the coast was the *Valencia* on a stormy day on January 22, 1906. The wreck prompted the placement of a lighthouse at Pachena Point and construction of the West Coast Life-saving Trail. The *Valencia* was a steamship bound for Victoria. It overshot the entrance to Juan de Fuca Strait and hit the rocks three miles southeast of Pachena Point. The shoreline was too rough for a safe landing or rescue, and 126 people died trying to get to safety.

Tsusiat Falls

The waterfall is just one attraction along this picturesque stretch of shoreline. The water cascades almost 20 m (65 feet) over a sheer rock wall to the beach. It's a popular camping location for hikers, and gray whales feed alongside the reefs just offshore from the falls. East of Tsusiat Falls, at Tsusiat Point, erosion has carved a huge natural arch—the largest on Vancouver Island's coast. Klanawa River, to the west of the falls, has created a notable sandbar blocking much of the river's mouth. Hikers must cross by a hand-operated cable car.

Nitinat Narrows

This wide river opens to the Pacific Ocean through a deep chasm that's invariably ringed by breaking waves. Here hikers must take a ferry across the narrows; tired or injured hikers can arrange for a boat

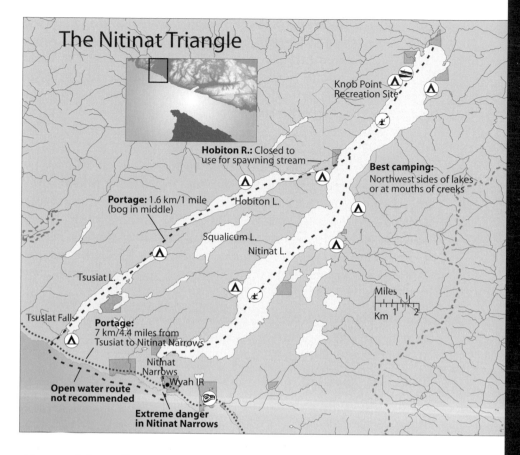

The Nitinat Triangle

Knob Point Recreation Site

Hobiton R.: Closed to use for spawning stream

Best camping: Northwest sides of lakes or at mouths of creeks

Portage: 1.6 km/1 mile (bog in middle)

Hobiton L.

Squalicum L.

Nitinat L.

Tsusiat L.

Miles

Km

Tsusiat Falls

Portage: 7 km/4.4 miles from Tsusiat to Nitinat Narrows

Nitinat Narrows

Wyah IR

Open water route not recommended

Extreme danger in Nitinat Narrows

ride out of the trail, courtesy of the Ditidaht band at Whyac. The narrows passes into Nitinat Lake, a mid-point entrance or exit to the West Coast Trail. Here Nitinat Lake is partly intertidal. Rising surf will rush up the narrows, blanketing the lake with a layer of salt water.

Caution: This passageway is often the terminus of the open-ocean portion of a paddling trip down the coast. But it comes with a risk. Strong currents from the river meet incoming surf and create dangerous conditions. The narrows itself can be a thundering maelstrom of water. It's best approached with expert local knowledge only. The narrows has a history of fatalities.

The Nitinat Triangle

The triangle is one of the most advanced canoe/kayak routes on the coast, notorious for its difficult portages. The triangle is from Nitinat Lake to Hobiton Lake to Tsusiat Lake. Then, depending on your map, your guide or your inspiration, it's an open water crossing along the coast or a portage back to Nitinat Lake. The first portage is to Hobiton Lake. The Hobiton River is a salmon spawning stream and is closed to marine use by the Department of Fisheries and Oceans. There are many obstructions and paddling through the shallows can damage spawning channels. The second portage is from Hobiton Lake to Tsusiat Lake—about 1.6 km (1 mile) with a bog in the middle. The portage will mean climbing over and under fallen trees. The route back to Nitinat Lake through the open Pacific isn't recommended. It's 6.5 km (4 miles) to Nitinat Narrows, and the narrows produce fast-running tidal channels and eddies. A round trip is approximately four to five days. This is an extremely difficult trip through rough terrain. You can launch from Knob Point on the northwest side of Nitinat Lake. A park use permit is required to canoe or kayak the triangle. Permits are available from the Pachena Bay or Port Renfrew information centres. Call **250-726-7721**.

Place names: Whyac comes from the Nitinaht word meaning 'open mouth,' referring to fish trap openings. The nearby canyon was thought to resemble a fish trap's mouth.

Launches: There's a boat launch at Knob Point on Nitinat Lake's northwestern end. It's accessible by logging road from Duncan.

Camping: There are numerous wilderness locations to camp on Nitinat Lake. For those keeping to the open ocean, there are several pocket beaches just east of the narrows. These are among the most sheltered on this stretch of coast, and I would recommend them over the beach at Clo-oose, which is quite open to surf.

Clo-oose

Clo-oose (generally pronounced "close") is an abandoned village, with buildings still visible. The beach in front of the village site, known locally as Stanley Beach, is well protected, but it's a First Nation reserve and access is restricted. Camping is clearly prohibited. The reserve extends past the mouth of the Cheewhat River. As well as abandoned houses, you can find surge channels, a blowhole and petroglyphs here. The petroglyphs face the ocean and are on a sandstone shelf at Stanley Beach. The glyphs include a mysterious masted ship. One author has speculated the ship petroglyph is from the wreck of the *John Bright*, a ship that went down in 1869 (see page 235).

Clo-oose was once the main village of the Ditidaht. It was marketed at the beginning of the 19th century as the new centre of Vancouver Island. With the promise of a road, people from the prairies fell for the sales pitch, and arrived to find not even a dock to unload their belongings. But until the 1950s it was indeed a bustling community. Census figures show that in 1881 the population was 271; in 1891 it was 278. The post office still stands.

Caution: Moderate to high surf tends to run across the entire mile-long stretch of white sand beach, including across the mouth of the Cheewhat River. Even if you can enter the Cheewhat River, you're still in a First Nation reserve unless you paddle upriver and camp on the shoals (not recommended). The beach here is used by band members as a surfing camp, an indication of the type of waves you'll have to battle to land.

Carmanah Point

This scenic area features a lighthouse, a rocky headland and a beautiful white sand beach. The surf on the main beach tends to be extremely high. The northernmost portion, Carmanah reserve, is comparitively sheltered. Carmanah Point is a significant groundfish area.

You can stop at the reserve for a burger or other treats in the unique setting of a plastic building. Chez Monique is operated by Monique, a French-Canadian who will be sure to update travellers on the news of the world. The food has a top-rated reputation.

The beach at Cheewhat River attracts a horde of gulls this day, but not many people.

The Carmanah Point Lighthouse began operating in September 1891. A steam whistle provided ship-to-shore communication in both the dark and fog by way of telegraph codes. Information to the lightkeeper was communicated to Victoria, then to Lloyd's of London. W. P. Daykin, the lightkeeper in 1891, recorded his 21 years of service in nine volumes, relating the hard weather, hard work and hard luck—including the loss of his wife and sons.

Camper Bay

East of Carmanah Point the indentations in the shoreline are so few that the existence of bays are greatly exaggerated. Cullite Cove and Camper Bay are generally non-existent when viewed from the ocean—and also in the sense of seeking shelter. The indentations are created by erosion from the associated creeks, and generally become rock platform at lower tide. Hikers will require cable cars to cross Walbran, Cullite and Camper creeks. For kayakers, however, this stretch will be easy paddling with very few reefs along pristine shoreline. But don't expect to be alone—off Owen Point is a popular recreational fishery, and on any given summer day several dozen boats can be out trolling.

Hiking the West Coast Trail: The trail began as the West Coast Life-saving Trail, built after the *Valencia* wrecked on the coast on January 22, 1906 just north of Klanawa River. The trail has since grown to become one of the most prestigious hikes in the world, causing Parks Canada to limit the use to 52 hikers per day during the season—26 from each trailhead. The trail is open between May 1 and September 30. The quota requires reservations, causing a flurry of calls to the reservation phone system three months prior to the opening (call **1-800-663-6000** in Canada and the U.S. or **1-250-387-1642** for international reservations). Phone any later and you're likely to be on a waiting list for the peak season. Fewer hikers use the trail in May and September. A fee is charged for a trail use permit, which is required for ferry use.

The trail runs from Pachena Bay to Port Renfrew, with a mid-point exit possible only at Whyac (Nitinat Narrows), where hikers can arrange transportation. Emergency evacuation service is provided by Parks Canada and helicopters regularly fly out injured hikers, but the wait can be long and the service costly.

As well as light, waterproof gear, a tide guide is a must. Many sections of the beachfront trail are accessible at low tide only; laggers can be caught in rising tides. Parks Canada provides detailed maps and an orientation session before hikers begin the trail. On the trail hikers will find sea arches, caves, breathtaking viewpoints, waterfalls, tough climbing, hand-operated cable cars over river gulleys and wonderful sand beaches. It's a five- to seven-day hike with many difficult stretches.

PORT SAN JUAN

This bay is similar to Pachena Bay, though larger. The western side has many intriguing sea caves backed by steep, mountainous and cliff-pocked terrain. The most interesting cave in the bay is tucked in just north of Owen Point behind Kellet Rock. For hikers it is accessible only at lower tides. Many hikers of the West Coast Trail say the highlight of the trip is this stretch of coast and the cave here. Port Renfrew, located on the east shore of the bay, is a trailhead for both the West Coast Trail and the Juan de Fuca Marine Trail. Many amenities are provided here for campers, day-use beach users and hikers.

Camping: Thrasher Cove is the only sand beach on the west shore of Port San Juan. The cove is small but picturesque—a rib of sand tucked in behind some reefs and backed by very steep terrain. The West Coast Trail passes through the cove, which tends to be an overnight stop for both westbound and eastbound hikers. Quite often by evening every sandy spot will be occupied, creating a tent city. Arrive early for the best spots (on the outside edges). Numerous small caves are located nearby. The beach is well sheltered for landing kayaks.

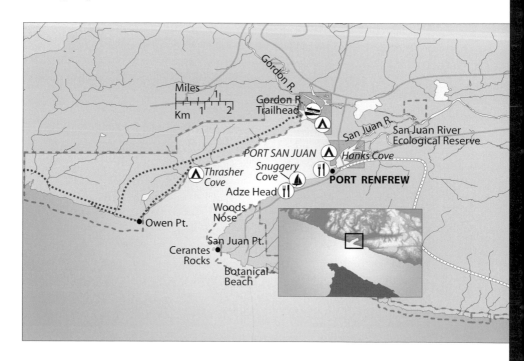

Port Renfrew

This small community is nestled on the southeast shore of the name-sake bay. It's accessible by road from Sooke or logging road from Lake Cowichan. Because it's the access point for hikers entering or exiting both the West Coast Trail and the Juan de Fuca Marine Trail, it has numerous amenities specifically designed for minimalist travellers: showers, cafés, hostels, campgrounds and outfitters.

Camping: At the head of Port San Juan is the Pacheena and Gordon River reserve. The beachfront is a campground. There are two main entrances—one just past the bridge near Port Renfrew and another next to the Gordon River. Amenities include a boat launch, a store and the Port Renfrew trailhead and park office for the West Coast Trail. The trail begins after a boat crossing of the Gordon River. The boats used to ferry hikers are operated by the reserve.

Launches: The Pacheedaht band charges for the use of the launch at Gordon River, which is located just inside the campground. A free option is in Harris Cove. To get there from Highway 14 exit into Port Renfrew on the turn just before the bridge. Follow the waterfront along Harris Cove Road. Watch for the turnoff to a rough gravel beach.

Caution: Outside Port Renfrew and the San Juan River estuary the water tends to shoal up with a long series of submerged or semi-submerged sandbars. This can lead to lines of breaking waves well

Thrasher Cove can be filled to overflowing with hikers.

out into Port San Juan. To leave the estuary and enter Port San Juan, boaters and kayakers must navigate the deepest channel between the beach and the sandbars parallel to the beach to avoid breaking waves. Generally it isn't dangerous, as the waves can be avoided, but it can be quite disconcerting to realize just how many breaking waves there are to avoid.

San Juan River

The San Juan River is part of a huge watershed covering 730 square km (282 square miles) that extends almost as far as Shawnigan Lake, 90 km (56 miles) away. The river subdivides into about a dozen channels before emptying into Port San Juan. In 1995 a B.C. government report blamed massive clearcutting by three forest companies—Pacific Forest Products, MacMillan Bloedel and TimberWest—for causing landslides that ruined fish habitat in the San Juan River. The companies paid $3.8 million in compensation.

The San Juan River Estuary Ecological Reserve is a 79-hectare (200-acre) reserve created in 1996 to protect the San Juan River flood plain and its examples of lower alluvial forest communities. The discovery of a patch of rare tooth-leaved monkey flowers the size of a tabletop stopped clear-cutting of the river. This rare flower is found nowhere else in Canada. The ecological reserve protects the flowers and the spawning ground for about 1,500 chinook. Passive pastimes, such as hiking, are permitted in this reserve, but more intrusive activities, such as camping, are prohibited.

JUAN DE FUCA PROVINCIAL PARK

Rarely considered a marine destination of its own, this stretch of coast contains many exotic features such as sea caves, sea stacks and rugged coast. The drawback for kayakers is the lack of places to find shelter once on the water. A series of provincial parks protect the shoreline, with the Juan de Fuca Trail running from Port Renfrew to China Beach.

Botanical Beach

Located at the western end of the Juan de Fuca Trail, a parking lot provides access to both Botany Bay and Botanical Beach. The Botanical Beach shoreline has ridges of shale and quartz thrust up through black basalt to form huge tableaus. The foreshore at

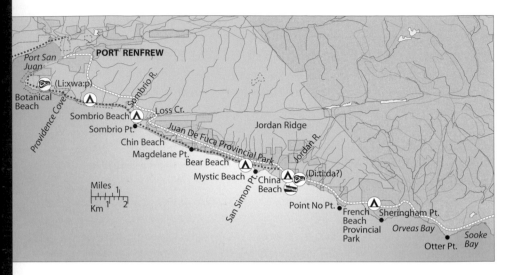

Botanical Beach is particularly rich; tide pools are home to a variety of flora and fauna such as starfish, sea urchins, periwinkles, chitons and sea stars. It served as the first marine research station in the Pacific Northwest, for the University of Minnesota, in 1901.

Sombrio Beach

Sombrio Beach is the first major beach east of Port San Juan that's easily accessible from land, making it a popular day-use beach and camping area. It's located at the 29-km (18-mile) point of the 47-km (29-mile) Juan de Fuca Marine Trail, and is accessed via a short trail from the parking lot off Highway 14. Kayakers probably won't want to land here. It's considered one of Vancouver Island's best surfing beaches.

Camping: There are two designated camping areas within the provincial park's jurisdiction, one at East Sombrio and one at West Sombrio.

China Beach

This is another popular camping and day-use area with public beach access.

Camping: The designated China Beach campground features 78 drive-in campsites available both by reservation and first-come, first-served. Amenities include pit toilets and water taps.

Hiking: A 1-km (.6-mile) trail leads from the campsites down stairs and on a steep gravel trail through a forest to Second Beach. Another 2.5-km (1.5-mile) trail leads to Mystic Beach, another popular recreation area.

Jordan River

The combination of wave action and river runoff has created a large gravel shoal, next to which Western Forest Products has created a forest recreation campground. At first it's easy to dismiss this site as unattractive, as much of the recreation site is designed for RVs and features a bleak stretch of open parking/camping stalls facing the beach. However, charming walk-in campsites are located in a forested section. In some ways Jordan River represents the end of the wild coast of Vancouver Island. East of Jordan River is the start of oceanfront development that will continually become heavier toward Sooke.

Camping: RV stalls face the water in an open stretch at the Jordan River Recreation Site. Other campsites in the neighbouring second-growth forest (planted in 1926) are pretty sites that either face the water or are set slightly back.

Launches: You can launch directly from the beach or use the boat ramp at Jordan River. The boat ramp is surrounded by a cobble beach that can be used for loading and unloading kayaks.

Hiking: A few miles east of Jordan River is Sandcut Beach. It's accessible from Highway 14 at a parking area 27 km (17 miles) from Sooke across from the logging road Spur D. The 330-metre (1,083-foot) trail criss-crosses through second-growth forest (planted in 1899) to the old-growth forest along the waterfront and finally to the beach.

A pair of hikers tackle the West Coast Trail, one of the world's premiere hiking destinations.

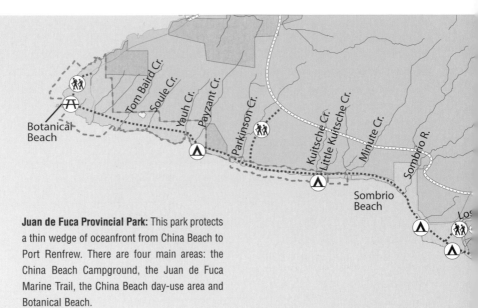

Juan de Fuca Provincial Park: This park protects a thin wedge of oceanfront from China Beach to Port Renfrew. There are four main areas: the China Beach Campground, the Juan de Fuca Marine Trail, the China Beach day-use area and Botanical Beach.

THE JUAN DE FUCA MARINE TRAIL

The Juan de Fuca Marine Trail traverses 47 km (29 miles) of wilderness along Juan de Fuca Strait. Four trailheads provide access to the trail: at China Beach, Sombrio Beach, Parkinson Creek and Botanical Beach, allowing a mix of multi-day hiking excursions and moderate day hikes. One of the best day hikes leads to Botanical Beach, a rich tidal marine environment best visited at low tide to view the tide pools. Reservation camping with vehicle access is available at China Beach.

This trail doesn't have the reputation of the West Coast Trail but provides just as beautiful an experience, with natural features including waterfalls, old-growth forests, tide pools and unusual rock formations. Unlike the West Coast Trail, reservations aren't necessary. Some portions of the trail cannot be passed at high tide and it's necessary to use tide tables (use the Port Renfrew tide listing). Maps are posted at trailhead locations. Orange balls are used to mark exits from the beach to the trail. A small cabin is provided at 20.5 km for emergency use only.

Botanical Beach: km 47
Parking lot provides day-use access to Botany Bay and Botanical Beach. No camping.

Payzant Creek: km 40
Designated wilderness camping with bear cache.

Parkinson Creek Trailhead: km 37.6
Trail access through some old-growth forest.

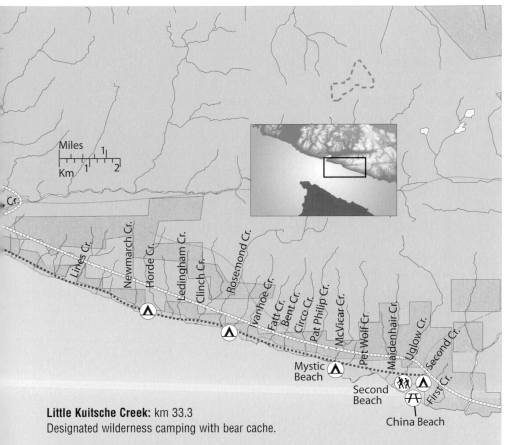

Little Kuitsche Creek: km 33.3
Designated wilderness camping with bear cache.

Sombrio Beach: km 29
Designated wilderness camping at both East and West Sombrio beaches. A 250-m
(820-foot) trail leads from parking to the cobble beach. Sombrio Beach is considered a
world-class surfing area.

Mystic Beach: km 2.5
A popular day trip from the China Beach Trailhead.

Second Beach: km 1
Can be reached from a 1-km (.6-mile) trail from the China Beach provincial park
campsite near the highway (see page 346) via stairs and a steep gravel trail. It's a
15- to 20-minute hike through mature forest.

China Beach: km 0
A popular day-use area. A waterfall is at the west end of the beach. Hiking is possible
to Second Beach.

Jordan River was home to the village called Di:ti:da?, the original "Nitinat."

French Beach

This beautiful beach stretches almost 2 km (1.2 miles), offering a great opportunity for hiking and beachcombing. It can be prone to moderate surf.

Point No Point was known as Ke:?ishadl, meaning 'neck cocked to one side.' It was the traditional boundary between the Pachenaht and T'sou-ke territories.

The Sheringham Point Lighthouse was built in 1912, and the original hexagonal concrete tower is still used today. The fresnel lens was replaced by a revolving beacon in 1976. The lighthouse is fenced off.

Camping: French Beach Provincial Park offers year-round, vehicle-accessible camping in a forested area in the beach's uplands. Amenities include picnic tables, day-use areas, a sani-station, pit toilets and fresh water.

Place names: James French was an early settler of Sooke who took two years to travel from New Brunswick to Victoria in 1885. He was a naturalist who travelled the world to bring exotic animals to zoos. One such animal was a small African elephant that spent some time

The Sheringham Point Lighthouse is set on a rocky bluff in an area that becomes increasingly developed as you head east.

here before it was sold to Woodland Park Zoo in Seattle. French died in 1952, and his home and beach would become a provincial park in 1974. Nearby Point No Point received its name for its deceiving look—from some angles it's clearly a point, while from others it's indistinguishable from the shore.

SOOKE (AND CIVILIZATION)

Here the wilderness comes to an end and is replaced by development broken only by a few regional parks. The most significant is East Sooke Regional Park, which protects much of the peninsula between Sooke Basin and Becher Bay. The Department of National Defence's Rocky Point Training Area marks the most southeasterly point of Vancouver Island. From there development increases toward Victoria, the exception being Witty's Lagoon and its waterfall.

Sooke Harbour

The town of Sooke, with its multitude of docks and marinas, is located on the northwest shore of the harbour. Sooke Harbour is divided from Sooke Basin by Billings Spit, a sandbar that extends well into the harbour. It's developed with residential properties that include apartment buildings. The area is a busy corridor for recreational boaters. Sooke River can be paddled quite a distance from the mouth just northwest of Billings Spit. Whiffen Spit Park is a narrow, natural

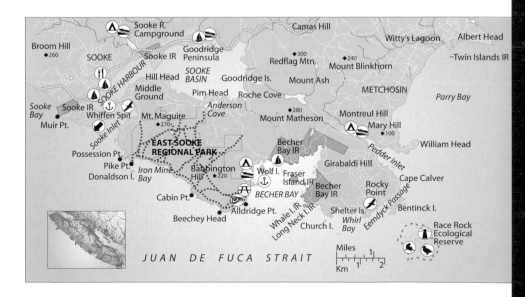

spit that extends over a kilometre (about 4,000 feet) into Sooke Inlet and protects Sooke Harbour. It has been reinforced to add to its permanence. A parking lot is located at the shore end of the spit. It's popular for hikers and joggers, but also with bird life. Seabirds are attracted to the intertidal shallows of Sooke Inlet just northeast of the spit.

The T'sou-ke First Nation has two reserves in the area. The T'sou-ke were nearly annihilated in an attack by the combined forces of the Cowichans, Clallams (U.S.) and Ditidahts in 1848.

Launches: Whiffen Spit offers the most convenient access for kayaks to Sooke's outer coast. Launching is possible from the parking lot to either side of the spit—the more exposed Juan de Fuca side or the more sheltered side facing Sooke Harbour. Sooke River Campground is another launch option. A fee applies.

Camping: Sooke River Campground, a community-owned camping area, is located in the flats on the western shore of Sooke River. For a fee there are showers, flush toilets, firewood and a boat ramp. Call **250-642-6076**.

Sooke Basin

This adjunct to Sooke Harbour would make a fine paddling destination for novice kayakers seeking sheltered waters near Victoria. It has a nice shoreline and a variety of coves to explore, but no outstanding features like those on the outer coast. Much of the shoreline is residential (generally on acreage), with some industrial sites, particularly on Goodridge Peninsula.

Launches: The most popular launch location for kayakers tends to be at Rush Adventures, a kayaking school and tour company located on the waterfront in a commercial complex that includes a waterfront pub. Rentals and guided kayaking tours are also available through Rush Adventures. Call **250-642-2159**.

East Sooke Regional Park

This pleasant waterfront park protects 1,400 hectares (3,460 acres) of coast. It's criss-crossed by trails that range from those that are well groomed and graded to difficult wilderness paths. Probably the most popular trail fronts the coastline from Becher Bay to Pike Point. The park extends north to Anderson Cove in Sooke Basin. A challenging trail leads up Babbington Hill, while another leads up Mt. Maguire. A petroglyph is carved onto a rock facing out to the ocean at Alldridge Point (on the east side of the point). The large etching depicts a mythical sea monster. It was made a heritage site in 1927.

Camping: North of Alldridge Point is a beautiful and expansive sandy beach. Camping would be possible on the beach above the high tide line, though it's prohibited by non-explicit park rules. Short trails from the beach lead to a flat, open, grassy meadow. Amenities here include a covered picnic shelter (it can be reserved by calling 250-478-3344) and out-

A view toward the beach near Alldridge Point in East Sooke Regional Park.

houses. The beach is generally quite well protected from the westerly swells, making it ideal for a stop during a coastal expedition by paddle. This location is significant because it's one of the few protected stops between Port Renfrew and Victoria for those paddling down the coast.

Becher Bay

This interesting bay is dominated by a marina and the Becher Bay reserve, which is in the process of adding more residences. The bay contains many interesting islands and rocks worth exploring. Wolfe Island is vacant but privately owned.

There are two marinas in Becher Bay. The Cheanuh Marina is operated by Becher Bay First Nation and has fuel, a small store, boat rentals, moorage and a launch ramp. Pacific Lions Marina has a sani-dump, electricity and a concrete boat ramp.

Camping: Sites are available at Pacific Lions Marina. The grass sites are suitable for RVs, trailers and tents. Reservations are required, along with a four-day minimum. Call 250-642-3816 or visit www.pacificlions.bc.ca.

Rocky Point

This point is significant as the southeasternmost point of Vancouver Island. Thus here ends (or begins) the west coast of Vancouver Island. Rocky Point's cape is Department of National Defence property known as the Rocky Point Training Area. The national defence property dominates the headland, which is mostly undeveloped except for numerous warnings that trespassing won't be tolerated, including on several attractive beaches. Rocky Point is a significant birding area, with fall migration including Wilson's warbler, Pacific-slope flycatcher, orange-crowned warbler, Lincoln's sparrow, Savannah sparrow and ruby-crowned kinglet. About 245 bird species have been recorded at the Rocky Point Bird Observatory.

Rocky Point replaced Colwood as the site for the West Coast Ammunition Depot after 1943. Rocky Point is part of a major military presence on the south coast of Vancouver Island that dates back to military tensions between the U.S. and Great Britain in the late 1840s.

Bentinck Island

This picturesque island is located off the Rocky Point Training Area. A narrow channel between the island and Rocky Point is filled with rocks and reefs, and is a favoured seal haulout. Bentinck Island is Department of National Defence property, and has been used for explosives blasting for decades.

Bentinck Island once housed a leper colony. Originally the colony was located at D'Arcy Island, a few miles north of Victoria. It was relocated to Bentinck Island in 1924, where it continued to operate until 1956.

Race Rocks

This collection of about eight rocks is set in open waters in Juan de Fuca Strait. Cliffs, chasms and surge channels dot the shoreline. A live webcam of Race Rocks can be seen at **www.racerocks.com**.

High currents and clear water near Race Rocks translate into energy and nutrients, leading to a high production of algae and invertebrates. Bull kelp and another 20 species of algae have been recorded here, along with mussels, anemones, sponges, ascidians, soft pink coral and the basket star. The area is frequented by marine mammals such as steller and California sea lions, elephant seals and fur seals. As many as 70 steller sea lions and 800 California seal lions have been recorded here. Seabirds nest on seven rocks, and include over 200 pairs of pelagic cormorants, 180 pairs of glaucous-winged gulls and four pairs of black oystercatchers.

Race Rocks Lighthouse is the second-oldest lighthouse in Western Canada. It opened in 1860 just after the Fisgard Lighthouse in Esquimalt Harbour. Just three days before the lighthouse was to begin operating the 385-ton *Nanette* ran aground here.

Race Rocks Ecological Reserve was created in 1980 to protect the rich intertidal and subtidal environment. The reserve includes the islets and the subtidal zones to the 20-fathom contour.

Caution: The exposed location off the southern tip of Vancouver Island and a shallow sea bottom result in very strong currents (up to 7 knots), eddies and generally turbulent waters around Race Rocks. Wind waves and swell can add to the difficulties. Public access to land isn't allowed.

Pedder Bay

This long, narrow bay is bordered by steep shoreline culminating in Pedder Bay Marina. The north shore is the William Head Correctional Centre. Pedder Bay Marina offers a boat ramp for a fee as well as RV sites and field camping. Showers and laundry are available. Call 250-478-1771.

Witty's Lagoon Regional Park

This stretch north of William Head has a few nice beaches backed by the residential community of Metchosin, but by far the nicest is Witty's Lagoon Regional Park. The lagoon is enclosed by a sandbar that's a popular day-use beach. The prettiest feature is Sitting Lady Falls, a small waterfall that plummets into the lagoon. If you're kayaking southwest past Witty's Lagoon, you'll pass a clothing-optional beach. An overhanging tree marks the boundary between the clothing-required and clothing-optional beaches.

Albert Head

Albert Head is Department of National Defence land, with a lagoon tucked into the north side of the peninsula. A Capital Regional District park, the lagoon is a wildlife sanctuary and reserve for a variety of migrating birds plus ducks, geese and swans. A nice cobble beach with some sand portions stretches north past the lagoon. If you're paddling around Albert Head Lagoon, you might notice that between the lagoon and the gravel loading dock there's a lack of bathing outfits. This is another clothing-optional beach on south Vancouver Island. The Albert Head Cadet Summer Training Centre serves as the Department of National Defence's regional cadet instructor school and an air cadet summer training camp. A basic officer training course for reserve naval officers also takes place here, as well as regular forces basic recruit training.

Looking across Becher Bay from Alldridge Point.

BIBLIOGRAPHY

Between Ports Alberni and Renfrew: Notes on West Coast Peoples, E. Y. Arima, Denis St. Claire, Louis Clamhouse, Joshua Edgar, Charles Jones and John Thomas (Canadian Ethnology Service Mercury Series Paper 121, Canadian Museum of Civilization, 1991).

Brooks Peninsula: an Ice Age Refugium on Vancouver Island (BC Ministry of Environment, Lands, and Parks, BC Parks Division, 1997).

British Columbia Coast Names: Their Origin and History, Capt. John T. Walbran (Douglas and McIntyre, Toronto, 1971).

BC Marine Parks Guide: The Official Guide to B.C.'s Coastal Marine Parks (undated).

"Canadian Important Bird Areas database" (Canadian Nature Federation, 2003).

"Che:k'tles7et'h' First Nation Offer to the Governments of Canada and British Columbia" signed by Frances Gillette, William Oscar and Mike Oscar, c2000, courtesy Nuu-Chah-Nulth Tribal Council.

Clayoquot Soundings, a History of Clayoquot Sound, 1880s to 1980s (Walter Guppy, 1997).

Cultural Heritage Background Study, Clayoquot Sound, Ian R. Wilson, Randy Bouchard, Dorothy Kennedy and Nicholas Heap (I. R. Wilson Consultants Ltd. for Clayoquot Sound Sustainable Development Strategy, 1991).

"Field Protocol For Migrating Monitoring at Rocky Point Bird Observatory," Ver. 1.3 (2000).

First Nations' Perspectives Relating to Forest Practices Standards in Clayoquot Sound, Appendix VI (Clayoquot Sound Scientific Panel, Coast and Marine Planning Branch, 1995).

"Forest Watch Update," Vol. 1, Issue 3, Feb. 2001, Forest Watch of British Columbia.

Guide to British Columbia Ecological Reserves (BC Ministry of Environment Lands and Parks, 1993).

"The Intertidal and Subtidal Macroflora and Macrofauna in the Proposed Juan de Fuca National Marine Park Near Victoria," James M. Goddard (Report to the National Parks Branch, Department of Indian and Northern Development, 1975).

"Issue Analysis for Strathcona Park Master Plan Update" (BC Ministry of Environment, Lands and Parks, BC Parks Division, 1999).

"Ka:'yu:'k't'h' First Nation Offer to the Governments of Canada and British Columbia" signed by Tyee Hawilthe, Hawilthe and Hawilthe, c2000, courtesy Nuu-Chah-Nulth Tribal Council.

"The Kyuquot Sound Coastal Plan, Draft" (Coastal Planning, Projects and Marine Initiatives, Ministry of Sustainable Resource Management, 2002).

"Land & Coastal Resource Management Plan, Socio-Economic & Environmental/Marine Base Case: Final Report," by Eliot Terry and Jacqueline Bothemp (Ministry of Employment & Investment, Economics Branch, 2000).

"Nootka Coastal Land Use Plan" (Nootka Resource Board, Land Use Coordination Office, 2001).

Nootka: Regreso a Una Historia Olvidada, Mercedes Palau, Carisa Cales and Araceli Sanchez (Lunwerg, 1999).

The Nootka: Scenes and Studies of Savage Life, by Gilbert Malcolm Sproat (Sono Nis Press, Victoria, 1987).

"North Island Heritage: Inventory and Evaluation" (Insight Consultants, undated).

"North Island Straits Coastal Plan" (Coastal Planning, Projects and Marine Initiatives, Ministry of Sustainable Resource Management, 2002).

Notes and Observations of the Kwakiool People of the Northern Part of Vancouver Island and Adjacent Coasts, George Dawson, 1885.

The Northern and Central Nootkan Tribes, Philip Drucker (Smithsonian Institution, 1949).

Nuu-Chah-Nulth Voices, Histories Objects and Journeys, edited by Alan L. Hoover (Royal B.C. Museum, 2000).

The Quatsino Chronicle, 1895–1995, compiled by Gwen Handsen.

"Quatsino Sound Coastal Management Plan, Draft" (British Columba Coast and Marine Planning Branch, 2003).

"Quatsino Sound—North Vancouver Island Sustainable Forest Management Plan, Draft Management Plan 9" (May 1, 2001 to April 30, 2006).

Quatsino-San Josef Map Area, Northern Vancouver Island: Geological Overview (92L/12W, 1021/8, 9), G. T. Nixon, J. L. Hammack, G. J. Payie, L. D. Snyder (Geological Survey Branch, undated).

"Quatsino Sound Project (92L/5, 6, 11, 12)," N. W. D. Massey and D. M. Melville (Geological Fieldwork 1990 Paper British Columbia Geological Survey Branch, 1990–91).

"Raft Cove Provincial Park Master Plan" (BC Parks South Coast Region, 1993).

"Surficial Geology and Drift Exploration: Mahatta Creek Map Area (92L/5)," David H. Huntley and Peter T. Bobrowsky (Paper 1995-1, British Columbia Geological Survey Branch, 1995).

Vancouver Island Summary Land Use Plan Appendices (2000).

Vancouver Island's West Coast, George Nicholson, (1962).

Index

ABOUT THE AUTHOR

John Kimantas grew up in Oakville, Ontario. He has worked as an editor at several Canadian newspapers, including the *Opasquia Times* and *Interlake Spectator* in Manitoba, the *Guelph Mercury* in Ontario, the *Nanaimo Daily Free Press* and most recently the *Nanaimo News Bulletin* on Vancouver Island. His writing credits include five environmental writing awards.

An avid outdoorsman and hiker, John, while watching killer whales with his son on Johnstone Strait, noticed a pod of orcas surfacing around two kayakers. Kayaking looked so peaceful that he was inspired to try it. It has become his favourite way to explore the beautiful and remote coastline of Vancouver Island.

He is currently working on the second volume, featuring Desolation Sound, in *The Wild Coast* series.